JOHN DUDLEY

Christine Hartweg

JOHN DUDLEY

The Life of

Lady Jane Grey's Father-in-Law

John Dudley

The Life of Lady Jane Grey's Father-in-Law

First published in 2016

Copyright © 2016 Christine Hartweg

All rights reserved.
No part of this publication may be reproduced or transmitted in any form or by any means without prior permission of the author.

ISBN 978-1517648411

Cover photo: Detail of *Edward VI as a Child* by Hans Holbein the Younger, 1538.
Courtesy The National Gallery of Art, Washington

Author's address: Königsweg 208 f, 14129 Berlin, Germany
e-mail: allthingsrd@t-online.de

http://www.allthingsrobertdudley.wordpress.com

Contents

Preface 7
1. A London Childhood 9
2. Kent and the Court 14
3. Family Business 19
4. Voyage to Spain 27
5. Lord Admiral 31
6. Companion of Kings 43
7. My Lord Protector 53
8. Rebellion 67
9. Coup d'Etat 75
10. Lord President 88
11. A Fraudulent Scheme 123
12. Riches upon Riches 138
13. Obstinate Doctors 156
14. The King's Will 165
15. Jane the Queen 191
16. My Deadly Stroke 206
17. There Hath Lacked a Northumberland 230
    Tables 247
    Bibliography 252
    Index 263

Die Geschichte eines Hypochonders,

für

Dr. Trabulsi

Preface

A mid-20th century biographer once wrote that the Dudleys "might have become as famous and terrible a dynasty as the Borgias" if the Duke of Northumberland's plot of 1553 had succeeded. Well, it did not succeed and the duke lost his head, but the Dudleys are still very interesting people, though they cannot quite compete with the Borgias; but then perhaps Tudor England cannot quite compare with the Italian Renaissance.

John Dudley, Viscount Lisle, Earl of Warwick, and finally, Duke of Northumberland, was the son of a traitor and rose to the heights of power at the courts of Henry VIII and Edward VI. He must have been a talented man, or Henry VIII would not have employed him in building up his navy. John succeeded brilliantly and achieved real power during the reign of the boy king, Edward VI. For three and a half years he ruled England. His tragedy was the youthful king's early death. Edward did not want to see his Catholic sister Mary on the throne and willed that his Protestant cousin Jane Grey should inherit the crown. Supposedly, this was John Dudley's one-man-plot, for Jane happened to be his daughter-in-law. Naturally, such a plan could not succeed and John paid with his life, returning to the Catholic faith before his execution, an act good for his soul, though not so good for his reputation.

Supposedly "the most evil statesman to govern England during the sixteenth century", in the words of a bestselling author, and "one of the most remarkably able governors of any European state during the sixteenth century", in the words of a professor, John Dudley without doubt is one of the most interesting figures of Tudor England. In recent decades, he has received a considerable amount of rehabilitation, including two academic biographies, but likewise he continues as the pantomime villain in many books, novels, and films.

I first read about John Dudley in any notable sense in one of the latter sort of books, Hester W. Chapman's 1962 biography, *Lady*

Jane Grey – and could not help but feel an intense liking for him. By a different avenue, I also became fascinated with his son, Robert, who survived his father's political adventures to become Elizabeth I's great favourite and lifelong friend. I have since done a lot of research into both Dudleys and written about them on several places on the internet. Naturally, some of this material has gone into this biography, but the book is a fresh project, with a narrative approach. Feeling that a new book never needs an excuse, I would like to thank fellow Dudley and Lady Jane enthusiasts for insisting that I should write one and/or encouraging me in the process – especially: Carol Dennis, Anne Tudor, Nora Platt, Geanine Teramani-Cruz, Tamise Hills, Claire Ridgway, Susan Higginbotham, and Susan Abernethy.

My aim has been to tell the story of John Dudley and his family, using his own words and other contemporary and near-contemporary sources. The quotations from John Dudley's letters are 99% his own words, the exception being quotes taken from Knighton 1992, which are close paraphrases. I have deliberately left many quotations in original spelling; I have, however, corrected the interchangeable use of *v* and *u* in 16th century printed texts to modern usage, as these were mere printer's conventions.

Since John Dudley was a man with many titles, I have decided to simply call him *John* or *John Dudley* throughout the book; however, now and then I refer to him as *Lisle*, *Warwick*, or *Northumberland* (and very rarely *Dudley*). A particular challenge has been his son and heir, the younger John Dudley, who also carried the titles of Lisle and Warwick, as courtesy titles. I hope it's always clear who is who.

Christine Hartweg,
Berlin, January 2016

1.
A London Childhood

John Dudley was born between February 1504 and February 1505,[1] probably in London, Candlewick Street. Apparently, he was named after his grandfather, Sir John Dudley of Atherington, himself a younger son of another John, the formidable first Baron of Dudley Castle who had always managed to be on the right side of the Wars of the Roses.

Baby John was the first child of Edmund Dudley, esquire, by his second wife, Elizabeth Grey. In 1505 Elizabeth was described as in her early twenties and she would have married Edmund around 1502/1503. She came from the nobility, her father being Edward Grey, 4th Viscount Lisle, and later in life she became Baroness Lisle in her own right as her brother's co-heir. After John, she bore her husband two more sons, Jerome and Andrew. From his father's first marriage John had a half-sister who in 1500 was described as "little Elizabeth Dudley", indicating that she was still very young.[2]

---

1   Loades 1996 p. 8. In a parliamentary statute of February 1512 John Dudley was described as "not yet eight years old", which indicates he was born between February 1504 and February 1505. There is no basis for the dates 1501 and 1502, found in some encyclopedias.
2   Loades 1996 pp. 7–8, 1, 2. Edmund Dudley's first wife was Anne Windsor, daughter of Thomas Windsor of Stanwell; the dates of the wedding and of her death are unknown. There is confusion about Edmund Dudley's age. According to the 17th century antiquarian William Dugdale he was born in 1462, but an inquisition post mortem concerning his mother's death on 12 October 1498 states Edmund was then "aged twenty six and more"; since this

She would have been something between five and eight years older than John.

In 1504 Edmund Dudley served as Speaker of the House of Commons, and later in the year he entered the council and counsels of King Henry VII. In 1506, when little John was about two, Edmund was appointed President of the King's Council. A brilliant lawyer, he had worked for the City of London, including as under-sheriff, and in the king's service he put his accumulated inside knowledge about the merchant class into practice: He and his colleague Sir Richard Empson became notorious collectors of fines and other "contributions". The centre of Edmund's activities was his house in Candlewick Street, positioned in the heart of London's commercial hub, and especially its textile trade. Edmund Dudley, like Thomas Cromwell decades later, was not just an administrator but a draper or cloth trader as well.[1] His first years John Dudley passed surrounded by beautiful fabrics.

The house stretched over 180 feet along the street, but as one Venetian visitor wrote, merchant houses "do not seem very large from the outside", but "they contain a great number of rooms ... and are quite considerable".[2] It boasted a hall with a dais and a large old arras behind it, a "great parlour", a "little parlour", and, importantly, a "counting house in the little parlour". There was a great chamber and many smaller chambers, an armoury, and "the long gallery leading to the garden", "the low gallery by the garden", as well as "the great gallery at the end of that".[3] When John was about three, his father obtained permission to build a private "current of water" to his house, leading off the public conduit at Cheapside. Such luxury was copied from Italian

---

is to mean "more than twenty six and less than twenty seven" (rather than "any age over twenty six"), he would have been born between 13 October 1471 and 12 October 1472 provided the inquisition is correct (which cannot be taken for granted). His educational progress at Oxford and the Inns of Court, in the 1470s and 1480s, has been hypothesized on the basis of the year of birth given by Dugdale, while his public career in parliament and on peace commissions (jointly with his father) is traceable since 1491 (Gunn 2008). Thus, he may or may not have been a very young MP.

1 Penn 2012 p. 266; Loades 2013c p. 23
2 Penn 2012 p. 266
3 L&P I No. 146

palazzi,[1] and indeed one of the people most often seen in Candlewick Street would have been the Genoese banker Battista Grimaldi who collaborated intensely with Edmund. The interior of the house was luxurious with "fine arras" on the walls, exquisite furniture, and glassware of "beyond sea making".[2]

Like all parents, Edmund Dudley was concerned that his children might be spoilt, growing up "among the women": "Let not the feminine pity of your wives destroy your children, pamper them not at home in furred coats and their shirts to be warmed ... Dandle them not too dearly lest folly fasten on them."[3] In fact, it was normal even for four-year-olds to be spanked by their doting mothers, and moral education started early. Four- and five-year-olds had to learn the Ten Commandments and the Lord's Prayer by heart. In 1500 the Bible was still the basis of literacy, favourite passages being taken from the Book of Proverbs and Ecclesiasticus. These texts also served to instil good manners in children.[4]

In the eyes of their contemporaries Empson and Dudley were "ravening wolves" who squeezed the last penny out of the poor rich and the unfortunate well-to-do. So there was great rejoicing when the two ministers, and some of their agents, were arrested in the early hours of 24 April 1509, three days after Henry VII's death. To young John the events were unforgettable. In August royal commissioners descended on Candlewick Street to confiscate and inventory the movables and papers of Edmund Dudley. How long John and his siblings were allowed to remain with their mother and how long they continued to live in Candlewick Street is unknown.

In the Tower, his father could regain some hope when parliament did not pass his attainder despite his conviction for treason months earlier. He even dropped his plan to escape from prison[5] and turned to writing a book, *The Tree of Commonwealth*, a treatise on good government: "Its detailed prescriptions for the

---

1   Penn 2012 p. 314
2   Penn 2012 p. 266
3   Brigden 2001 p. 56
4   Brigden 2001 p. 56; Smith 2013 pp. 27–28
5   Loades 1996 p. 11

judicial system and its suspicion of noble self-assertion, mercantile chicanery, and popular idleness and disorder look very like those pursued by Henry VII's regime. Reflections upon the previous reign and forebodings for the new meet in warnings against royal covetousness, fleshliness, warmongering, and indulgence in dangerous sports."[1]

That all collaborators of Empson and Dudley, even the most notorious, had meanwhile been released must have been comforting to Edmund and his family. Battista Grimaldi's cousin now even served one of Katherine of Aragon's Spanish ladies – after all the Grimaldi bank had processed the queen's dowry. However, this very reinstatement of the Grimaldis caused a new outcry among the London merchants and probably contributed to Edmund's end.[2]

In mid-August 1510, well over a year after their trial, Henry VIII ordered Sir Richard Empson and Edmund Dudley to be beheaded on Tower Hill. Edmund turned to writing his will. In it he mentioned his children; Andrew and Jerome were mere toddlers or infants in 1510, and Jerome he destined to the church. Edmund had been one of the executors of Henry VII's will and while awaiting his fate he drew up a list in which he detailed his actions for his late master; it was a catalogue of the persons Henry VII had wronged "contrary to his laws", compiled at his request so that restitution could be made for the benefit of the king's soul. Edmund admitted that people had been imprisoned for "light matters", that inordinate fines had been levied, that some had had a "very hard end", and that many proceedings had been "contrary to conscience".[3]

That the ministers had operated under the close scrutiny and direction of Henry VII is apparent from the king's own personal notes, including in Edmund's account book.[4] After Henry VIII had ascended the throne and summarily dealt with his father's "enforcers" this became a moot point, however. It was only then that the most graphic stories were written down by Polydore Vergil

---

[1] Gunn 2008
[2] Penn 2012 p. 373
[3] Brigden 2001 p. 37
[4] Brigden 2001 p. 36; Penn 2012 p. 262

and the London chroniclers, and they represented the point of view of what today would be called tax evaders, whether clerical (like the Bishop of London) or civic (like the City merchants); when they write of Empson's and Dudley's "poor" victims some scepticism is in order.

2.
Kent and the Court

Edmund Dudley's decapitated body was buried in the precincts of the Blackfriars monastery in the west of the City of London. Fifteen months later, in November 1511, his widow remarried, on the king's command; the lucky bridegroom was Arthur Plantagenet, Henry VIII's uncle of illegitimate birth. He received a good share of Edmund's confiscated lands but did not succeed in becoming his stepchildren's guardian, a circumstance which left him somewhat disgruntled.[1] Instead Sir Edward Guildford petitioned for and received John's wardship. At the same time, in February 1512, Edmund's attainder was annulled by parliamentary statute and his son was restored "in name and blood". The king was hoping for the good services "which the said John Dudley is likely to do".[2]

The Guildfords had been loyal to the House of Tudor from the start and Sir Edward and his half-brother Sir Henry belonged to the circle of Henry VIII's personal favourites. Now about seven years old, John would possibly have left his home to live in another family's household, anyway; as it came, he moved to Kent to live with the Guildfords. We do not know how much he saw of his mother or his little brothers, Jerome and Andrew, in the ensuing years; we do not know where they grew up while Elizabeth Grey,

---
1 Loades 2008a
2 Loades 1996 pp. 17–18

now Plantagenet, bore her second husband three daughters who survived. She died, probably in childbirth, in 1525 or 1526.[1]

Sir Edward Guildford's principal residence was at Halden in Kent. He married twice, and his two children were born of his first marriage:[2] Richard, whose date of birth is unknown, and Jane, who would have been three years old when John was added to the household. The date of Edward Guildford's second marriage being unknown, it is possible that the Lady Guildford of 1512 was Richard's and Jane's stepmother. The children doubtless became John's playmates and their schooling probably occurred at home under the direction of a private tutor. As his letters show, John Dudley became perfectly literate in English. In 1552, having received one of the youthful Edward VI's drafts for reform, he complained that it was written "all in latin, I can but guess at it", a remark which would support the assumption that he had no Latin. However, the truth is more complicated. On the one hand it was "polite convention" to underplay one's capacities in this respect,[3] and on the other he was quite capable to understand the meaning of Edward's text, so he must have learnt his "grammar" as a youth and simply forgotten most of it.[4]

Sir Edward, in 1514, was appointed Master of the Tower Armouries and thus became responsible for the king's personal body armour. He organized jousts and tournaments, and served as marshal in many festivities held to impress foreign ambassadors.[5] It seems likely that he introduced John to the court as a page during these years.[6] John's education was certainly that of a courtier and knight, comprising training with horses and weapons such as daggers, swords, and pikes. He soon would also have opportunity to brush up his French.

In May 1519 Edward Guildford was appointed Marshal of Calais, and it has been speculated that John Dudley, now about 15,

---

1 Grummitt 2008
2 His first wife was Eleanor West, daughter of Thomas West, 8th Baron West and 9th Baron De La Warr.
3 Ives 2005 p. 45
4 Loades 1996 p. 203; Loades 2008a. Roger Ascham, in 1547, also expected him to understand his Latin letter (Ascham I Pt. 1 p. 125).
5 Lehmberg 2008
6 Loades 2008a

went with his guardian to serve there at the garrison.[1] Guildford was still at Calais in June 1520 when he was responsible for arranging the elaborate pavilions and lodgings for the Field of Cloth of Gold, where Henry VIII and Francis I met to celebrate their somewhat hollow friendship. In July 1520 Calais also saw the visit of the Emperor Charles V, Edward Guildford again being involved in the preparations.[2] It is unknown whether young John saw some glimpses of all this splendour, but quite possible.

The next year, 1521, Sir Edward served as Constable of Dover Castle and became Lord Warden of the Cinque Ports. His ward John, whom he seems to have always preferred before his son Richard,[3] meanwhile entered the entourage of Cardinal Wolsey on a mission to France. The cardinal, who was wont to tour Europe with a huge following, was to help negotiate a peace between the French king and the emperor; nothing came of it, though. We next find John (once again?) at Calais, in his first ever command at the garrison. War between England and France had resumed, and, towards the end of 1522, he gained his first experience of military action in skirmishes around Calais.[4] He was 18 years old.

In August 1523 he got his first military post, again at Calais, as Lieutenant of the Spears. "As that position was in the gift of the Lord Deputy rather than the Marshall [Sir Edward Guildford], his advancement cannot be attributed to mere nepotism. He was a very promising young soldier."[5]

A few weeks later he took part in the Duke of Suffolk's campaign in France. This was meant to support the emperor and the Duke of Bourbon, who had recently switched sides and was now fighting against his master the King of France. However, Bourbon turned up at Marseille instead of in the northwest of France, and the English army, about 11,000 men, soon got bogged down at the Somme. The October weather was terrible and many English soldiers succumbed to sickness. Nonetheless, towns and fortified places were taken in the revived cause of an English

---

1   Loades 1996 p. 20
2   Lehmberg 2008
3   Loades 2008a
4   Lehmberg 2008; Loades 2008a
5   Loades 1996 p. 22

"empire" on French soil.[1] The exploits of John Dudley's guardian stood out:

> Sir Edward Gyldford capitaine of the horsmen vewed the castle of Bowhen or Boghan, whiche ever was thought to be impregnable, but he iudged it might be wonne, for the castle was invironed with Marryses [marshes], so that to no mans judgement it was possible to wynne it: But nowe he perceived that the frost was so great and strong that it might be beseaged, & all that night it fresed againe: wherfore he desired the Duke to geve him leave to assaute it whiche thereto agreed. Then he caused the ordinance to be set furth over the marrish. When they within the castle perceived that the marrishe fayled theim, they were sore dismayed. Then sir Edward Guildeford shot thre great pieces at the castle, and the castilian shot thre pieces againe. Then as the Englishe gunners wer preparing to the battery, the capitain seyng his castle could not hold, by reason that the marishe failed, and that he could defende none assault, delivered the castle to him to the behofe of the Emperor and the kyng of England, and after a small communicacion had betwene the sayd sir Edwarde Guyldforde and the capitaine, the capitaine with all his retinue departed levyng behynd the ordinaunce of bombardes, curtawes, & demy curtaux, slinges, canons, volgers, and other ordinaunce, there were lxxvi. pieces, plentie of pellettes & pouder.[2]

In early November the Duke of Suffolk in person made "Sir Edw. Semer" and "Sir John Dudlay" into knights,[3] the first evidence of a close if ultimately tragic relationship. A friendship from boyhood was that between John Dudley and Thomas Wyatt, who was John's exact contemporary. John was Edward Guildford's ward, Thomas

---
1 Loades 1996 p. 21
2 Hall p. 671
3 L&P III No. 3516. "Sir Edw. Semer" is Edward Seymour.

Henry Guildford's *protégé*. Both the Wyatts and the Guildfords resided in Kent, and so did the antiquarian John Leland, who during the 1520s enjoyed John Dudley's patronage.[1] In 1527, when John once again accompanied the cardinal to Europe – as one of over 900 attendants – Leland composed a Latin poem for his friend Wyatt, who had remained in England; the piece was carried home by Dudley:

> Dudley, about to arrange a journey from here to his native shores, advised that I should remember to present you, my familiar and old companion, with a greeting.[2]

John Dudley, by his 18th birthday, was firmly integrated into a Kentish network of intellectual friends; in July 1522 one of the group, writing from Louvain, desired "remembrance" to, among others, Dudley.[3] By 1524 Sir John had also gained the king's personal favour; he was now a Knight of the Body, which meant a lot of jousting and things like archery and wrestling, sports he still excelled in many years later.[4] He was also about to become a married man.

---

1 Brigden 2012 pp. 80, 130
2 Brigden 2012 pp. 129, 130; Loades 1996 p. 24
3 Brigden 2012 pp. 89–90; L&P III No. 2390
4 Loades 1996 p. 22. A French summary of his life claimed that he was "the most skilful of his generation, both on foot and on horseback" (Ives 2009 p. 99).

3.
Family Business

John's intended bride was Jane Guildford, Sir Edward's only daughter. The arrangement had been agreed upon between John's mother and his guardian,[1] possibly many years before the consummation of the marriage. The wedding may have occurred in 1524, perhaps after John's return from campaigning in France. Born in 1508 or 1509,[2] Jane would have been about 16 and in time would give birth to 13 children, eight boys and five girls.[3] It is nearly impossible to establish their birth dates. The first child, unsurprisingly named Henry, was born not later than 1525; the second son, perhaps equally unsurprisingly called Thomas,[4] died at age two. Next came either the eldest daughter, Mary, or the third son, John, quickly followed by Ambrose and Robert.[5] Robert, the

---

1   Loades 2008a
2   Loades 2008a. The 1508/9 date is derived from her epitaph, which states that she was 46 at her death in January 1555. The inquisition post mortem of her uncle, Thomas West, Baron West and De La Warr, on the other hand, claims she was 50 in September 1554 (IPMs Sussex p. 236). However, the epitaph would have been commissioned by her children, who were more likely to know her exact age than her uncle.
3   For all children see Tables 1 and 2. The number of her children is also derived from her epitaph. It is confirmed by a number of pedigrees.
4   The king was of course Henry VIII, while his chief minister was Thomas Wolsey.
5   The birth year of John is variously given as 1527, 1528, and 1530. However the first two dates seem to be inferred from his parents' assumed marriage date around 1525, and there is no reason why the couple's third son – but not necessarily the third child – must have been born within two or three years after their marriage. The year 1530 is given by at least one of the surviving manuscript pedigrees, one made for Robert Dudley when Earl of Leicester, and it is confirmed by a statement in John Dee's dedication of his *Mathematicall Praeface* (1570): "This noble earl died Anno 1554 scarce of 24

fifth son, is in fact the only child whose exact birthday can be established with confidence: he almost certainly was born on 24 June 1532, a great feast day in England.[1] Depending on whether Mary was born before or after Robert, Jane Dudley had seven or eight more children until early 1547, when the last seems to have been born.[2]

The next son after Robert was Guildford, probably named for his grandfather, Sir Edward Guildford, and born in March 1537.[3] In between Robert and Guildford there may have come Margaret, after them another Henry as well as the eighth boy, Charles, who would have been born around 1540 and died eight years later. Charles was followed by two Katherines; the result of at least one of the godmothers being a Katherine.[4] It is unclear who was the last child, but it was probably daughter Temperance who died one year old.[5]

---

    years of age" (see Table 1). John Dudley junior died on 21 October 1554 and John Dee had been his close friend.

1 Adams 2008b. William Camden believed that Robert was born on the same day as Queen Elizabeth, which is however contradicted by a letter in which Robert named 24 June as his birthday. From a description on a miniature by Nicholas Hilliard it is possible to calculate the year of his birth.

2 Beer 1973 p. 59; CSP Span 10 February 1547

3 Higginbotham 2011a; de Lisle 2013 pp. 261, 492. There is no evidence for Guildford being born in 1534, 1535, or 1536. He was likely born in 1537, as his godfather Diego Hurtado de Mendoza arrived only in May 1537. Children had three godparents in all and one of them played his or her part in the confirmation, which could take place together with the baptism or later. Mendoza stayed until August 1538, Jane Dudley having been delivered of a son in March 1537.

4 Adams 1995 p. 44. Katherine Brandon, Duchess of Suffolk, stood godmother to a Dudley daughter in 1545; this was most probably the Katherine who "died aged vii", almost certainly in June 1552 (see below p. 141). The elder Katherine, the later Katherine Hastings, Countess of Huntingdon, was under twelve years old when Jane Dudley made her will in early 1555.

5 It cannot have been the youngest son, Charles, since he would then have survived both his father and mother, the latter of whom would have mentioned him in her will. The heralds who made the family pedigrees seem not to have been sure about the birth order of the daughters, except that Mary was the eldest. Although one pedigree describes her as such, neither of the two Katherines was probably the youngest daughter, so there remain Margaret and Temperance. However, the name Temperance is rather unusual and it was probably given in the same intellectual climate where the young Edward VI

Sir Edward Guildford died in 1534 before he could draw up his last will. His son Richard had predeceased him, and his next male heir was his nephew, John Guildford. John Guildford almost immediately turned up at the manor house of Halden (where John Dudley lived with his wife and children) and asserted that his uncle had intended him to inherit. The inheritance included Halden. The Dudleys' stance, on the other hand, was that Jane as Guildford's daughter was the natural heir, and so, despite Thomas Cromwell's good services at reconciliation, the parties ended up at court. The Dudleys won the case. John had secured Cromwell's patronage early on, writing: "I beg you to be my good master in this, that my enemies may take no advantage against me."[1]

From Sir Edward Guildford John Dudley also inherited the post of Master of the Tower Armouries, as well as a seat in the so-called Reformation parliament. He sat as a Knight of the Shire for Kent and became responsible for the king's body armour.[2] In October 1532, John travelled to Calais to take part in the reception of Henry VIII and Anne Boleyn by Francis I. He also attended the new queen's coronation, serving as Archbishop Cranmer's cupbearer at the "queen's board", and at the christening of Princess Elizabeth in September 1533 he was listed as bearing gifts.[3]

John Dudley had also inherited from his mother the reversion of most of her lands, which means he was entitled to receive said lands after the death of his stepfather, Arthur Plantagenet. In 1532 he began to sell these reversions to third parties, among them his fellow courtier, Sir Edward Seymour. A dispute now arose between Lord Lisle (as Arthur Plantagenet had become via his first wife, John's mother) and Seymour. In this seemingly endless affair John sided with Seymour rather than with his stepfather. As it turned out, Seymour and Dudley "very craftily" deprived Lisle of £60 p.a.[4]

Lisle complained to Cromwell that "Sir John Dudley may see that I have rather used him like a father than a father-in-law, as the

---

addressed his sister Elizabeth as "sweet sister Temperance".
1 Loades 1996 pp. 30–31, 32
2 Loades 1996 p. 31; Ives 2009 p. 99
3 Beer 1973 pp. 8–9
4 Loades 1996 pp. 28–29; Beer 1973 p. 8

King and the Council know."[1] We do not know whether John would have shared this opinion; on the whole, relations with his stepfather and his half-sisters Frances, Elizabeth, and Bridget were friendly enough. Elizabeth Plantagenet lived with John and his family for some years, and John very outspokenly defended his sister's interests. Having heard that Lord Lisle was planning to leave his entire estate to his eldest daughter, thereby jeopardizing Elizabeth's marriage prospects, he informed him: "for my part I have and will do as becomes a brother to do to his sister".[2] Elizabeth later married Francis Jobson, one of her brother's cronies.

Elizabeth Dudley, John's elder half-sister, was less fortunate. She married William, 7th Lord Stourton. Her husband evicted her from home as he wanted to live with his mistress, whom in 1547 he married bigamously. Elizabeth took refuge in the house of her neighbours and after her husband's death her son tried to force her into an agreement never to marry again and to deprive her of her property. Charles, 8th Lord Stourton, was largely successful in this except that his mother did marry again.[3] John's niece, Ursula Stourton, married Edward, 9th Lord Clinton, and seems to have been a regular guest of the Dudleys.[4] Intriguingly, Lord Clinton was to profit more than almost anybody else from John's patronage in years to come.[5]

We do not know whether John's brothers lived in his household in those years. Andrew never married, but later we find him in his own house in London. Jerome, originally being destined for the church by his father, appears next in the wills of his sister-in-law and his brother. From these it seems clear that, though apparently not bed-ridden, he needed care. He was relatively helpless and probably mentally disabled; significantly he had no household of his own, which a person of his station could otherwise have maintained even if suffering from a physical ailment.

---

1   L&P 10 March 1534
2   Ives 2009 p. 106; Loades 1996 pp. 33, 38
3   Bellamy 2005 pp. 146–147, 228
4   Higginbotham 2012a
5   Loades 1996 p. 226

*

John Dudley and his wife moved in reform-friendly circles,[1] which were also the circles of Anne Boleyn. The French humanist Nicolas Bourbon, a Boleyn *protégé*, counted the ten-year-old Henry Dudley among his pupils and exhorted his parents "to continue to follow the banners of Christ".[2] John indeed tried his best, suggesting to the queen reformed clergy for vacant positions.[3] However this world soon came crushing down; on 10 May 1536 he informed Lady Lisle at Calais:

> As touching the news that are here, I am sure it needeth not to write to you nor to my lord of them, for all the world knoweth them by this time. This day was indicted Mr. Norris, Mr. Weston, William Brereton, Markes[4] and my Lord of Rochford. And upon Friday next they shall be arraigned at Westminster. And the Queen herself shall be condemned by Parliament.[5]

Within days John could demonstrate his loyalty to the king by once again sitting in parliament for Kent. He was also assigned a contingent, under Thomas Howard, 3rd Duke of Norfolk, against the Pilgrimage of Grace later in the year. His task, though, was chiefly to carry letters between king and commander-in-chief and there was no fighting. In October 1536 he was made Sheriff for Staffordshire.[6] In July and August 1536 we find him at Calais visiting the Lord Deputy, his stepfather. On the way home John was assaulted by some Frenchmen who "took away his purse and letters."[7]

---

1 Loades 2008a. Robert Dudley later reminded a friend that he had always adhered to the reformed faith: "you know I was ever from my cradle brought up in it." (Adams 2008b).
2 Loades 2008a; Ives 2005 p. 287
3 Ives 2012 p. 143
4 Mark Smeaton.
5 Wilson 2005 p. 91
6 Loades 1996 pp. 33–34.
7 Loades 1996 p. 33; L&P 24 August 1536

Though John rented a London house at Holborn, he did not acquire a grand property of his own until 1550. Apart from Haldon in Kent, which he sold to Thomas Cromwell (who had twice earmarked him for the office of Vice-Chamberlain), the Dudleys possessed lands in Sussex and by the 1530s John had his eye firmly on Dudley Castle in Staffordshire. This ancient seat of his clan was owned by his second cousin, Baron Dudley, a man hopelessly in debt through his ancestors' great spending and his own financial incompetence.[1] John Dudley scratched up the huge sum of £7,500 through his City contacts and lent it to his relative who in turn mortgaged his castle to him. And Lord Dudley never paid a penny back; so John foreclosed after half a decade, and thus came into possession of Dudley Castle, where he immediately started impressive building works. It is likely that Jane and the children lived mostly at the castle during the late 1530s. The new Renaissance wing was a beautiful structure:

> a flight of steps leading up to a loggia fronted by a row of ionic columns ... gave unto a porch from which a door led into the great hall, twenty-four metres in length ... Morning and evening light streamed into this impressive space through large rectangular windows.[2]

John also built more private quarters: a great chamber and four or five bed chambers located over the large kitchen and bakery (so the family had it always warm). The other branch of the Dudley family were not amused by this change in their fortunes; their efforts to avoid the consequences of financial ruin (in the form of pleas to Henry VIII) having failed, they resorted to burglary: Lord Dudley's brother Arthur, a priest, "wrongfully entered into the castle of Dudley and thereupon brake up certain chests and coffers, then being in the said castle, wherein remained divers evidences, charters, writings, court rolls, ... etc. ... and took them away with him and keepeth them in his possession and custody".

---

1 Loades 2008a; Hawkyard 1982
2 Wilson 2005 p. 108

Unsurprisingly, he "at all times denied and utterly refused to return them".[1]

The dangers of 16th century life were not confined to robbery and burglary. Plague and smallpox were a constant threat, as John found out on a rare visit to his seat and family. Thomas Cromwell, the king's secretary, was immediately informed:

> Please it your Lordship; so it is that within two or three days after my coming home to Dudley, Andrew Flamoke and his son came thither to me, and the same night sickened both in a bed in my house, and by the next day at night, the son was dead full of the marks, and the father hath a blain ... they came both out of Gloucestershire from Mr. Poyntz, and whether they brought it from thence or by the way, God knoweth, for this country was as clear before their coming as any county in England.

Since Andrew Flamock was also keeper of Kenilworth Castle, another beautiful place John had a distinct liking for, he asked straightaway for the (possibly) now vacant office for himself:

> If it might please your good Lordship to be so good Lord unto me to be a mean for me to the King's highness for the office of Kenilworth, I were much bound to your Lordship, if not, your Lordship may do your pleasure for any other that you shall think meeter for it, for no man hath knowledge hereof by me but your Lordship. And sorry I am (as knoweth God) to send you word of such news, for the King's highness shall lose a tall man of him. His son died this last night, and he himself both raveth and hath the blain. No more to your Lordship at this time, but the merciful Lord have you in his merciful keeping, and all yours.

---

1 Wilson 2005 pp. 80–81

Scribbled in haste, as appeareth, the 21st of March in the morning, with the rude hand of your most bounden through life.

John Dudley[1]

*

The Dudleys' family life was absolutely scandal-free, and John was by all accounts a model husband. A poem of 1535 praised "the love and devotion with which you and your noble wife adorn the ties of marriage".[2] Still, the Dudley household was not a dour or dull place, nor was Jane only concerned with her pregnancies. In September 1537 she "feasted" at the court, "with right good dishes and great cheer", Anne and Katherine, Lord Lisle's stepdaughters.[3] Only a few weeks later "a book of the Quenes juelles" was compiled after Jane Seymour's death in childbirth; among the items listed were some beads given to "Lady Duddeley".[4]

---

1 Adlard 1870 p. 105
2 Ives 2009 p. 307
3 St. Clare Byrne 1983 p. 209
4 L&P XII Part 2 No. 973

4.
Voyage to Spain

In May 1537 arrived in England Don Diego de Mendoza, a Spanish diplomat and poet from a most illustrious house. Charles V had sent his new ambassador, temporarily replacing Eustace Chapuys, to negotiate a marriage for his cousin Mary. Nothing came of this project, but at some point during his 15-month stay in England, Mendoza stood godfather to Guildford Dudley,[1] the sixth son of John and Jane Dudley. On 12 October 1537 Henry VIII was likewise blessed with a son, the prince he and the country had yearned for so long. Three days later, among "all estates and gentlemen present at the christening", was listed "Sir John Dudley",[2] and he was chosen to bring the glad tidings to the emperor.

He travelled to Spain not by sea, but through France. This was not for lack of experience on the waters, for in January John had been appointed Vice-Admiral, and he did his job, which consisted chiefly of clearing the Channel from Breton pirates, with great diligence.[3]

> On coming to Boleyn [Boulogne] I chanced to find the Bretons that I took upon the sea, who tried to impeach me for the things my mariners took from them; whereupon the captain came out of the castle and beat them with his sword that it would have pitied a man to have seen it, and caused them to be put into a dungeon

---

1 Higginbotham 2011a; Loades 2013 p. 72
2 L&P XII Pt. 2 No. 911
3 Loades 1996 pp. 34–36

within the castle, although they had only come wandering about me, asking for some compensation.[1]

John clearly was a man with a heart. His diplomatic immunity spared him any further inconvenience, and he proceeded to Paris. At this juncture France and the Empire were drawing nearer together, even talking of peace (as John informed Cromwell); this alarmed Henry VIII, who feared to be left isolated, and so he offered himself as peace broker. In early November 1537 Charles V was staying in the northeast of Spain, at the former Templar castle of Monzón in Aragón. Sir Thomas Wyatt, Henry's resident ambassador, had just been in trouble for promoting the new faith – through distributing his own pamphlets – and for speaking bad of the pope in the emperor's presence.[2] Wyatt was now happy to greet his old friend and their audience with the emperor occurred around 8 November. Of this event John penned his own "Memorye":

> After the King's effectuous recommendations to the Emperor's Majesty by me declared and his Highness' letters delivered, the Emperor thanked God of the news, of which he was no less glad than he was of his own child which was born 20 Oct.,[3] the same present month that the King his brother's son was born in. Although he would have been glad if the benefit had been to his own blood, he was as rejoiced as if it had been by his aunt.[4] He had always a good opinion of the King's last marriage,[5] as much as he was cloyed with the other.[6] He trusted that things between the King and him would go the better for this, and prayed God to send the King's son long life.

---

1 L&P XII Pt. 2 No. 987
2 Brigden 2012 p. 347
3 Juan, who lived only five months.
4 Katherine of Aragon.
5 Jane Seymour.
6 Anne Boleyn.

When we perceived he had finished his answer and showed gladness we declared the stature and goodliness of the child, and who were the godfathers and godmothers. I declared I was sorry he had made no better answer to the King's ambassador[1] touching the overture for peace between him and the Most Christian King, which would have been acceptable to God and laudable to himself.

"Mr. Wiat" now interjected that "my fellow Mr. Dudeley here present hath the like commandment as I had", and that Henry VIII "would be right glad of a peace", yet that Charles seemed to doubt it as the English overture was not embraced. Charles replied that he had news that the King of France was amenable to peace. This, however, was just what John had been sent to prevent, an agreement between Charles and Francis without Henry: "I said I saw no great appearance of peace considering the French king's passing the mountains with so great an army". Dismissing this, the emperor pointed out that "the best men of war that ever he had" were already waiting for Francis should he cross into Italy. Charles assured Wyatt and Dudley that he would not make peace without consulting Henry first, then he was finished: "He asked how his cousin the lady Mary did."[2]

It was uppermost on Charles' agenda to achieve England's return to Rome, to end the "English schism". He offered to mediate between Henry and the Holy See, "if the king would". Wyatt and Dudley made clear to him that, quite apart from King Henry, the English people would never return to "the yoke … and that that mediation should be but vain". – That was Wyatt's version of their words, yet Charles got the impression that "nevertheless, the proposal did not seem altogether distasteful to them".[3] The papal nuncio was very hopeful and excited, praising the two English diplomats as "fine men". It was always clear to Wyatt and Dudley, however, that Henry's reconciliation to the papacy was not an option and, more importantly, that they could not afford to let

---
1 Wyatt.
2 L&P XII Pt. 2 No. 1053
3 Brigden 2012 pp. 347–348

anyone in England think that they had wavered on this issue for a second. Still, keen to defuse the notion of England's isolation, they somehow managed to leave Charles dreaming of King Henry contributing to Christianity's crusade against the Turk.[1] This particular chimera lasted less than a fortnight; Charles threatened to withdraw his ambassador from England a few days after John Dudley had left the Imperial court, leaving Wyatt on his own again.

On arriving in Lyon, John heard rumours that Wyatt had been arrested on the emperor's orders; this was not true, but John himself was now taken prisoner by the Chancellor of France and the Cardinal of Tournon, who had been expecting him on the orders of the French king. Having smelt the rat, John had already sent his own messenger to Paris in guise of a merchant, so that the most important news should reach England. Francis' comment on hearing this was that Dudley "had perhaps learnt some subtlety in Spain".[2] But all English messengers were being stopped now, as John wrote home on 26 November, still detained in Lyon. He complained that his news would be "cold" by now and that his treatment by the French, so dishonourable to the King of England, was in "every mouth".[3]

He was back in England for Christmas, and Henry VIII himself informed Sir Thomas Wyatt of how the issue had played out: "Sir John Dudley, late ambassador to the Emperor," had reported the emperor's kind entertainment of him. But if Charles was wondering why he had not heard from the King of England recently, Wyatt was to explain that Dudley had been held up at Lyon for 12 days by Cardinal Tournon, to the great displeasure of the French king.[4]

---

1 Brigden 2012 pp. 348–349
2 Brigden 2012 p. 349; L&P XII Pt. 2 No. 1253
3 Brigden 2012 p. 349; L&P XII Pt. 2 No. 1133
4 L&P XII Pt. 2 No. 1249

5.
Lord Admiral

In June 1539 we find John Dudley busy extracting Wyatt's arrears in ambassadorial diets from the Exchequer.[1] At the end of the year, towards the coming of Anne of Cleves, John got a new appointment, that of Master of the Queen's Horse; his wife continued as lady-in-waiting, as she had done with some of the earlier queens. On 3 January 1540 Henry's new consort arrived at London, "syr Iohan Dudley Master of her horses leadynge her spare palfrey".[2] Then, on 1 May, at Anne's last performance as queen, he fell from his horse:

> This yeare, on Maie daie, their was a great triumphe of j[o]usting at the Kinges place at Westminster, which said j[o]ustes had bene proclaymed in Fraunce, Flanders, Scotland, and Spaine, for all commers that will come against the chalenges of England, which were Sir John Dudley, knight, Sir Thomas Seymor, knight, Sir Thomas Poyninges, knight, Sir George Carow, knight, Anthony Kingston, esquier, and Richard Crumwell, esquier, which said chalengers came into the listes that daie rytchlie apparayled and their horses trapped, all in white velvett, with certaine knightes and gentlemen riding afore them apparayled all in white velvett and white sarcenett, and all their servantes in white sarcenet dobletts and hosin, after the Burgonion[3] fashion; and their came in to just

---

1 Loades 1996 p. 41
2 Loades 1996 p. 42
3 Burgundian.

against them the said Maie daie of defendantes: the Earle of Surrey being the furmost, Lord William Haywarde, and Lord Crumwell, sonne and heire of Thomas Crumwell, Earle of Essex, and Chamberlaine of Englande, with other, which were [all] rytchlie apparayled; and that daie Sir John Dudley was overthrowen in the fielde by mischance of his horse by one Mr. Breme defendant; nevertheles, he brake many speares valiantlie after that; and after the said j[o]ustes were donne the said chalengers rode to Durham Place, where they kept open howseholde, which said place was richlie behanged, and great cubbordes of plate, where they feasted the Kinges Majestie, the Queenes Grace and her ladies, with all the court, and for all other commers that would resort to their said place, where they had all delicious meates and drinckes so plenteouslie as might be, and such melodie of minstrelsey, and were served everie meale with their owne servantes after the manner of warr, their drume warning all the officers of householde against everie meale which was donne, to the great honor of this realme.[1]

Within weeks the queen, Anne of Cleves, had turned into the king's sister and the Chamberlain of England, Thomas Cromwell, had lost his head. John continued to serve as Master of the Horse, to Katherine Howard.[2] This young queen fell victim to her love life, the religious reformers jumping at the opportunity to destroy the traditionally-minded Howards. Katherine was brought to Syon House, a former monastery and now property of Edward Seymour, now Earl of Hertford, where she was interrogated by Thomas Cranmer. John was present at this interview and then delivered her written confession to Henry. He also informed the king of what else had happened – verbally, for Cranmer had lacked time "to write everything" and left it "to the bearer, Sir John Dudlay, to relate." John was certainly trusted by the reformers, as well as the

---
1   Wriothesley I pp. 116–117
2   Warnicke 2012 p. 64; Loades 2013a p. 201

king.[1] His next task was to bring the Lady Mary, the king's daughter, to her brother the prince, the queen's household being on the point of dissolution.[2] It was about the last thing he did in capacity of his office. About this time his nine-year-old son, Robert, must have met the Lady Elizabeth, the king's other daughter, "for they had first become friends before she was eight years old".[3] Their favourite topic of conversation was marriage.

In the parliament that condemned Katherine Howard John Dudley sat for Staffordshire, while Thomas Wyatt had succeeded him in Kent as Knight of the Shire.[4] Henry's fifth queen lost her pretty head on 13 February 1542, and two and a half weeks later Arthur Plantagenet also died in the Tower. A religious conservative, John's stepfather had not managed to stay clear of several suspected conspiracies. After nearly two years of imprisonment, he suffered a heart attack on receiving the news that the king had ordered his release. John could now realistically hope to become a viscount, as his patent read, "by the right of his mother Lady Elizabeth, sister and heir to Sir John Grey, Viscount Lisle, who was late wife to Arthur Plantagenet, Viscount Lisle, deceased". The ceremony was held on 12 March 1542, John being supported by the Earl of Hertford (Edward Seymour) on the right and the Lord Admiral (Sir John Russell) on the left. The patent was read by Thomas Wriothesley, the king's secretary: "and at the words Creamus etc. the king put on his mantel and robe assisted with the other lords and then … all things done the King delivered the patent to the said Viscount, who gave his Majesty most humble thanks."[5]

John also sought to advance his brother Andrew in the king's service. Having transacted business with Thomas Howard, Duke of Norfolk,[6] he had found Andrew a place in Norfolk's household, who in his turn took him on as an officer of the Exchequer. When Lord Treasurer Norfolk answered complaints of corruption, the

---

1 L&P XVI No. 1325; Loades 1996 pp. 47–48; Wilson 2005 pp. 117–118
2 L&P 11 November 1541
3 Adams 2008b
4 Ives 2009 p. 103; Miller 1982. Wyatt died in October 1542 on another diplomatic trip.
5 Loades 1996 pp. 48–49
6 Byrne 2014 p. 78. He bought a manor from the duke for £98 in 1538.

33

duke maintained that he had "never taken bribes for these offices, though all his predecessors did," nor employed any servant of his own, except Andrew Dudley and Edward Bellingham.[1]

Only a month after his ennoblement, John Dudley was sent with Sir Richard Southwell to the north to inspect the fortress at Berwick-on-Tweed. They found the building works to be unsatisfactory.[2] In June, Henry VIII signed another treaty with the emperor, Charles V; this meant a new war with France, after nearly 20 years. It also meant new hostilities with Scotland, so Henry sent the Duke of Norfolk to the north to find a pretext for some pre-emptive action. 10,000 men were sent over the border under Edward Seymour, Earl of Hertford, in an "immensely destructive" raid.[3] Hertford was to be the new Warden General of the Marches but refused the appointment on the grounds of his "unsuitability". So, Henry selected John Dudley to serve as Warden General and sent him from Hampton Court to Newcastle.[4] John was to find his "predecessor" in place, but he had not arrived yet when he heard of a Scottish defeat at Solway Moss. – The King of Scots, James V, had retaliated by sending 20,000 men into Northwest England.[5] On 8 December, the child's actual birthday, John heard that the Scottish queen, Mary of Guise, had given birth to a son; on 12 December he corrected this to a daughter, "a very weak child", not likely to live, he thought.[6] Within a fortnight, however, the news was that the King of Scots himself was dead, and that his baby daughter would succeed him. "But seing nowe that God hath thus disposed his will of the said Kinge of Skottes, I thought yt shuld not be your majesties honor, that we your souldiors shuld make warre or ynvade upon a dedd bodye or uppon a wydowe, or on a yonge sucling his daughter," John Dudley informed his sovereign, thinking it right to give the Scots some respite, "specially upon the tyme of the fyneralles of the said kinge, whiche tyme all his realme muste lament the same. Wherfore considering the same, and also

---

1   L&P 16 October 1540
2   Loades 1996 p. 49
3   Loades 2015 p. 117
4   Loades 2015 p. 117
5   Loades 2015 pp. 117–118; Loades 1996 p. 51
6   Loades 1996 p. 52.

knowing the valyant courage that ys in your moste roiall and kinglye harte ... I have thought good to staye the stroke of your sworde untill your majesties pleasure be ferther knowen to me in that bihalf."[1]

"This night at midnight, oon of myne owne espielles [spies] came unto me out of Scotland". The man reported that the King of Scots was not only dead, but had died of poison and been secretly buried, and that the earls of Huntly, Moray, and Arran had taken upon them the government of the realm. Scotland, surely, posed no danger to England in these times: The Laird of Fernherst, John wrote, on hearing of the king's death, went straight to Jedburgh to remove "two grett pecys of ordenaunce, and brought theym to his owne house"; the Abbot of Jedburgh took the rest of the cannons, likewise carrying them "to his owne house." – "Yt apeyreth by this that they mynde not somoche the defence of the countrey as they do to defend oon agaynst an other."[2]

There was even better news: "The pryncers lately borne ys a lyve, and good liking; ... I wolde she and her nourse were in my lorde prynce house."[3] – Edward need look no further for his bride.

*

Scotland indeed was in disarray, "wonderfully consumed and wasted, especially hay and corn", John observed.[4] The political situation was fluid amid night time raids, squabbling Scottish nobles, and a regency council that was not very much in charge. On the other side of the border, Henry's representatives had no real influence, lacking a natural following in the north parts. This made them trustworthy in Henry's eyes, but it did not solve the problem.[5] John had as little experience on the borders as had Edward Seymour, therefore Henry had charged the Bishop of Durham, Cuthbert Tunstall, to assist him, and John was grateful of his counsel. But Tunstall was summoned away in January 1543.

1 Hamilton Papers I p. 342
2 Hamilton Papers I p. 342
3 Hamilton Papers I p. 342
4 Loades 1996 p. 52
5 Merriman 2000 p. 68

35

Viscount Lisle did not feel entirely confident in his position.[1] He warned the English council that "your lordships dothe knowe my bringing up; I have never byn practysed nor experymented in no mattiers of counsaill before this tyme". He conceded that it was "more esyer to conduce those affaires" in "open warr" than in the current situation.[2] Still, Lisle and Hertford did not lose all humanity before Henry's commandments: When Lisle received orders to sent Scottish prisoners to the galleys (which in effect was little better than a death penalty) they thought it better "not to put into execution the said proclamations"; they had given the issue lots of "consultation, reasoning, and debating" and probably concluded that the danger of Scottish and French reprisals was considerable.[3]

In his appraisal of the Scottish situation, John Dudley's evangelical outlook also showed: He suggested to the Earl of Arran, the current Scottish regent, that

> yt wold not do amisse, yf your lordship did lett slipp emonges the people in this tyme, the Bible and New Testament in Englishe, wherby they may perceyve the truthe, ... and if you have non in your own tonge, I will help to gett you som out of England.[4]

In February 1543 the religiously conservative Duke of Suffolk, Charles Brandon, arrived in the north as the king's lieutenant, and it was enclosed in a letter to Suffolk that John sent his letter to the Regent Arran. Henry VIII, meanwhile, reshuffled offices. He appointed Edward Seymour, Earl of Hertford, Lord Admiral; it occurred to him, however, that Hertford was Prince Edward's uncle and that there was a better post for him, that of Great Chamberlain of England (which was entirely ceremonial). So, after only three weeks Henry needed another Lord Admiral, and Viscount Lisle came to mind.[5]

---

1 Beer 1973 pp. 14, 17–18
2 Hamilton Papers I p. 394
3 Beer 1973 p. 15
4 Hamilton Papers I p. 424
5 L&P XVIII Pt. 1 No. 19

Only in April John returned to the south, when he was admitted to the Privy Council. He also received the Order of the Garter and soon travelled to Windsor with his fellow new knights, Sir William Parr and Sir William Paulet. On 6 May 1543 they were invested in a mantle of dark blue velvet lined with white satin in a ceremony overseen by the Earl of Hertford.[1]

King Henry had decided that his six-year-old son, Edward, should wed the Scottish queen, Mary, who was about six months old, thereby uniting the British kingdoms to England's advantage. In July 1543 this was agreed in the Treaty of Greenwich. However, by the end of the year the Scottish regent, Arran, had shown his sense of political survival by changing sides and the Scottish parliament turned pro-French, repudiating the Treaty of Greenwich. This meant another war; Henry's wooing would be rough.[2]

In the 1544 campaign against Scotland the English force under Edward Seymour was supported by a fleet commanded by John Dudley. John sailed north with 68 ships, 11 of them warships, the remaining 57 transport vessels. He landed the troops near Leith on 3 May, joining Hertford's main army.[3] After plundering Leith and taking two of their ships, the *Salamander* and the *Unicorn*, several heralds from Edinburgh turned up, offering surrender on terms. Hertford declined, promising good treatment on unconditional surrender and threatening utter destruction in case of resistance. The intimidated provost and council of Edinburgh agreed to let the English in, but when the soldiers arrived before the gates there was fire from some of the houses, the burghers having resolved to defend their city.[4] The main gate was made of iron. But "the ... lord admyrall ... caused to lay ordenaunce to the said gate" and "after three or four shottes of a culveryn, the gate flewe oppen, and

---

1 Loades 1996 p. 57; Scard 2011 p. 93
2 Loades 2015 pp. 118–119
3 Loades 2015 pp. 119–120
4 Hamilton Papers II pp. 364–367

our men entred the towne with suche good courage, as all the enemyes fled awaye".[1]

The English troops sacked the city, including the church and royal palace of Holyrood, but they could not get at the castle, and even had to take cannon fire from there. Within ten days the whole expedition plundered its way back to Berwick, loading the looted treasures and guns on their ships. The Lord Admiral set sails for London,[2] carrying a letter of recommendation by the Earl of Hertford full of praise and with a somewhat surprising request:

> Pleasith Your Highness to be advised that, for as much as my Lord Admiral repaireth unto your Majesty, I can do no less than to recommend him unto your Highness as one that hath served you hardly, wisely, diligently, painfully, and as obediently as any that I have seen, most humbly beseeching your Majesty, that he may perceive by Your Highness that I have not forgotten him.[3]

*

Henry was pleased and as John returned the king was busy preparing his next war, an invasion of France led by himself. John was to oversee the English build-up of forces and over 30,000 men were shipped to Calais under his watch.[4] The military advance started in June 1544, and on 14 September the town of Boulogne capitulated before Henry VIII. On the 30th, the king returned to England, but not before dubbing John's eldest son, Henry, a knight. The king left the dukes of Suffolk and Norfolk behind and appointed his Lord Admiral Captain of Boulogne and Senechal of the Boulonnais.[5] His tasks were to rebuild the fortifications to King Henry's design and to fend off French attacks by sea and land.[6] But

---

1 Hamilton Papers II p. 367
2 Loades 1996 p. 63
3 Wilson 1981 p. 21
4 Ives 2009 p. 101; Loades 1996 p. 64
5 Ives 2009 p. 101; Loades 1996 pp. 65, 67
6 Ives 2009 p. 101

John was not particularly happy with his new position, and he was especially concerned to retain the admiralty. The latter, he thought, was "an office of honour, of estimation and of profit, and within the realm". Still, he apparently planned for an extended stay in France, requesting "to have some arable land, pasture, mead and woods for the provision of my house at reasonable rent." He also wanted those provisions custom free and was already asking for the use of country estates and parks "for recreation in time of peace".[1] However, it was not all sweet life in France, and while he may have been glad to see the back of the two dukes who had left him in command, he was faced with a disgruntled king and council over his repeated demands for more supplies. In a drawn-out correspondence, which was at least in part handled by Bishop Stephen Gardiner, he was told to be more careful and consume less.[2]

John also lost his eldest son at this time. Henry Dudley died 19 years old, either at the siege of Boulogne or from disease.[3] His next son, John, was a boy of 14 and possibly still at home with his grieving mother. The elder John Dudley's intellectual friend, John Leland, composed a Latin epitaph on Henry Dudley, which his father had printed in London the next year.[4]

*

Unsurprisingly, the Lord Admiral's brother, Andrew Dudley, served in the royal navy as well, and in 1545 he was entrusted with the command of a new ship of 300 tonnes and a crew of 160 men, the *Swallow*.[5] In June the French navy was busy in the Channel disrupting the English reinforcement of Boulogne. The Lord Admiral's plan was to confront the French navy in the Seine and to destroy a large part of it with fire-ships, but the attempt misfired: His 160 ships with 12,000 men on board had to retreat before the weather. John Dudley's French counterpart, Admiral Claude

---

1 Loades 1996 pp. 65–66
2 Loades 1996 pp. 66–67
3 Genelogies of the Erles of Lecestre f. 18r; Loades 1996 p. 67
4 L&P XX Pt. 2 Appendix 1
5 Löwe 2004; Moorhouse 2006 p. 324

d'Annebault, answered the attack by sending no less than 324 ships in July. The English fleet was still in the harbour of Portsmouth when the French vessels appeared in the Solent on 19 July.[1] On the 17th, King Henry, who was inspecting his forces and fortresses, had shown the new Imperial ambassador, François van der Delft, his biggest ship, the *Henri Grace a Dieu*. Popularly known as *Great Harry*, it was the Lord Admiral's flagship and had once upon a time carried the Emperor Charles V. Van der Delft reported how "the admiral received me very civilly, and asked me to dinner for the following day, where I was very handsomely entertained with three or four Knights of the Garter."[2] The next day, Sunday the 19th, the French fleet deployed in battle array.

English resistance was successful, wiping out a French landing force on the Isle of Wight; and d'Annebault started to retreat on watching Henry's fleet coming out in full fighting order. Amid changeable winds, fire was opened from both sides. Within minutes the Vice-Admiral's flagship, the *Mary Rose,* sank when her opened lower gun ports were flooded as she suddenly keeled over in a gust of wind. Some 400 men were drowned, among them Sir George Carew, the Vice-Admiral, who had been appointed only the other day.[3]

Henry had seen it all from his recently built fort, Southsea Castle. The *Mary Rose* was in full view, and the *Great Harry* was next seaward, so John Dudley would also have been in a position to oversee the tragedy. His first duty was the pursuit of the French fleet as the threat of an invasion was not over yet. But first on his mind was probably the salvage of the *Mary Rose*; it was hoped that the ship could be raised from the shallow water and re-used again. Henry's old friend, the Duke of Suffolk, whom the king had entrusted with the operation, hired a group of Venetian experts. Some three weeks later, though, they told the Lord Admiral that they could not raise the ship and, worse, they had broken the

---

[1] Ives 2009; Loades 1996 p. 69; Hutchinson 2006 p. 117
[2] CSP Span 24 July 1545. While Henry showed van der Delft around the *Great Harry*, it clearly appears from the report that the ambassador did not dine with the king on board, as claimed in several modern accounts.
[3] Ives 2009 p. 101; Loades 1996 p. 70; Hutchinson 2006 pp. 117–118; Moorhouse 2006 p. 253

mainmast on trying. They were now asking for six more days to try another method. John Dudley was not inclined to lose more time and money on the *Mary Rose*, but he understood how much the king treasured her, and so gave them green light. He was also keen on securing the precious guns and the rigging. Having got a good part of these, he "postponed" the salvage of the wreck for good.[1]

*

Henry stayed a little longer at the Hampshire coast, mourning the loss of his favourite ship and, always the king, poking his nose into everything. He gave a lot of thought to a list of his navy's captains and John described to William Paget, the king's secretary, how Peter Carew "with piteous moan besought me that he might not be shifted out of his ship." The Lord Admiral also had to deal with an epidemic of "the bloody flux" among his men.[2] But on 11 August 1545 he finally took up the pursuit of d'Annebault's fleet, which had sporadically, and ineffectually, been raiding the English coast. On 15 August there was an exchange of fire of over 200 shots, but it did not result in any real damage. Nothing much happened the next day, Sunday, both fleets anchoring within a league. Then John reported angrily from the "*Harry*" on Monday, 17 Aug. at 9 p.m." how on daybreak the French had been "as far into the wind of us as we might escry them out of my main top," vanishing into "the seaward."[3]

It was somewhat mysterious why the French had returned to home waters so quickly, but when the Lord Admiral's ships followed them to the coast of Normandy, it became obvious that the French crews were suffering from the "plague". John returned to Portsmouth, but he was back in Normandy in September, where his troops burned the fishing port of Le Tréport, killing "all the men and women they could catch." Meanwhile, the "plague" was now decimating the English fleet, some dying literally before

---

1 Moorhouse 2006 pp. 252, 257–258; Loades 1996 p. 70–71. The salvage of precious materials from the ship was taken up again in 1549 and 1552, and £559 8s 7d were spent on it in total (Clabby 2015).
2 Moorhouse 2006 p. 259; L&P 7 August 1545
3 L&P XX Pt. 2 No. 151; Loades 1996 p. 71; Ives 2009 p. 101

John's eyes "when they have come to receive their money full of the marks." Back in Portsmouth, he left for the court on 18 September, leaving the new Vice-Admiral, Sir Thomas Seymour – who had had a bad night and was "evill at ease" – in place.[1]

*

As Lord Admiral, John Dudley was responsible for creating the so-called Council for Marine Causes, the later Navy Board, which for the first time co-ordinated the various tasks of maintaining the navy functioning; thus English naval administration became the most efficient in Europe.[2] Of course, a perennial problem was to extract enough provisions and money out of a watchful and sometimes stingy central government; when £2,000 were missing in April 1546, Secretary Paget demanded of the Lord Admiral that "if you know where it is bestowed, you will do well to write to me thereof."[3] John's answer was that he had borrowed this amount "in his own name" and the council had countersigned it and that it had been repaid, and "other than this I never meddled with his Majesty's money, nor never desired to meddle with any of his Highness' money, I can so evil keep my own."[4]

As is shown by the fighting orders he gave out in August 1545, as a commander at sea John was abreast of the most advanced developments: Squadrons of ships, ordered by size and firepower, were to manoeuvre in formation, using co-ordinated gunfire. – "It is to be considered that the ranks must keep such order in sailing that none impeach another." – Henry's navy had caught up with France and the Empire.[5]

---

1   L&P XX Pt. 2 No. 391; Loades 1996 p. 72; Moorhouse 2006 p. 267–268
2   Loades 1996 p. 85
3   L&P XXI Pt. 1 No. 527; Beer 1973 p. 33
4   L&P XXI Pt. 1 No. 553
5   Loades 1996 pp. 71

6.
Companion of Kings

On 22 August 1545 Henry VIII lost his brother-in-law and best friend, Charles Brandon, Duke of Suffolk. Since 1540, Suffolk had been the Great Master of the Household, a position modelled on its French equivalent,[1] but akin to the former post of Lord Steward with extended powers. John Dudley clearly felt he should fill the void caused by the duke's death, although he wrote to Paget, the Secretary, that "I would the king had appointed me to serve in the meanest room under some nobleman of reputation, for all the world knows I am not of estimation for so weighty a charge."[2]

Yet only five days later he thanked Paget for helping him obtain some exchange of lands with the king, it did not matter where, for "all places in the realm are indifferent to me", but "I must be holpen or sink." He had also found a document Paget had asked for, concerning the Earl of Hertford's land transactions, and while there, he had also found "the gift of the house from the King to the Earl of Hartforde and his wife." He went on hinting broadly at his wish for the Great Mastership, and we learn how the angling for a great court position was done in practice:

> As touching the words ... which you understood not, I trust there is nor shall be occasion to give you any further understanding; but the meaning was that, at

---
1 L&P XIII Pt. 1 No. 503
2 Loades 1996 p. 72

our last being togethers, at which time I moved you of a matter concerning an office *in commendam*, which you thought to be no great advancement in it, and, upon further communication between us, you moved a question unto me what I thought by such a thing, touching that which was lately in a great man's hands[1] and now is determined upon one that at our then communing was said to be sore sick,[2] if such an alteration should eftsoons happen again, which God forbid, in case you thought it a convenient suit for your friend and could bring it to pass, I might then leave this which I have, &c., as it is further in my said letter. Whether to move or omit it I leave to your discretion. Albeit the thing is no higher than what I have, its being before occupied by such a personage[3] would give it more estimation to the world. Take not this for ambition, for, were it not my duty to offer continual service, I had rather seek no promotion.[4]

It was indeed William Paulet, Lord St. John, who became the next Great Master of the Household, not John Dudley, Viscount Lisle. However, it was not just John himself who believed in his growing prestige. A high-ranking servant of the emperor who had just paid a visit to England, the President of the Council of Flanders, Sieur d'Eyck, also expected John Dudley to step into the Duke of Suffolk's feet.[5] On a purely personal and very limited level this appears to have happened, for Henry around this time selected John as his preferred partner in playing cards.[6] Presumably, this was an expensive occupation, but Henry had placed his Lord Admiral in a position to afford it. With lands worth £1,376 the Viscount Lisle was among the richest people of the realm, straight behind the Earl of Hertford.[7]

1   The Great Mastership.
2   William Paulet, Lord St. John.
3   Such as the Duke of Suffolk.
4   L&P XX Pt. 2 No. 427
5   Loades 1996 p. 73
6   CSP Span 12 March 1546
7   Loades 1996 p. 73

His standing was also apparent from the godparents he managed to win for his children: on 26 November François van der Delft stood sponsor to John's 12th child, a daughter, almost certainly called Katherine; the godmothers, who attended in person, were the Lady Mary and the Duchess of Suffolk, recently widowed.[1] John and Jane Dudley were also good friends of Queen Katherine Parr, Henry's sixth wife. On 20 June 1543 John informed William Parr that William's sisters, Katherine and Anne, had been seen in the company of "my Lady Mary's Grace and my Lady Elizabeth", and that other news "is none". Only three weeks later, his wife, Jane, was among Katherine's three favourite ladies when she married Henry, the other ladies being Edward Seymour's wife, Anne, and Katherine Brandon, Duchess of Suffolk.[2]

As appeared from the guests at his daughter's christening, John was highly acceptable to the Imperial party, and so in March 1546 Andrew Dudley, by now Equerry of the Stable, made a trip to the Habsburg regent in Brussels, Mary of Hungary, to deliver Henry's gift of hackney horses, greyhounds and running dogs.[3]

In April John himself went to France for peace negotiations. His fellow diplomat was Sir William Paget, who according to John was "no seaman".[4] Henry's delegates did well. In the Peace of Camp, concluded on 7 June 1546, the French king acknowledged Henry's title of Supreme Head of the Church of England, no mean achievement. An even greater was that Henry could keep Boulogne for the next eight years! (The English would then have to hand it back, but only for a recompense of 2,000,000 gold crowns, a sum the French were unlikely ever to find in their treasury).[5] Both things, the title and Boulogne, were hugely important to Henry.

John Dudley got on famously with Claude d'Annebault, who had greeted him saying that God had preserved them for better things than war, such as making peace.[6] John thought his counterpart to be "a right proper man, and very gentle and well

---

1 CSP Span 30 November 1545
2 Starkey 2003 pp. 713, 714
3 L&P XXI Pt. 1 No. 437, 444
4 Gammon 1973 p. 170. Paget was known to get always seasick.
5 Beer 1973 pp. 35–36; Moorhouse 2006 p. 278
6 Moorhouse 2006 p. 265

spoken, and very fine in his apparel."[1] Yet, success was not all about niceties; when John suspected the Admiral of France of manoeuvres which might have led to a renewal of hostilities, he suddenly put to sea and made a show of English strength before returning to the negotiating table a few days later. Paget was annoyed by this unforeseen interruption of proceedings, but King Henry was very pleased and the snubbed Secretary had to accept that the Lord Admiral now effectively took the lead.[2] John still had to learn the business of the diplomat: He had made some remarks about his sovereign he feared could be ill construed. Immediately he wrote to Secretary Petre to ask him to "wropp upp my follys to gythers and kepe theym to your selffe."[3]

On the whole, life as the king's peace commissioner was not bad, though, he and Paget enjoying red deer and delicious puddings, the latter being especially to John's taste. Paget may have overindulged, as he became sick; when he was better, John wrote: "I am glad you have taken the purge. The ladies and all the rest … long for your return".[4]

*

Paget and Dudley returned to England on 14 June, but John was back in July, and the good life started afresh. He led a delegation of thirty who were to witness the ratification of the Treaty of Camp by Francis I. The party included the venerable Bishop Tunstall of Durham, as well as Andrew Dudley. After some delays caused by protocol, they were wined and dined wherever they went. On 25 July they were welcomed at St. Denis by Monsieur de Laval, "one of the greatest inheritors of all France", as John noted. At St. Denis alone they had to endure three banquets: one at the famous abbey (the kings' of France final resting place); "a great supper" at their lodgings; and one the next day, "all at the town's cost".[5] On 26 July

---

1   L&P XXI Pt. 1 No. 837
2   Loades 1996 pp. 77–78
3   Beer 1973 pp. 34–35
4   Beer 1973 pp. 34, 35
5   Beer 1973 p. 35

the party proceeded to Paris, where they were welcomed to the Louvre in the evening:

> The Cardinal of Meudon made us great cheer last night, with meat and drink, and good company of ladies and gentlewomen, but the plays and pastime were spoilt by the crowd.[1]

The English guests lived on Francis' expenses, who provided them with a "maistre dostell" for their table.[2] On 30 July they arrived at Fontainebleau, where they were to meet the king and the Dauphin. John and his fellow commissioners got "richly appointed chambers", the lesser dignitaries were "well lodged in the house". Their first glimpse of the king was in the evening, watching "the dancing and pastime" in his presence. Francis invited them to the hunt in the morning, where they dined at a cottage in the forest. Back at the château, after supper they "were desired" to attend at the dance, "finding a chamber richly hanged and the young noblemen and young ladies wonderful richly apparelled."[3]

The treaty was ratified by Francis early next morning, Sunday, 1 August 1546. In the château's chapel the French king read the oath in a loud voice, declaring the English king "Defender of the Faith and Supreme Head of the Church of England and Ireland" in the presence of six cardinals. The only point he had objected to was Henry's claim to be King of France.

There followed dinner with the king and the cardinals of Lorraine and Ferrara. Francis then talked about his library, and John Dudley, Claude d'Annebault, and Nicholas Wotton, appointed Henry's new ambassador, were called up, "and the conversation was of books which the King had caused to be translated out of Greek." (If John did understand little of the Greek, at least his French must have been excellent). The king next showed John round his château, leading him by the hand. They inspected "a very fair great gallery" as well as the baths with a sauna-like implementation. In the afternoon there was "great jousting"

---
1 Beer 1973 pp. 35–36
2 L&P XXI Pt. 1 No. 1406. Maître d'Hôtel.
3 L&P XXI Pt. 1 No. 1405

arranged by the "Dolphin", Henri. He sent for John, "to do him the honour to give him a staff, the which I did"; in recompense the Dauphin sent him a jennet in harness. The night saw another great banquet, "given to the Queen and ladies, followed by two rich masques, the King being in the one and the Dolphyn in the other." The next day the King insisted on taking them to hunt the hare and the boar.[1]

On 3 August the English party left "Fountayn le Bleau"; back in "Parrys", they received diplomatic presents sent by the King of France and met up with the French Admiral, who would sail from Rouen to England in order to witness Henry's ratification of the peace. Another dinner, at the Admiral's house and on behalf of the French king, was scheduled for the next day. Meanwhile, John reported, they had "exceeding great" cheer and they were well provided for by the "master dotelles". John planned to be back with Henry two or three days before d'Annebault would turn up at the English court and so had to return post haste. The French Admiral, he wrote, would only stay for three or four days;[2] enough time for another round of banquets.

Meanwhile, his wife Jane had asked John for some "goldsmith's work from Parys", but

> I pray God I may have enough to bring home myself. I assure you this journey hath been extremely chargeable, after such sort as I think I shall be fain to hide me in a corner for vii year after. I have borrowed here in Parrys almost 500*l*., and all little enough.

Clearly, he had bought so many presents already that he could not afford any more, and anyway:

> The great ladies of this Court which be young, and also the young noblemen, be exceeding rich in apparel. The ladies that be anything in years weareth

---
1 L&P XXI Pt. 1 No. 1405
2 L&P XXI Pt. 1 No. 1405

neither goldsmith work neither jewels, nor none other but those which be duchess, marquess or princess.[1]

All this he did rather write to Paget than his wife – "lack[ing] leisure to write to my wife" – after all, Jane was now 38 and "only" a viscountess.

*

John returned from France on 12 August, eight days before d'Annebault arrived at Greenwich. Despite all the "plentifulness, magnificence, riches and also the good order" of the festivities, the two admirals managed to quarrel over the restitution of a captured French galley, exchanging hot words but remaining friends.[2]

The leaders of the religious reform party were now Edward Seymour, Earl of Hertford, and John Dudley, Viscount Lisle.[3] There was also William Parr, Earl of Essex, the queen's brother. At the court of Katherine Parr the reformers' influence naturally was on the increase, and in the summer of 1546 the conservatives around Stephen Gardiner, the Bishop of Winchester, sought to regain some of their former strength when they took up the case of Anne Askew, an outspoken, "heretical" former housewife with excellent court contacts. The proceedings against her were already well advanced when William Parr and John Dudley – nervous that she should name the ladies that had befriended her – tried to convince her to adopt the doctrines of the Henrician church:

> Then came my lord Lisle, my lord Essex, and the bishop of Winchester, requiring me earnestly that I should confess the sacrament to be flesh, blood, and bone. Then, said I, to my lord Parr and my lord Lisle, that it was a great shame for them to counsel contrary to their knowledge. Whereunto, in few words, they did say, that they would gladly all things were well.[4]

---

1 L&P XXI Pt. 1 No. 1406
2 Beer 1973 p. 38; L&P XXI Pt. 1 No. 1530
3 CSP Span VIII No. 386
4 Foxe V p. 544

Obviously, Dudley and Parr were not made of the stuff of martyrs, but they tried to rescue Anne from the terrible torture and death that lay ahead of her. In September, as the French ambassador informed Admiral d'Annebault, John struck Gardiner in the face during a full meeting of the council. This was a grave offence, and he was lucky to escape with a month's leave from court, supposedly being ill.[1] A reason may have been that he was counted among "certain persons [who] had come into great favour with the King". He was allegedly so ill he could not "peruse a letter", though. Intriguingly, the privy council held meetings at his home.[2]

*

As the king's health declined in late 1546, Edward Seymour and John Dudley played their parts in Henry's strike against the conservative Howards, whose ambition, he felt, jeopardized his heir's future. Thomas Howard, Earl of Surrey, the Duke of Norfolk's heir, a great poet and haughty man, looked down on Henry's supposedly low-born ministers. Despite his undoubtedly noble decent, John, Viscount Lisle, was such a self-made man in Surrey's eyes, although not to the extent of Sir William Paget, whom he called a "catchpole" to his face.[3] On 12 July 1546 John had received a letter from the earl, who was one of his fellow commanders in Henry's army. John told Paget how perplexed he was by this peace of writing by a poet:

> I do send you herewith a letter which my Lord of Surrey sent unto my lodging this morning, wherein is contained so many parables that I do not understand it; which letter (if you think it meet), I require you to show unto the King's Majesty ... also to send me your

---

[1] Loades 1996 pp. 81–82
[2] Beer 1973 pp. 39–40
[3] Spanish Chronicle p. 147. "He called him catchpole (which means bailiff) because his father had been a constable, and Paget was very much abashed, and hold his peace."

advice touching an answer, which I have briefly made unto the same letter, the copy whereof I do send you.[1]

On 2 December, Henry Howard, Earl of Surrey, was arrested for supposed heraldic offences. His servant, Ellis, said to his interrogator, Thomas Wriothesley, that the letter had been about "a discord" between his master and "my Lord Admiral"; also, Ellis explained, Surrey had never spoken against any of the Lords of the Council, with the exception of John Dudley. To him "he did write his mind in a letter".[2]

Surrey had quartered the royal arms with his own, which could be interpreted as entertaining ambitions for the crown. At some point he seems to have obliterated the offensive evidence, and apparently at some point tried to escape from the Tower, unsuccessfully. At his trial, before his peers, on 13 January 1547, Surrey's defence was interrupted by John Dudley, who asked him two questions and received a reply he would not forget:

> "If you be not guilty and meant no ill, why did you put the cover over the painting, and why did you attempt to break out of prison?" – "I tried to get out", said the Earl, "to prevent myself from coming to pass in which I am now; and you my lord, know well that however right a man may be they always find the fallen one guilty."[3]

After six hours of consultation by the jury, William Paget slipped out of the Guildhall and on his return brought a message from the king which he passed to the jurors. After another hour, the Earl of Hertford pronounced the guilty verdict.[4] The previous day,

---

1 Childs 2006 p. 255. Neither Surrey's letter nor John Dudley's reply survives.
2 Childs 2006 pp. 256, 269, 278
3 Spanish Chronicle p. 147. This source must be taken with a pinch of salt; however it does narrate recent events in a tabloid manner, as understood by a foreigner of low birth, probably a mercenary soldier. From internal evidence it was composed in early 1552 and thus cannot be referring to John Dudley's downfall from hindsight. It may well be alluding to Edmund Dudley's fate, though.
4 Spanish Chronicle p. 147

Wriothesley, Hertford, Dudley, and Paget had secured the Duke of Norfolk's confession, who had also been imprisoned in the Tower of London.[1] Surrey was beheaded on 19 January, while his father's attainder (he did not get a trial) was passed by parliament on 27 January. On 28 January, Henry VIII died in his bed. This saved Norfolk's life.

The king had passed his last Christmas alone in his chamber, brooding intensely over the witness depositions against the Howards; his jottings on these papers survive and betray his deep suspicion.[2] Notwithstanding, François van der Delft suspected that the downfall of the Howards was engineered by Seymour and Dudley, for "nothing is done at Court without their intervention".[3] Eustace Chapuys, from his retirement in Louvain, was of similar opinion: "And if (which God forbid) the King should die … it is probable that these two men will have the management of affairs, because, apart from the King's affection for them, and other reasons, there are no other nobles of a fit age and ability for the task."[4]

---

1 Childs 2006 p. 302
2 Hutchinson 2006 pp. 196–197
3 Childs 2006 p. 310
4 CSP Span VIII No. 386

7.
My Lord Protector

The 16 executors of Henry's will, one of whom was John Dudley, also embodied the regency council appointed to rule collectively until Edward VI reached his 18th birthday. Within days of Henry VIII's death, on 31 January 1547, the new council agreed on making Edward Seymour, Earl of Hertford, Lord Protector and Governor of the King's Person, with full powers, which in effect were those of a prince.[1] On 1 February, the nine-year-old king received his nobles as he sat in a chair of state in his presence chamber; each of them knelt before Edward, kissed his hands, and said, "God save your Grace."[2]

The council's next major item of business was to award themselves a round of promotions based on a list presented by Secretary Paget. He swore he had prepared it according to Henry's wishes.[3] The Earl of Hertford became the Duke of Somerset and John Dudley was raised from Viscount Lisle to Earl of Warwick.[4] This was because, later claims that he was the grandson of a carpenter notwithstanding, John was a direct descendant of Richard Beauchamp, 13th Earl of Warwick, who had served in the

---

1   Loach 2002 p. 25; Alford 2002 pp. 29, 69–70
2   Loach 2002 p. 29
3   Loades 1996 pp. 89–90
4   On Paget's list John Dudley had been proposed for the earldoms of Coventry or Leicester (Wilson 1981 p. 26). He had close connections to Coventry and was popular in the town (Beer 1979 p. 5).

Hundred Years War and as governor for the young King Henry VI. The new Earl of Warwick accordingly assumed the arms of the medieval earls of Warwick, the bear and the ragged staff.[1] He also wanted the castle, because "it is a stately castle, and a goodly park and a great royalty." It was basically a ruin, he told Paget, "not able to lodge a good baron with his train", but he feared what people might think if he did not get it. – "Because of the name, I am the more desirous to have the thing."[2]

The coronation was scheduled for 20 February. A special court was appointed which was to decide who was allowed to take part and which role to perform in the great ceremony. John Dudley was one of the judges, alongside his friends William Parr and Thomas Wriothesley and, among others, Chief Justice Edward Montague. John himself was to bear one of the swords of state at the coronation and take part as chief pantler at the feast afterwards. He was also to carry Edward's train; fully dressed in his robe of state of crimson velvet furred with ermine and wearing his cap of maintenance, he was to appear at seven in the morning at Westminster Palace. The men scheduled to assist him in carrying the heavy train were William Parr, now Marquess of Northampton, and Thomas Seymour, recently created Baron Seymour of Sudeley.[3] John's son John, now known as the Viscount Lisle, was to be made a Knight of the Bath the night before the coronation.[4]

Meanwhile, the reshuffling of offices was observed and expertly commented by François van der Delft, who informed Charles V about the chief power brokers, who were "the earl of Hertford, the Lord Chancellor, the Lord Admiral and Paget".

---

1 Adams 2002 pp. 312–314. This descent was from his mother's side, by whom he was also a direct descendant of the famous John Talbot, 1st Earl of Shrewsbury (see Table 5).
2 Tytler I p. 28
3 Loach 2002 pp. 30–32, 34; Bernard 2010 p. 70. The office of pantler, panterer, or panter had originally been associated with the pantry and would have entailed the serving of bread and cakes at the feast; it was now entirely ceremonial. John Dudley also held another ceremonial office of the table, that of chief trencher, from 1537 till 1552.
4 Loades 2008a

Each one of these will strive his best for his own advancement, and it is already evident that this is the case by the action of the earl of Hertford himself. ... He causes to be borne before him two gilt maces, and his intention is to create his brother Lord Admiral, the object of this apparently being the more firmly to consolidate his authority, whilst the present Lord Admiral aspires to be Lord Chamberlain and Commander in Chief, which office was held previously by Hertford himself. ... It is, of course, quite likely that some jealousy or rivalry may arise between the earl of Hertford and the Lord Admiral, because, although they both belong to the same sect they are nevertheless widely different in character: the Lord Admiral being of high courage will not willingly submit to his colleague. He is, moreover, in higher favour both with the people and with the nobles than the earl of Hertford, owing to his liberality and splendour. The Protector, on the other hand, is not so accomplished in this respect, and is indeed looked down upon by everybody as a dry, sour, opinionated man.[1]

It may indeed have come hard upon John Dudley to part with his cherished office of Lord Admiral, however at least it passed to someone with naval experience, Thomas Seymour having served as Vice-Admiral under him. Apparently, John was happy with the arrangements in the government, for five months later van der Delft sent the emperor an update:

If your Majesty will please pardon me for doing so I will change the opinion I formerly held, namely that the Earl of Warwick, as he is the most splendid and haughty by nature and in high reputation would probably determine not to give way to the Protector. I think now that, contenting himself with the preeminence he at present enjoys, before all the others

---
1   CSP Span 10 February 1547

except the Protector, he will not persevere in the management of affairs, nor is he, indeed, so able to support the work, which appears to be unable to tire the Protector.[1]

If John Dudley was lazy paperwork-wise, he soon had opportunity to exercise his body in a new Scottish campaign. Protector Somerset was contemplating to take up the "Rough Wooing" once more, pressing home the marriage agreed between Edward VI and Mary of Scotland. On 27 February 1547 Andrew Dudley was appointed admiral of the fleet.[2] He was to oversee the "annoyance of the Scots" in the North Sea and to interrupt the shipping of munition from France to Scotland.[3] In March he captured one of the Scots navy's principal ships, the *Great Lion*, giving her a broadside from his flagship, the *Pauncey*.[4] Unfortunately, while being towed to Yarmouth the *Great Lion* was stranded on a sandbank; he still received a letter from the privy council, commending "his hardy enterprise against the Scots".[5]

Andrew then sailed north to negotiate with the rebellious lairds who had killed the Francophile Cardinal Beaton and were now holding St. Andrews Castle against the Regent Arran, with Arran's eldest son, James Hamilton, as hostage. The lairds signed a contract with Dudley, according to which they were to receive English aid to hold the castle against the Scottish government

> for the better staye and suryte of themselfes and his Majesties freendis in Scotland and thadvancement and perfection of the said mariage [and] a perpetualle peax, unite and hardy naturall love between both the Realms.[6]

---

1 CSP Span 10 July 1547
2 Löwe 2004
3 Loades 1996 p. 96
4 Cameron 1927 pp. 176, 180, 186; Strype Memorials II Pt. 2 pp. 14–15
5 Lefèvre-Pontalis 1888 pp. 117–119; APC II pp. 451–452
6 Merriman 2000 p. 226

The lairds promised to surrender St. Andrews Castle and Arran's son to the English on arrival. Andrew also struck a deal with Patrick, Lord Gray, the owner of Broughty Castle, a fortress of great strategic importance at the mouth of the river Tay. According to the agreement, Lord Gray was to surrender his castle and help the English take Perth.[1]

Meanwhile, John was engaged in negotiations for a defensive league between France and England, which however came to nothing with the death of Francis I on 31 March 1547, his son and successor, Henry II, refusing the ratification. St. Andrews Castle fell in July 1547, which greatly strengthened French influence in Scotland and triggered the next English invasion. John Dudley, Earl of Warwick, was ordered to assemble a force at Berwick before 31 August, and a week later an army of 10,000 men crossed into Scotland. Warwick led a vanguard of 3,000 footsoldiers, and, as the eyewitness and chronicler William Patten observed, "did camp with the field in the army".[2]

On 7 September, "did there arise a very thick mist, [and] my Lord the Earl of Warwick, then Lord Lieutenant, as I told you, of the Army, did so nobly quit himself upon an adventure that chanced then to fall, as that his accustomed valiance might well be acknowledged":[3] Having fought his way out of an ambush John shouted, "Why … will not these knaves be ruled? Give me my staff!" – Spear in hand, he chased his Scottish counterpart for some 250 yards, nearly running him through.[4] Two days later the Earl of Huntly put a challenge to the Duke of Somerset, to decide the war by personal combat. The duke declined on grounds of his superior rank, however John Dudley, like Huntly an earl, immediately stepped in and offered himself for a duel. But Somerset would have none of it:

> "Nay," quoth my Lord's Grace, "the Earl Huntley is not meet in estate with you, my Lord!" … This said, my Lord Lieutenant continued his requests that he

---

[1] Merriman 2000 p. 226
[2] Beer 1973 pp. 61–62
[3] Tudor Tracts p. 91
[4] Tudor Tracts p. 93

might receive this challenge: but my Lord's Grace would, in no wise, grant to it.[1]

In the morning of Saturday, 10 September, the Scottish army was in the process of occupying an impregnable place on top of the slope of Fawside Brae near Musselburgh. Somerset was moving his right wing to position his cannons when the Regent Arran suddenly decided to descend on the English flank. For a moment Somerset nearly lost his nerve; it was also the moment of the Earl of Warwick, who rallied his troops with a battle cry. They should "pluck up their hearts", and "he himself, even there, would live and die among them!"[2] – A furious cavalry charge stopped the Scots, who were then worn down by superior English gunfire, which came partly from the English navy lying offshore. As the Scottish army disintegrated, the Earl of Arran fled and the Earl of Huntly became an English prisoner. The Scots had lost some 10,000 men, chiefly butchered at the last stage of the battle, in the rout.[3] The scene was grisly:

> Some with legs off, some ... left lying half dead; other, with the arms cut off; divers, their necks half asunder; many, their heads cloven; of sundry, the brains pasht out; some others again, their heads quite off.[4]

*

Somerset marched up his victorious army to Leith, but did not attack nearby Edinburgh, his objective being to install a chain of English garrisons in Scotland. Andrew Dudley again served in the campaign at sea, which was led by his nephew-by marriage, Lord Clinton.[5] A week after the Battle of Pinkie Andrew was knighted

---

1 Tudor Tracts p. 103
2 Tudor Tracts p. 121; Merriman 2000 p. 234
3 Merriman 2000 p. 234
4 Beer 1973 p. 63
5 Beer 1973 p. 62

by the Duke of Somerset, who "despatched my Lord Admiral[1] and him, with ships full fraught with men and munition, towards the winning of a Hold in the east side of Scotland, called Broughty Crak."[2] True to his word of five months ago, Lord Gray gave up the castle after three cannon shots from the English ships. On 20 September Andrew Dudley became captain of the new English garrison.[3]

He soon informed Somerset that "never had a man had so weak a company of soldiers given to drinking, eating and slothfulness [though] the house stands well";[4] however, it had "scant window to shut, nor door, nor bolt, ... nor nail".[5] Andrew hired Master John Rossetti, an Italian engineer, for re-fortification of the place.[6] He also secured a bond of alliance from the town of Dundee by firing on the town from his two ships, the *Bark Ager* and the *Mary Hambroughe*. He believed the Reformation in Scotland was making progress, for the Tyndale Bible and "other good English books" were in much demand.[7]

Weeks after Pinkie, Somerset returned to London, declining the city's offer of a triumphal entry; there was also "great praise" of the Earl of Warwick in town.[8] John had stayed behind for talks as the king's "lieutenant"; however the Scottish lords with whom he was supposed to negotiate would not turn up, being too busy with their feuds against each other.[9] One of the more illustrious prisoners, the Earl of Bothwell, was prepared to hand over his formidable border castle, Hermitage, in exchange for an English bride. The earl suggested he might choose between the Duchess of Suffolk, the Lady Mary, and the Lady Elizabeth, "as though if he liked them, they would not mislike him", John explained.[10]

---

1 Thomas Seymour.
2 Tudor Tracts p. 141
3 Merriman 2000 p. 250
4 CSP Scotland I p. 24
5 Merriman 2000 p. 250
6 Merriman 2000 p. 250
7 Donaldson 1987 p. 77; CSP Scotland I pp. 21, 35
8 Beer 1973 p. 64; CSP Span 19 September 1547
9 Loades 1996 pp. 101–102
10 Beer 1973 p. 64. Patrick Hepburn, 3rd Earl of Bothwell, was the father of Mary Stuart's third husband, James Hepburn, 4th Earl of Bothwell.

The first parliament of Edward VI convened on 4 November 1547, among its business being some Protestant reforms and the repeal of Henry VIII's treason laws. It is not at all clear whether John was present at the sessions or even back in London.[1] However, before the end of the year his household had stopped hearing mass, a sure sign of the Protestantism that came to dominate English life over the next years. In the last days of Henry's reign, Eustace Chapuys had already described Edward Seymour and John Dudley as the "stirrers-up of heresy", who via their wives (and the Duchess of Suffolk) had also "infected" the queen, Katherine Parr, "the malady being one of those incurable mental ones into which they have fallen by natural inclination".[2]

During 1548 John and his wife also suffered from other illnesses. In March the French ambassador, de Selve, reported about John's leg which for months had caused him so much trouble that he needed a doctor. He was still ill in May. Having just returned from war, it is possible that he was treating some injury. In September he rather stayed at his new London home, Ely Place, than return to court after a long absence, for "my wyfe hath hadd herr Fytt agayne more extremer then she hadd any tyme yet".[3] John was obviously an attentive husband, but his own ailments have been suspected of being cases of hypochondria.[4] – Whatever the diagnosis, he was lucky, as he wrote, to have "escaped the Fytt which I dyd loke for yester daye".[5] He also helped other people. In July he was asked by a lady, a victim of the surgeons of London, to be allowed to keep her surgeon of Boulogne. He decided to write to William Cecil, the Protector's de facto secretary: "Please have my lord let him remain or she may lose a leg."[6]

John and Jane Dudley's circle included Sir William Cavendish and his wife Bess,[7] a couple they visited several times and to whose children they repeatedly stood as godparents; John's fellow godfather at the christening of Bess' fourth child, Henry, was

---

1 Beer 1973 pp. 65–66; Loades 1996 p. 102
2 CSP Spanish 29 January 1547
3 Higginbotham 2012a; Beer 1973 pp. 66, 68
4 Loades 1996 pp. 104, 155; Ives 2009 p. 125
5 Higginbotham 2012a
6 Knighton 1992 p. 53
7 Elizabeth Cavendish is better known as Bess of Hardwick.

Henry Grey, Marquess of Dorset, the father of a bookish girl named Jane.[1] The Cavendishes being clients of the Dorsets, John and his wife may have seen rather a lot of Henry Grey and his family. Unsurprisingly, among the friends of the rising royal servant Cavendish we find the other marquess, William Parr. Northampton's sister, the Dowager Queen Katherine and her new husband, Thomas Seymour, still were in friendly contact with John and Jane Dudley. In a letter to his brother the Lord Protector, who was on campaign in Scotland with John, Thomas included his greetings to the Earl of Warwick and reported that "my Lady [of Warwick] is also merry."[2]

Around 1 July 1548, John was appointed President of the Council of Wales, a position he was able to fill reasonably well, as his frequent abode Dudley Castle was not far from Ludlow, the council's seat. He was concerned, however, that "without honest and sound associates" he "could do little good".[3] Only days later, he complained to Cecil that Somerset had let him down respecting the removal of a corrupt judge and some unsuitable councillors – "By whose persuasion this happens I know not, but I am sure I have base friends who smile to see me so used."[4]

Throughout 1548, John did not attend the privy council's meetings, and he did not return until January 1549. One of his pastimes was to increase his collection of houses and in 1548 his eye fell on Hatfield, the Lady Elizabeth's residence, for whom, he suggested, "some other place agreeable to her desire" should be found.[5] In December he did sit in the House of Lords when parliament discussed and ultimately passed the Bill of Uniformity, legislation that placed England firmly into the Protestant camp, of a decidedly Swiss persuasion. John Dudley certainly shared this outlook, supporting Somerset and Cranmer in the debates. This occurred rather robustly, in his entirely common sense style. His sparring partners, so to speak, were Bishops Thomas Thirlby of

---

1   Lovell 2006 pp. 57, 70
2   Beer 1973 p. 73
3   Loades 1996 p. 103
4   Loades 1996 p. 104
5   Beer 1973 p. 76. He did not get Hatfield, of course.

Westminster and Nicholas Heath of Worcester,[1] the latter of whom he would meet again in very different circumstances.

*

King Edward's relationship with his Seymour uncles was at best distanced.[2] The Lord Protector not only used the royal "we",[3] but used the title of "Edward by the grace of god Duke of Somersett".[4] He was stingy, too: "My Unkell off Sumerset dealeth very hardly with me and keepeth me so strait that I cannot have money at my will."[5] Though Thomas Seymour was different ("my Lord Admiral both sends me money and gives me money"[6]), he broke into the king's bedchamber at night, killing Edward's dog.[7]

Protector Somerset and his wife also loved to appear bedecked with royal jewels.[8] Some of these had belonged to Katherine Parr, and she had not at all been happy to part with them; she fought over them until the very end. She died on 5 September 1548. It had not helped her relations with the first couple that she had married Thomas Seymour, the Protector's younger brother – within a few months of Henry's death, causing raised eyebrows and widespread frowning. Thomas held his own grievances against his brother: Never before had a Protector of the Realm held both the offices of Protector and governor of the king's person, and Somerset had made Sir Michael Stanhope, his wife's half-brother, de facto governor of the king – a position of enormous influence and opportunities for patronage.

Thomas Seymour felt that he, another uncle of the king, should be in such a position rather than Stanhope and his assistant Sir Richard Page, mere relations of the Duchess of Somerset.[9] John

1 MacCulloch 1996 pp. 406, 407; Loades 1996 p. 105
2 Edward had a third uncle, Sir Henry Seymour; rarely seen at court, Henry lived to an old age (Loades 2015 pp. 198–199).
3 Loach 2002 p. 40
4 Hoak 1976 p. 153
5 Loach 2002 p. 55
6 Loach 2002 p. 55
7 CSP Span 27 January 1549
8 Loach 2002 p. 40
9 Hoak 2008

may have supported him in this; in the early days of the reign it would have been entirely reasonable to suggest to Thomas that he apply for Edward's governorship. However, he was first and foremost Somerset's ally and seems to have warned Thomas at some point, "using strong language to the Admiral, remonstrating with him that he had come to occupy such a high position through the favour of his brother and the council ... 'Be content, therefore.'"[1] Later, John confirmed before the privy council that he had warned Thomas that his brother would put him "fast in the Tower" if he did not mend his ways.[2]

An Elizabethan source later claimed, in hindsight, that John did all this with a sinister purpose:

> How after it was concluded by the council that the duke of Somerset should be protector and governor of the king, the earl of Warwick said to the admiral, Sir Thomas Seymour, that he should do well to move in council that his brother being protector, he might be the king's governor, ... and promised the admiral all his help and furtherance, and that if he would it, he would declare it he meant as he said. The admiral accordingly did move it in the council which as soon as the duke heard, he suddenly arose and spake not one word, and so the council was dissolved. After, Warwick came unto the duke and said thus, your grace may see this man's [Thomas'] ambition. After such sort he procured and maintained hatred between the brethren, that so he might the rather dispatch one and at length the other, and in the end rule alone himself.[3]

---

1 CSP Span 8 February 1549
2 Beer 1973 p. 74
3 Adams, Archer, Bernard 2003a pp. 53–54. The unknown author jotted down notes for a history that was never written. A man with a grudge against the Dudleys, he wrote in about 1562 and presumably had been a member of Somerset's household in the function of a clerk but had not been a privy councillor. It has been suggested that he was John Hales, MP, chief ideologue of Somerset's agrarian policy and correspondent of John Dudley (Adams, Archer, Bernard 2003a pp. 41, 45–46; see below p. 67).

On the next page the same writer offered rather different reasons for the troubles between the duke and his younger brother:

> The cause of the falling out of the protector and the admiral was ambition of the admiral and the envy he had that his brother should be more advanced than he.
> ...
>
> Of the hatred between the queen and the duchess of Somerset, and how the duchess hated the admiral, and contrariwise, and how the admiral sought the disinheritance of her children and would have had the duke's children by his first wife to be his heirs. How the brethren were once pacified but the love continued not.[1]

And so, in early 1549, Thomas Seymour tried to obtain the young king's help (and signatures) in a wild scheme to gain more power. Edward had been sympathetic to his marriage, but now he was more cautious:

> In the month of September, Anno Dom. 1547, the lord admiral told me that my lord protector went to Scotland ... and ... that he spent a great sum of money in vain. At the return of my lord my uncle, the lord admiral said, I was too bashful in mine own matters, and asked me why I did not speak to bear rule, as other kings do.

Edward replied that "I needed not, for I was well enough."[2] But Thomas Seymour would not give up so easily:

> The lord admiral came to me in the time of the last parliament at Westminster, and desired me to write a thing for him. I asked him what: He said it was none ill thing; ... I said, if it were good, the lords would

---

1 Adams, Archer, Bernard 2003a pp. 54–55
2 Literary Remains I pp. 58–59

allow it; if it were ill, I would not write in it. Then he said they would take it in better part if I would write. I desired him to let me alone in that matter. ... At another time ... he said, ye must take upon you yourself to rule, for ye shall be able enough as well as other kings ... for your uncle is old, and I trust will not live long. I answered, it were better that he should die.[1]

Thomas took the hint and went on with his plotting: He planned to kidnap Edward and marry the Lady Elizabeth and remove the Lord Protector, he also piled up weapons and fortified his houses. Evidently concerned about John Dudley's power, he asked Henry Grey, Marquess of Dorset, "to kepe my house in Warwikeshire ... to match with my lorde of Warwike, so as he should not be hable to matche with me there".[2]

On 25 January 1549 William Paget reminded Somerset to order "the committinge of thadmiral and his complices".[3] It was later claimed that John lived in the duke's house during the crisis, being "always at hand" until Seymour's death, when he moved out, the implication being a sinister one.[4] It is somewhat unlikely that John was so physically close to the Protector, though, for he wrote letters intended for the duke's attention in March and April 1549,[5] at the same time he was supposed to have urged Seymour's execution on Somerset in person.[6] John no longer addressed his

---

1 Literary Remains I pp. 57–58
2 Bernard 2008
3 Hoak 1976 p. 190
4 Adams, Archer, Bernard 2003b pp. 124–125
5 Letters to John Thynne preserved at Longleat (Beer 1973 p. 75; Alford 2002 p. 82).
6 Some historians have blamed John Dudley for Thomas Seymour's death, building on the Black Legend which evolved about the time of his downfall (see below p. 230). Chapman 1958 p. 136–137 claims that the French ambassador "De Noailles, joining de Selve's embassy, reported to Henry II that as soon as Seymour had irrevocably compromised himself, Warwick first urged Somerset to arrest him ... and then demanded his death ... *'Il poussa l'affaire'*, was the Frenchmen's summing up; and it is the only one that is historically acceptable."; Skidmore 2007 p. 108 writes that "the French ambassador had perceived that it was the earl who had first urged Somerset to

letters to the duke personally, but always to men like William Cecil and Sir John Thynne, Somerset's "familiars"; he did so even when suggesting solutions to policy and military matters that greatly alarmed him.[1] The Protector had become almost unapproachable by 1548/1549, as appears also from one of John's letters: "for my meaning towards his Grace, I would his Grace knew it as God doth."[2]

The attainder and execution of Thomas Seymour was strongly backed by the privy council and parliament; still, it rested on the Duke of Somerset's will. The Lord Protector consulted crown jurists about whether his brother's doings amounted to treason: Two of three judges giving a negative answer, he arranged for Seymour's attainder in parliament rather than for a trial. The result was of course a death sentence for treason, described as "indifferent justice" by Somerset.[3] The indiscriminate condemnation he left to Hugh Latimer, who preached a series of vitriolic sermons in front of the eleven-year-old king and the court, both before and after Thomas Seymour's execution on 20 March 1549.[4]

---

arrest his brother, before demanding his death". However, both authors quote from the first volume of the edition of Noailles' dispatches by the Abbé Vertot, which is a *secondary source*, a narrative of English history in the 16th century penned by Vertot in the early 18th century. As Vertot's own editors put it in 1763: "Il composa, sur ces dépêches, une introduction historique, qui forme le premier volume" (Vertot I p. 6). As for Ambassador Noailles, he first set foot in England in May 1553, more than four years after his supposed observations.

Exonerating the Duchess of Somerset, Warnicke 2012 pp. 93, 212 is eager to shift the blame onto John Dudley instead. She cites the Spanish merchant, Antonio de Guaras, who according to her wrote *in 1549* that Thomas Seymour was executed on Dudley's "contrivance". However, Guaras' account is from *September 1553* and not about the realities of 1549, but about the triumph of Queen Mary over the forces of evil and heresy – as well as about the rise and fall of the monstrous Duke of Northumberland, on whom Guaras blames every notable death from Henry Howard, Earl of Surrey, to Edward VI.

1   Alford 2002 pp. 81–82; Loades 2004 pp. 44–45
2   Loades 2004 p. 57; Hoak 1976 pp. 167–190
3   Hoak 2008
4   MacCulloch 1996 p. 408

8.

Rebellion

In his proclamations the Lord Protector liked to appeal to the common people, becoming increasingly arrogant to his colleagues.[1] Somerset's agrarian policy was inspired by a group of intellectuals highly critical of landlords;[2] commissions meant to investigate enclosures of common land by greedy landlords were set up,[3] but only one actually got to work, under the MP John Hales. The landowners, unsurprisingly, refused to be told what to do with their property, and after being cowed into passing the respective legislation in parliament they did not implement it at home.[4] The only thing achieved by Hales was to plough "a symbolic furrow across the Earl of Warwick's parkland".[5] In July 1548 John Dudley wrote angrily to Hales, accusing him of "stirring up" the people against the natural order. However, as one of England's major landowners, John was also seriously concerned that Hales' activities would lead to serious trouble.[6] The next year he also tried to warn Somerset, writing to the duke's familiar, John Thynne:

---

1 MacCulloch 2001 pp. 50–51; Loades 2004 p. 43
2 Loades 1996 p. 107
3 Enclosures were not the big problem made out by 16th century moralists. Most of the conversion of arable land into pasture had occurred already during the 15th century (Loach 2002 pp. 59–60). By the mid-16th century the population had increased substantially, however, and there were far more potential tenants than there were landholdings available, so that even old enclosures came "to be regarded as a grievance" (Loades 2015 p. 148).
4 Dawson 1993 p. 237; Loades 2004 pp. 43–44
5 Dawson 1993 p. 237
6 Loades 1996 pp. 107–108

Mr. Thynne, I received your letters, being very sorry to hear the continual trouble of my Lord's Grace with these uproars. And wherein I do perceive my Lord's Grace would have had mine advice ... I do intend to adventure tomorrow to come to his grace.[1]

Though he was "ill in my stomach" and said "I would me to be in my grave", he was very concerned that Somerset's plan to send him with more troops to Scotland would deprive England of the necessary forces to deal with the unrest in the Midlands. He was even worried about his ability to keep Warwick Castle in safe hands.[2] At the time he was writing there was already widespread unrest in all parts of England, Somerset having to abandon his Scottish plans for the 1549 season and instead sent troops to the West Country, where a major rebellion had broken out at Exeter. Andrew Dudley was one of the minor commanders employed there in the punitive expedition led by John Russell.[3] Now it dawned even on Somerset that "sharpe justice must be executed upon those traytors which will learne by nothing but by the sword."[4]

Meanwhile, the tanner and yeoman landowner Robert Kett of Wymondham, Norfolk, had embarked on his own rebellion. The Lord Protector sent William Parr, Marquess of Northampton, to deal with it; he arrived as the rebels were about to take over the city of Norwich. On 1 August Northampton's men suffered a humiliating defeat in a battle that saw the captured Lord Sheffield butchered by "a butcherly knave ... who by occupation was both a carpenter and a butcher", the marquess being distracted by a feint petition for pardon.[5]

Somerset himself had judged the Norfolk "commotion" a minor affair, to be dealt with a small contingent of troops. Now, he blamed Northampton for tactical errors and poor leadership, while remaining undecided how to proceed further. After a few days, he decided that Northampton was to be replaced with Warwick. John's

---

1 Loades 1996 p. 119
2 Loades 1996 p. 119; Loades 2004 pp. 44–45
3 Beer 1973 p. 83
4 Dawson 1993 p. 239
5 Beer 1982 p. 123

letter of thanks, once again not addressed to the Protector but to Cecil, was almost entirely concerned with the psychological well-being of William Parr, his old friend:

> I do think myself much bounden to my Lord's Grace and the Council to receive so great a charge, so I cannot but wish that it might please the same to permit and suffer my Lord Marquis of Northampton to continue still in the force of his commission, ... forasmuch, the nobleman having lately by misfortune received discomfort enough, haply this might give him occasion to think himself utterly discredited, and so for ever discourage him; which, in my opinion, were great pity. Wherefore, if it might please his Grace to use his services again, I shall be as glad for my part to join with him, yea, rather than fail, with all my heart to serve under him, for this journey, as I would be to have the whole authority myself; and by this means his Grace shall preserve his heart, and hable him to serve hereafter, which, otherwise, he shall be utterly in himself discouraged – I would wish that no man for one mischance or evil hap, to the which we be all subject that must serve, should be utterly abject; for, if it should be so, it were almost a present discomfort to all men before they go to it, since those things lie in God's hand. Therefore, good Mr. Cecill, use your accustomed wisdom, and good heart that you bear to my Lord's Grace, in declaring this matter with effect to the same, and with diligence let me hear from you again ... Fare you well.[1]

As it turned out, Northampton served as John's second-in-command in the second attempt to deal with the rebel host, this time with a much larger force. The campaign was still no easy affair. On 13 August 1549 John met up with William Parr at Cambridge. A delegation of citizens from Norwich also arrived, "falling down upon their knees before him". They "besought" the

---
1   Tytler I pp. 193–194

earl "to be good Lord unto them," declaring "their miserable state, great grief and sorrow". – "The Earl of Warwick told them, that he knew indeed in what danger they had been among those unruly ribalds."[1]

By 22 August the royal army was at Wymondham, where they rested overnight at the house of Sir John Robsart.[2] Robsart had a 17-year-old daughter, Amy, who took a lively interest in the Earl of Warwick's son, Robert. Robert and Ambrose Dudley, about 17 and 18 years old, accompanied their father in what was their first experience of military action. Ambrose later recalled the brutality of the battle, which he judged to be "manfullie fought on both sides".[3] The next day the Earl of Warwick marched over

> the playne, betwixte the Citie of Norwich, and Eyton wood, and lodged that night at Intwood, an houfe belonging to Sir Thomas Gresham Knighte,[4] a two myles distant from Norwiche.

> Heere they rested that daye and nighte following, not once putting off their armoure, but remayning still in a readynesse, if the enimies shoulde have made any suddaine invasion against them.[5]

John Dudley issued several offers of pardon, on the condition that the peasant army disband at once; they were all rejected. The last one with "a filthy act" by a youth who, with lowered breeches, pooped in the direction of Norroy King of Arms. The result, unfortunately, was that the boy was shot dead by an enraged soldier.[6] Now, Robert Kett suddenly decided that he should meet the Earl of Warwick personally, however as he came down from his camp on Mousehold Heath he was stopped by his own men.[7]

1   Holinshed IV 1.21.1.
2   Holinshed IV 1.21.1.; Skidmore 2010 p. 14
3   Wood 2007 p. 68
4   Thomas Gresham the financier. He was a good friend of John Dudley (see below p. 121).
5   Holinshed IV 1.21.1.
6   Holinshed IV 1.21.1.
7   Holinshed IV 1.21.1.

Intriguingly, Kett may have been an acquaintance of John Dudley, for only the previous year John had sold him a piece of land;[1] a fact which gives us a hint at how Kett came to be a rebel in the first place – he had started with tearing down his own fences out of sympathy with the protesters.[2]

Next to Mousehold Heath was the city of Norwich, now in the hands of the rebels. In the night of 24 August Warwick "determineth to proceede againste them by force" and as he came to St. Stephen's Gate, "whiche the Rebels stopped uppe with lettyng downe the portculice, he commanded those that hadde charge of the artillerie, to plant the same against the gate, and with batterie to break it open." – A contingent of foreign mercenary soldiers drove out most of the rebel force in heavy street fighting. John, having entered "with all his army, and finding in manner no resistance, came to the market place," where he immediately had hanged 49 rebels according to martial law.[3]

Remnants of the rebel force were still active, John coming under "a sharpe storme of arrowes" in John's Street. He then took "order for the safekeepyng of the Citie, appoyntyng watche and warde to be kept on the walles, and in every streete. Also that all the gates should be rammed up, excepte one or two that stoode towardes the enimies, at the whiche were planted certaine peces of the greate artillerie."[4]

---

1 Loades 1996 p. 126
2 Kett was not John Dudley's tenant, as claimed in Skidmore 2007 pp. 130–131 and Ackroyd 2012 p. 218. The same authors also suggest that John Dudley may have used Robert Kett as an agent to create Kett's Rebellion as an instrument to bring down Protector Somerset. This idea, which is preposterous, seems to go back to John Ponet's 1555 *Treatise of politike power*, a vitriolic accusation of Queen Mary, John Dudley, and others (MacCulloch 1996 pp. 451–452; see below p. 238). It is true that Sir Richard Southwell, a government official and Norfolk magnate, surreptitiously financed Kett's men from public funds. He was, however, punished for his misdemeanour when it came to light, and the claim in Skidmore 2007 p. 130 that he was John Dudley's friend rests on a single remark by the Imperial ambassador van der Delft, writing in the politically chaotic aftermath of Somerset's fall in October 1549. Van der Delft was not always correct, though; Richard Southwell belonged to the Catholic party around Mary.
3 Loades 1996 p. 127; Holinshed IV 1.21.1.
4 Holinshed IV 1.21.1.

Kett's men, meanwhile, were holding out on Mousehold Heath and continued their attacks as they knew Warwick "wanted powder and other things apperteyning to the use of the greate ordinance"; for they had managed to seize many carriages of munitions and even some of Warwick's cannons. Everything seemed "to chance and fall out in favour of the rebels," and some in the royal camp were "despairing of the whole success of their journey", suggesting to John to withdraw from the city thinking "it was unpossible to defend it against such an huge multitude." The Earl of Warwick,

> as he was of a noble & invincible courage ... and not able to abyde anye spotte of reproche, ... made this aunswer: why ... fayle you so soone? or are you so madde withall, to thinke that so long as anye lyfe resteth in me, that I will consent to suche dishonour? Should I leave the Citie? ... I will rather suffer whatsoever eyther fire or sword can worke agaynst mee.

With these words he drew his sword and commanded the others to do likewise and kiss each other's sword, according to ancient custom. They "made a solemne vowe" not to leave the battlefield "till they had either vanquished the enimies, or lost their lives in manful fight, for defence of the kings honour."[1]

*

On 26 August Kett broke up his fortified camp on the hill to entrench his forces in lower ground near Dussindale, making for an ideal target for Warwick's cavalry. They still had the captured ordnance to protect them, though.[2] They also brought gentlemen hostages in place, chaining them together in front of the camp to serve as human shields. Once again, John Dudley offered pardon, the message being delivered by Sir Thomas Palmer and Sir Edmund Knyvet. It was again refused, underscored by "one Myles, that was a very perfect gunner and marvellous skilfull in the feate

---
1 Holinshed IV 1.21.1.
2 Fletcher and MacCulloch 2008 p. 75

of shooting of great artillerie", firing at the royal standard bearer and killing his horse under him.[1] It was the sign for battle and for John to rally his men with a speech: The rebels were not men, but "brute beasts imbued with all cruelty" who "came not out to fight but to take punishment."[2]

The "punishment" turned into a slaughter of some 2,000 "peasants". Kett was not a soldier, let alone a commander, and his forces were no match against a professional army, reinforced only the day before by a contingent of "1400 Lansquenetz".[3] However, the government troops also suffered heavy losses, in their hundreds.[4] Before the end of the day, John had taken hundreds of prisoners, rescued most of the gentlemen hostages, and executed about a dozen peasant "captains".[5] Robert Kett had fled on his horse but was captured the next day, to be transferred to London for trial and brought back to Norwich again for his execution in December 1549. He was hanged in chains from the castle walls. Unlike their leader, some of Kett's men did make a last stand, entrenching themselves behind carts and carriages and armed to the teeth. John once again sent an offer of pardon, but the remaining rebels doubted his sincerity: "Utterly refusing the king's pardon", they chose "to try to quarrel with the extremity of the sword", an eyewitness recalled the scene.[6] John now inquired if they would lay down their weapons and accept the pardon from him in person, to which they agreed. So he came to them and had the pardon read by Norrey King of Arms, "which being read, every man throweth down his weapon, and with one whole and entier voyce crie, God save king Edward, God save king Edward."[7]

"The battaile being thus ended, all the spoyle gotten in the fielde was given to ye souldiers, who solde the most part thereof openly in the Market place of Norwich."[8] For the next two weeks John Dudley remained in Norwich to help in the clean-up

---

1 Holinshed IV 1.21.1.; Beer 1982 p. 136; Fletcher and MacCulloch 2008 p. 75
2 Skidmore 2007 p. 128
3 Holinshed IV 1.21.1. Landsknechts.
4 Wood 2007 p. 69. "On both sides, the casualties had been appalling".
5 Loades 1996 p. 127; Beer 1982 p. 136
6 Beer 1982 p. 137
7 Holinshed IV 1.21.1.
8 Holinshed IV 1.21.1.

operation, so to speak. Two days after his victory, he attended a church service in St. Peter Mancroft, raising his voice in person to praise the Lord. In the evening a masque was performed in his honour, and the City of Norwich ordered the Earl of Warwick's coat of arms, the bear and ragged staff, to be placed on every town gate.[1] Also on 29 August, some of the chief rebels were hanged outside Norwich on a tree they had dubbed the Oak of Reformation; they included Fulke the butcher (who had killed Lord Sheffield) and Miles the gunner (who had gunned down the royal standard bearer).[2] Later, "divers" others were hanged, drawn and quartered within the city. According to 16th century estimates, some 300 men were executed in total.[3] This, of course, was not enough for the humiliated local gentlemen. Those, John warned against excessive revenge:

> Is there no place for pardon? What shall we then do? Shall we hold the plough ourselves? Play the carters and labour the ground with our own hands?[4]

---

[1] Beer 1982 p. 137; Skidmore 2007 p. 129
[2] Wood 2007 p. 72
[3] Wood 2007 p. 72. Fletcher and MacCulloch 2008 p. 76. They were not hanged on a single day, as claimed in Skidmore 2007 p. 129.
[4] Holinshed IV 1.21.1.

9.
Coup d'Etat

The Earl of Warwick still had the troops from the Norfolk campaign at his disposal when he returned to the capital in late August 1549. Andrew Flamock, his old acquaintance, was mortally ill after serving valiantly in the Norwich campaign, and John felt that certain offices should go to Ambrose, his fourth son, after Flamock died; especially the keepership of Kenilworth Castle, a place he had long set his sights on. The Protector did not comply, but worse, he granted those offices to his secretary Thomas Fisher, a former servant of John Dudley but now his enemy: John took it "very evil".[1] Somerset's lack of generosity also showed when John called at the head of a number of captains, some of whom had not been paid for two months. When Somerset insisted there was no money left, John reminded the duke how much money he was "squandering in building" – a reference to the huge building site of Somerset House – and that he thought "much more of that than what is good for the King or the Kingdom." After this meeting John addressed the captains, telling them to hold themselves ready to strike at the stingy Lord Protector.[2]

Somerset had developed a very peculiar government style – not only had he "no care but to build houses for himself"[3] – but the king's councillors were only called in to lend their signatures to decisions already taken in the duke's small circle of his own household servants (like William Cecil). Senior royal councillors were in an awkward position when dealing with the Lord

---
1 Adams, Archer, Bernard 2003a p. 126
2 Spanish Chronicle pp. 185–186; Adams, Archer, Bernard 2003a p. 126; Ives 2009 p. 110
3 CSP Span 8 October 1549

Protector, whose "great colericke facions" erupted "when so ever you are contraried in … that which youe haue conceaved in your heade." So William Paget, who held a unique position of trust, reminded him. – "No man shall dare speake to youe what he thinckes, though yt were never so necessarye for youe to knowe yt."[1] Paget became seriously disillusioned at the Protector's aloofness as his frequent warnings went unheeded: "I was a Cassandra, I told your grace the truthe and was not beleved."[2]

*

In 1548 John had paid a visit to the former Lord Chancellor, Thomas Wriothesley, Earl of Southampton, who as a sceptic of Somerset's protectorate had lost both his post and his seat on the council a few weeks into the reign of Edward VI. At the time John had acquired his London town residence, Ely Place, a former episcopal palace, in a property exchange with Wriothesley.[3] While staying with his old friend he became ill: He felt "stricken to the heart" and his stomach was in such a state that he could not eat "so much meat as a little chicken."[4] John Dudley and Thomas Wriothesley also shared a friendship with John Leland, from their youthful days,[5] and they now shared a grievance against the Protector. It was by John's agency that the Earl of Southampton returned to the privy council in January 1549.[6] In September François van der Delft informed the emperor that

> The Lady Mary had received trustworthy information that there was much rivalry and division in the Council, for the Earls of Warwick, Southampton and Arundel, and the Great Master[7] were working against the Protector and his new Council and sending to sound her to see if she would lend her favour to an

1 Hoak 1976 pp. 178, 103
2 Hoak 1976 p. 182
3 Wilson 2005 p. 172; Rowse 1965 p. 23
4 Beer 1973 p. 68
5 Akrigg 1968 p. 5
6 Elton 1977 p. 346
7 Sir William Paulet.

76

attack on the Protector, whom they wished to impeach for lesemajestie. She therefore begged the ambassador to send his secretary to his Majesty in order to obtain his good advice as to how she was to behave if matters went further, as they doubtless would all the sooner if she were to lend an ear. However, if pressed, she would say as she had said before that she never interfered in government nor would she do so now, but was sad to see the realm going to perdition so fast that there was no longer any knowledge of God nor of reason, for which she could blame no man more than another, because by their common advice things had fallen into their present disorder and desperate condition.[1]

Thus, Mary may have lost her chance to become Edward's regent. Apart from Warwick and Southampton, the third principal plotter was the Earl of Arundel, who in the last year of Henry VIII had become Lord Chamberlain. His position at court had all but been usurped by Sir Michael Stanhope, the Lord Protector's brother-in-law who controlled Edward's privy chamber.[2] All three plotters were disillusioned by the Duke of Somerset's increasing aloofness and his mismanagement of the 1549 rebellions. The earls of Southampton and Arundel being conservatives (as long as convenient[3]), the Imperial party was naturally hoping for religious changes in the right direction and van der Delft was approached by William Paget, another conservative (as long as convenient), to contact the Earl of Warwick and "try to bring him round to a better disposition regarding religion, but I have not yet attempted to do so, as I am waiting for your Majesty's instructions".[4] Van der Delft needed not to worry, for "the Earl of Warwick ... on his way to Greenwich ... came to see me at a house I have in the country. But before his arrival I was told that he was coming by a trusty and

---

1 CSP Span September 1549
2 Lock 2004
3 Lock 2004
4 CSP Span 15 September 1549

secret friend of mine," a native from the emperor's dominions "and also a man in the earl's confidence". This man told van der Delft

> everything the earl had said about me, the upshot of which was that he doubted if he could trust me because he well knew I was a great friend of the Protector and of his party, which made him afraid that I would inform the Protector of what he should say to me. However, he would confide in the friendship I had always shown him, and come and converse with me.[1]

The upshot of the meeting was that after talking of "various subjects", John "displayed his discontent with the Protector", and, "as he put off our conversation until another day", van der Delft suppressed his urge to speak about religion, having hoped "to be able to sway" Warwick; he still believed, though, that John Dudley was much more amenable to Catholicism than Somerset, who, he thought, was egged on by his wife to persecute the true faith.[2]

In September 1549 Somerset was away hunting, just before "a great assemblie" of the disgruntled councillors

> was made at the Earle of Warwick's house in Ely Place, Holborne, whither all the confederates in this matter came privily armed, and finally concluded to possess the Tower of London, which, by the policy of Sir Wm. Paulet was peacefully obtayned for them … And after that the said counsayle was broken up at Ely Place, the Earle of Warwick removing forthwith into the City of London, and lay in the house of John Yorke, citizen of London, … which said Yorke was shortly after, by the aide of the Earl, made by the King a knight, by name of Sir John Yorke.[3]

Within days, the conspirators included the entire privy council, apart from William Paget, Thomas Smith, and Archbishop

---
1 CSP Span 23 September 1549
2 CSP Span 23 September 1549
3 Holinshed qu. in Spanish Chronicle pp. 186–187; Holinshed IV 1.21.1.

Cranmer, who remained with the Lord Protector. Somerset returned to Hampton Court and on 5 October issued a proclamation in which he accused the other councillors of treason; his recalcitrant colleagues he described as having "come up of late from the dunghill ... more meet to keep service than to occupy offices".[1] The rebellious council issued their own proclamation – "Let the people know the truth" – in which they claimed to safeguard the king's safety and condemned the Lord Protector for his "malice and evil government[,] ... pride, covetousness and extreme ambition".[2]

The duke, for his part, tried to raise a people's army and then fled to Windsor Castle, taking Edward with him. On the ride through the chilly autumn night the young king caught a cold, and at Windsor he complained: "Methinks I am in prison, here be no galleries nor no gardens to walk in."[3] The castle was not provisioned for harbouring the royal household and when the rebel lords heard that the king was without food, they, "most sorrowful for the same", immediately sent a large load of supplies to Windsor.[4] Somerset, sensing the moral high ground slip away under his feet, spectacularly claimed that the lords were seeking the king's life; he compared them to Richard III[5] – oddly enough, since he was the uncle. The people's army having materialized in the form of a few peasants with forks, Somerset had only the king's person and the royal sign manual to his advantage; as it stood, the Earl of Warwick and the rebellious council had the support of the City of London and of not one but two armies: the western army under Lord Russell had joined the lords' side. On 8 October the Protector wrote a letter to his old comrade in arms, the Earl of Warwick:

> My Lord, I cannot persuade my self that there is any ill conceived in your heart as of your self against me, for that the same seemeth impossible, that where there

---

1   Dawson 1993 p. 244; Beer 1973 p. 88
2   Dawson 1993 p. 244; Beer 1973 p. 88
3   Tytler I p. 242
4   Skidmore 2007 p. 141
5   Skidmore 2007 p. 137

hath been from your youth and mine so great a friendship and amity betwixt us, as never for my part to no man was greater, now so suddenly there should be hatred; and that without just cause, what soever rumours and bruits, or persuasions, of others have moved you to conceive. In the sight and judgement of Almighty God, I protest and affirm unto you, I never meant worse to you than to my self; wherefore, my lord, for God's sake, for friendship, for the love that hath ever betwixt us or that hereafter my be, persuade yourself with truth, and let this time declare to me and the world your just honour and perseverance in friendship, the which, God be my witness, who seeth all hearts, was never diminished, nor ever shall be whilest I live. And because my heart and mind shall be more plain and open than my writings: this bearer, Master Hoby, shall declare unto you the effect thereof at length, to whom I pray you give credit.[1]

Three days later, on 11 October, Somerset surrendered.[2] The council sent a delegation to Windsor, where they were welcomed by Edward "with a merry countenance and a loud voice". The young king asked how the lords in London did, "when he should see you, and that you should be welcome whensoever you come"; he then allowed the delegates to kiss his hands.[3] Edward's next task was to command the Duke of Somerset's conveyance to the Tower of London.[4] Also to the Tower went Sir Michael Stanhope, Sir Thomas Smith, Sir John Thynne, and William Cecil, all the Duke of Somerset's creatures,[5] and the last two intimate correspondents of John Dudley. On 17 October Edward returned to London, to his cheering subjects. The same day, he approved the patent re-

---

1 Stow p. 1008
2 Skidmore 2007 pp. 145–146
3 Tytler I p. 242
4 Loades 2004 p. 50
5 Loades 2004 p. 50

appointing John as Lord Admiral;[1] the office had been vacant for seven months, since Thomas Seymour's attainder.

*

The Protector's tyranny over, there was now the problem of who should govern; it was decided to return to the will of Henry VIII, to government by committee or ruling junta. And it appeared that the Earl of Warwick "was more forward in wanting to command than any of them."[2] It was also stipulated that it "should be requisite to have some noblemen appointed to be ordinarily attendant about his Majesty's person in the privy chamber, to give order for the good government of his most royal person, and for the honourable education of his highness in these tender years in learning and virtue". The peers selected were the Marquess of Northampton, the Earl of Arundel, the Earl of Warwick, as well as the Lords St. John, Russell, and Wentworth. The privy chamber was also reorganized, Edward's courtiers Sir Thomas Wroth, Sir Edward Rogers, Sir Thomas Darcy, and Sir Andrew Dudley coming to the forefront as "four principal gentlemen of His Highness' Privy Chamber".[3] These gentlemen received £100 p.a. and were entrusted with Edward's "singular care".[4] John and Andrew Dudley had always been among Edward's favourite courtiers, or generals, rather, and he enthusiastically described their exploits in Scotland in his diary.[5]

John was wise enough not to forget William Paget, his old correspondent and Somerset's best man:

> It is true that … first … they showed Paget no favourable countenance, which disturbed him greatly, but after he had been with them in Council he came out very joyful and showed quite a different face from

---

1 Wilson 1981 p. 41
2 Spanish Chronicle p. 190
3 APC II p. 345; Jordan 1970 p. 20; Skidmore 2007 p. 149
4 Jordan 1970 p. 20
5 Loach 2002 p. 54

before. Since then he has had long conversations with the Earl of Warwick.[1]

On 26 November 1549 Paget was once again found "in deep private conversation" at Warwick's house; the next week he was Baron Paget of Beaudesert.[2] Paget was another peer with Catholic sympathies and van der Delft was already full of hope of a Catholic restoration:

> The Archbishop of Canterbury still holds his place in the Council, but I do not believe they will leave him there ... and it is probable that they are now tolerating him merely that all may be done in proper order. For the same reason they are not yet making any show of intending to restore religion, in order that their first appearance in government may not disgust the people, who are totally infected. But every man among them is devoted to the old faith, except the Earl of Warwick, who nonetheless is taking up again the old observances day by day, and it seems probable that he will reform himself entirely, as he says he hopes his eldest son may obtain some post in your Majesty's court where he may serve you.[3]

At the French court it was even talked that John Dudley was attending mass, as was Edward![4] There were also rumours about new promotions: "my lord of Warrewyck is nomynated to be Marques of Pembroke, and also shalbe Tresorer of England. And the Erle of Arrundell shalbe lord greate Chamborleyn, and that my lord pagett shalbe lord Chamberleyn."[5]

Alas, within weeks the triumvirate of Warwick, Arundel, and Southampton was showing cracks, and – notwithstanding all three

---

1 CSP Span 17 October 1549
2 Gammon 1973 pp. 167–168
3 CSP Span 17 October 1549; CSP Span 8 October 1549
4 Beer 1973 p. 208
5 Brigden 1990 p. 98. These promotions never materialized.

men pleading illness during much of November and December[1] – a new conspiracy was rife. There was the problem of what to do with the former Protector who, it was widely believed, was doomed and likely to be executed:

> [E]very day four or five of them go to the Tower to examine him, and they say he is to be accused publicly this week, and heard in court in his own defence. Though the common rumour has it that he will run no danger of death, and that the Earl of Warwick, who is a very changeable and unstable person, now shows him favour and has been won over by the Protector's wife, who is always in his house, I believe he will not escape.[2]

As Arundel was busy examining the fallen Protector in the Tower – "concerning his treasons in his government" – it transpired, according to Somerset, "that they were done from article to article by the advice, consent, and counsel of the Earl of Warwick". Southampton,

> being hot to be revenged of them both for old grudges past when he lost his office said to my lords … I thought ever we should find them traitors both; and both is worthy to die for by my advice; my Lord of Arundel in like manner gave his consent that they were both worthy to die; and concluded there that the day of execution of the lord protector, the earl of Warwick should be sent to the Tower and have as he deserved.[3]

One witness to this meeting, however, William Paulet, Lord St. John, immediately went to Warwick "and told him of all was done".[4] John decided to invite his enemies to his house, "all the

---

1   Beer 1973 p. 99; CSP Span 19 December 1549
2   CSP Span 19 December 1549
3   Adams, Archer, Bernard 2003a p. 135
4   Adams, Archer, Bernard 2003a p. 135

council coming to Holborn Place where the earl of Warwick lay sick":[1]

> [M]y Lord Wriothesley began to declare how worthy the lord protector was to die and for how many high treasons; the earl of Warwick hearing his own condemnation to approach, with a warlike visage and a long fachell [sword] by his side laid his hand thereof and said; my lord, you seek his blood and he that seeketh his blood would have mine also.

His "great earnestness and sound speeches", "being so well assisted" by his sword, "put all the rest to silence."[2]

Within a few weeks of this dramatic scene, John consolidated his power by placing his "great friends about the king" and packing the privy council so that there was a balance between conservative and evangelical councillors.[3] Edward appointed the serious Protestants Henry Grey, Marquess of Dorset, and Thomas Goodrich, Bishop of Ely, to the council – on the prompting of Archbishop Cranmer and the Earl of Warwick, but also "by my consent", as he stressed.[4] Thus the reformed agenda was saved. The earls of Southampton and Arundel were no longer seen at council meetings and Arundel was also deprived of the office of Lord Chamberlain; "commanded to leave away his staff", he lost his privileged access to the king:

> What is laid to their charge is not openly known, but some imagineth that they went about the subversion of religion, and where there were bolts on the doors of the king's highness privy chamber the Earl of Arundel caused divers of them to be taken away. What he meant thereby I know not, but his answer was therein to Sir Andrew Dudley coming to him at the striking of

---

1 Adams, Archer, Bernard 2003a p. 136
2 Adams, Archer, Bernard 2003a p. 136
3 Adams, Archer, Bernard 2003a pp. 135–136
4 Skidmore 2007 p. 149; Adams, Archer, Bernard 2003a pp. 135–136

the bolts that he would not tarry at other men's pleasure to come to the king's chamber.[1]

Thus Richard Scudamore informed his friend Philip Hoby, now English ambassador at the Imperial court of Brussels.

Buckhounds, whose affairs at court were tended to by the Master of the Buckhounds, were not only participants in the royal hunting parties, the animals were also valued presents to foreign rulers. English diplomats abroad needed to be supplied with them on a regular basis. Throughout the crisis of late 1549 the use of fine hunting dogs as a diplomatic tool continued uninterrupted and John Dudley, Viscount Lisle, at 19 showed promising signs of a Master of the Buckhounds. Richard Scudamore updated Ambassador Hoby on 5 December 1549:

> I have put my Lord Lisle in remembrance for the chase dog that he promised you, who said that he marvelled much that the dog had not been sent unto him before this, alleging further that if it came not shortly that then he would send a servant of his own for him.[2]

In January the recent plot was still very fresh, and John Dudley was still very cautious: "this evening being of the 11th of this month my Lord of Warwick and my Lady his wife were carried in a litter from his house in Holborn to York the sheriff and as yet my Lord came not at the court, the which thing maketh men to judge that he dareth not to remain in his own house."[3] By 29 January 1550 John's power was firmly consolidated, though he was still only Earl of Warwick; on the same day was set free from the Tower, among others, "Mr Seycell",[4] and the next day, 30 January, there was

---

1   Brigden 1990 pp. 107–108
2   Brigden 1990 p. 96
3   Brigden 1990 p. 108
4   Brigden 1990 p. 114. William Cecil.

> a newe alteration of offycers amongst certeyn of the greate counsell, as the Erle of Wyllshyre and late lord greate master is nomynated to be lord hygh Treasourer of England, and my lord of Warrewyck ... shalbe Lorde greate master and president of the counsell.[1]

*

And on 6 February, Philip Hoby was still waiting for his hunting dogs:

> My Lord Lisle showed me that he looketh for the chase dog within these few a days. And when the dog cometh I know not how he shall be conveyed unto you, but in the mean time he shall be well kept. I have three fair young mastiffs for you, the which I leave in keeping in Paris Garden until I may have shipping for them.[2]

Paris Garden, a Southwark manor, was in the keepership of Scudamore's cousin. A week later, Hoby received the next update:

> My Lord Lisle looketh every day for the chase greyhound. And your mastiffs stayeth for the coming out of the ships.[3]

And on 23 February:

> My Lord Lisle looketh every day and hour for the chase dog, marvelling much that he is not brought before this unto him. My Lord of Warwick, Lord

---

[1] Brigden 1990 p. 116. For his good services in averting the Arundel-Southampton plot William Paulet, Lord St. John, had been elevated to Earl of Wiltshire and now became Lord Treasurer, a position held by Lord Protector Somerset while in power and recently suggested for John Dudley (see above p. 82). William Paulet had been Great Master of the Household and Lord President of the Council, offices now conferred on John Dudley.
[2] Brigden 1990 p. 118
[3] Brigden 1990 p. 119

Great Master, hath been this sevennight at the court already metely well amended.[1]

Hopefully, about the end of February, the chase dog finally materialized, as we hear no more about it. In April 1551, Lisle finally became Master of the Buckhounds. And while, early in 1550, the earls of Arundel and Southampton were commanded to keep to their palaces and later to their "countries", the Duke of Somerset's rehabilitation made great progress.[2]

---

1 Brigden 1990 p. 121
2 Adams, Archer, Bernard 2003a p. 135–136

10.
Lord President

On 6 February 1550 the Duke of Somerset was released from the Tower. There were even expectations and rumours that Somerset would regain the title of Lord Protector, which had only just been abolished by parliament, however the new ruler was undoubtedly the Earl of Warwick. During the spring Somerset was received back into the privy council and the privy chamber; now without a major office, he was still the senior peer of the realm, as well as the richest. His rehabilitation was complete by 26 April, when he returned to court, where "all men seeketh upon him".[1]

The plot against himself had convinced John Dudley that it would be better to work Somerset's release, and it was observed that John had "bent himself all he could for his life".[2] – Yet these times of intrigue were really the hour of the ladies; "their wives exchange banquets and festivities daily", François van der Delft described the Duchess of Somerset's and the Countess of Warwick's activities.[3] There was even a funny story of how the Duchess, "a very prudent woman", at the time when "everyday it was said that either on that or the next day" the Duke of Somerset "would be let out to have his head cut off, ... went one morning to the Earl of Warwick's house" to plead with him for her husband's life. John had great difficulties convincing her to rise up from her kneeling position and take a seat and finally promised that he "would do his best"; she then passed into the Countess of Warwick's chamber, "where they talked for a long time, and the Duchess begged the Countess to speak that night to her husband in

---
1 Brigden 1990 p. 130
2 Adams, Archer, Bernard 2003a p. 135
3 CSP Span 18 January 1550

favour of the Duke, and at the same time she took out a very rich jewel of diamonds, and gave it to the Countess, and begged her to take it to remind her of her promise. The Countess refused it at first, but afterwards accepted it." The next morning, when the Earl of Warwick

> went to the Council he repeated the request of the Duchess, and the lords, who thought more of the Earl than of anybody else, told him he could order as he thought best. Great is the power of gifts; for from the very night that the Countess spoke to her husband in favour of the Duke he lost all rancour against him.[1]

*

In March van der Delft wrote that it was rumoured that the Earl of Warwick had "gone into the country for a change of air", yet that he had really set out for Somerset's house to discuss the marriage between his heir, John, and Somerset's eldest daughter, Anne.[2] Somerset, it seems, at first was not very interested in the match, as John later suggested that Somerset's daughter marry the young Duke of Suffolk, Katherine Brandon's son. Katherine was categorically against arranged marriages, however – she did not want young persons to "marry by our orders and without their consent".[3] Thus, the young Viscount Lisle was only a second choice, although he had apparently lived for some time in Somerset's household, making gifts of fine clothes to the duke's cooks and kitchen boys; and he would also have met his future bride.[4]

The wedding took place at Somerset's palace at Sheen on 3 June 1550; in the presence of King Edward there was "a fair dinner made" among plenty of other entertainments. The next day saw the marriage of Amy Robsart and Robert Dudley, and again Edward

---

1 Spanish Chronicle pp. 190–192
2 CSP Span 8 March 1550
3 Knighton 1992 p. 163
4 HMC Second Report pp. 101–102; Loades 1996 p. 224

89

amused himself.[1] Notably absent from the festivities was the elder John Dudley who, it was later claimed, feared to be poisoned.[2]

*

Between 12 and 14 years old at the time of her marriage, Anne Seymour was a learned young lady, a correspondent of Continental reformers, who was, with her sisters, eulogized by the French poet Ronsard.[3] In view of the younger John Dudley's collection of books of Greek and Latin classics she may not have been an unsuitable wife for him, but nothing has survived as to the material settlement for the young couple. It cannot have been overwhelming, as the younger John always seems to have had difficulties to support himself out of his own pocket. He lived in style, as is shown by "a note of all the velvet shoes that my Lord Lisle hath had since [December 1545] which are in number 46 pair, and 2 pair of velvet slippers."[4] He may also have been a bit careless, as no less than "4 buttons were cut off my Lord's gown in the privy chamber by Mr. Fitzwilliam, and never gotten again".[5] This happened on 29 June 1550, a few weeks after his wedding, and yet four days before a rather more serious mishap had occurred:

> 36 buttons of gold, six-cornered and black enamelled changed for 31 pairs of black enamelled aglets: which aglets and 8 pair more of the same making and bought the same time, and 39 enamelled buttons, all set on a velvet cap, were stolen, cap and all, at Hatfield.[6]

How good that he also received valuable stuff, although he had a tendency to give such things away; this is what happened to "a rapier, dagger, and girdle" given to him by his father-in-law, the

---

1   Literary Remains II pp. 273–275
2   Adams, Archer, Bernard 2003b p. 52
3   Stevenson 2004
4   HMC Second Report p. 101
5   HMC Second Report p. 102
6   HMC Second Report p. 102

Duke of Somerset, as well as to "a sword which Doctor Cox gave my Lord, and my Lord gave the same to Sir Andrew Dudley."[1] Even the mysteriously high number of velvet shoes needed over the years may be explained by gift giving: "9 pair of white velvet shoes; whereof Mr. Anglionby had a pair, Mr. Verney a pair, Mr. Granado a pair, Mr. Guildford Dudley a pair, a pair left at Mr. Williams, and so there is 3 pair remaining in the wardrobe."[2]

Before John and Robert Dudley's marriages there had been Ambrose's wedding in about December 1549 to Anne Whorwood, daughter and co-heiress of a wealthy London lawyer, after he and Robert had returned with their father from the suppression of Kett's Rebellion. At that time Ambrose also received his keepership of Kenilworth Castle. The 18-year-old Amy Robsart, bride of the equally 18-year-old Robert Dudley, seems to have been Robert's sweetheart and it looks like John was happy with a love match for his fifth son; he signed an agreement with her father, 11 days before the marriage. Amy was her father's heiress, though only after the death of both her parents, and Sir John Robsart was wealthy but not spectacularly so. Presumably, the Earl of Warwick was happy to acquire a relative in the troubled county of Norfolk, where he had little personal influence, and he was willing to pay handsomely for his son Robert's "dowry", the young couple living chiefly from his gifts.[3]

The brothers John, Ambrose, and Robert were all tutored by England's foremost classical rhetorician, Thomas Wilson, as well as by Roger Ascham,[4] Cambridge's best man for the instruction of Greek. In 1547, Ascham reminded the Earl of Warwick how "your mind is wonderfully influenced by the love of letters in that you take so much care in educating all your sons."[5] The younger John Dudley called his own a precious collection of books: Apart from Cicero, there were to be found Horace, Terence, and Virgil's *Aeneid*. He had a Greek grammar, a "King's grammar", "a boke to

---

1 HMC Second Report p. 102. Richard Cox was one of Edward VI's tutors.
2 HMC Second Report p. 102. Edward Aglionby was the younger John Dudley's chaplain (Alford 2002 p. 130). He also received two pairs of boots.
3 Loades 1996 p. 222; Skidmore 2010 p. 24; Jackson 1878 p. 84
4 Ascham I Pt. 1 p. 125; Chamberlin 1939 pp. 55–57
5 Chamberlin 1939 p. 55

write the Roman hand", as well as a "boke to speake and write Frenche"; next two "bokes of cosmografye" and a number of plays by John Heywood, there were two volumes in Italian and "the Debate between Heraldes", a medieval work from the times of Richard II, recently printed. There were also religious works like "a Testament in Frenche, covered with black velvet", an "Anglishe Testamente", "Aurilius Augustinus", "a Frenche boke of Christ and the Pope", and "a Tragidie in Anglishe of the unjust supremicie of the Bisshope of Rome" by the Italian reformer Bernardino Occhino.[1]

Considerably younger than their older brothers, the younger sons Guildford and Harry, and perhaps Charles until his death at the age of eight, seem to have received a slightly different education. The boys may well have passed time in the household of their uncle by marriage, Francis Jobson, for Jobson spent some money for the "board of [John's] children".[2] Nevertheless, now and then all the brothers were in each other's company, as appears from inventories of Viscount Lisle's goods. In September 1550 the younger John took his brothers Robert and Guildford on a trip to Warwick Castle, and on the way he presented them with "a pair of red boot hose" and "a hat of unshorn velvet", respectively. Recently, Robert had also received one pair of "white freeze buskins", and on 18 May 1550 there were "4 dozen and 8 Damascene buttons, six-cornered, whereof 2 dozen were given to Mr. Guildford Dudley at Westminster". In 1545 young Harry, perhaps six years old, received "a white satin coat" from his 14-year-old big brother. On other occasions young "Master Harry Duddely" gave the presents: a sword, and another time "a fine rapier, dagger, and girdle of Damascene work".[3]

*

Instead of taking the title of Lord Protector, John Dudley set out to rule as *primus inter pares*, reinstituting the privy council as the

---

1   HMC Second Report p. 102; MacCulloch 2001 pp. 52–53
2   Adams 2008b
3   HMC Second Report pp. 101–102

actual governing body.[1] The new Lord President of the Council was in effect the new regent, even before he officially took office on 2 February. François van der Delft, who could see no signs of the religious *volte-face* he had been hoping for, commented sourly:

> The Earl of Warwick is absolute master here, and the Lords of the Council are under his orders. They go daily to his house to learn his pleasure; nothing is done except by his command. He hardly ever appears in public, but by shamming illness he attempts to hide his pride and ambition.[2]

By Edward's appointment finally Great Master of the Household, John also controlled the king's surroundings. His powers included debarring councillors from the privy council as well as appointing new ones, and he proceeded to exclude the earls of Arundel and Southampton.[3] But John also recruited new personnel; he availed himself of the services of William Cecil, who was still in the Duke of Somerset's service but gradually shifted his loyalty to the new ruler. In a very short time, John Dudley judged Cecil to be "such a faithful servant and by that term most witty councillor ... unto the king's majesty and his proceedings, as was scarce the like within this realm".[4] On 5 September 1550 Cecil was appointed Edward's junior Principal Secretary. In this position he became John's trusted right hand, who primed the privy council according to the Lord President's wishes. At the same time Cecil had intimate contact with the king because Edward worked closely with the secretaries of state.[5]

Sharing power with the Earl of Warwick were not just a few of the ex-Protector's former friends, but also some of his enemies. William Parr, Marquess of Northampton, was one such. At the age

---

1 MacCulloch 2001 p. 55; Loades 2004 p. 88, "Working hand in glove with Cecil, he rationalized the procedures of government by council, which became central to the conduct of affairs ... and in the process created the 'system' which Cecil reinstituted under Elizabeth I." (Hoak 2008).
2 CSP Span 8 March 1550
3 Hoak 1980 pp. 36–39
4 Alford 2002 p. 140. Words reported by Richard Whalley.
5 Hoak1980 p. 40; Alford 2002 pp. 139–141; Hoak 1976 p. 63

of 13 he had been married to the 12-year-old Lady Anne Bourchier, heiress of the Earl of Essex; however, when the earldom became vacant in 1540, the title was secured by Thomas Cromwell, Parr having to wait for his sister to become queen to obtain it. His wife, meanwhile, eloped with a lover and started a family with him. William Parr obtained a formal separation, but no divorce, a situation that left him unable to remarry. He hoped to change this after Edward VI's accession; an undeniably Protestant regime could not ignore that a divorce and remarriage of the wronged partner in cases of adultery was biblical and accepted by most reformers. Unfortunately, when Archbishop Cranmer, after endless delays, decided in his favour, Parr had already married his lover Elizabeth Brooke in secret, and the prim Lord Protector expelled him from the privy council as well as ordering him to separate permanently from his new wife.

John Dudley passed on his office of Lord Chamberlain to his old friend as he himself rose to Great Master of the Household. Sharing the two positions between them, Dudley and Parr in effect ruled the court. In March 1551, parliament finally passed a private bill which allowed Northampton to legalize his current marriage (and to hold on to most of his first wife's property and inheritance).[1] The third prominent man in the ruling junta was Katherine Parr's brother-in-law, Sir William Herbert. From the very start of the new administration William Herbert sat with John Dudley on key commissions. It is intriguing that both Parr and Herbert seem to have taken ill the removal of Thomas Seymour. Shortly after John Dudley's takeover of power they met the Imperial ambassador over some complaints about piracy, which the late Lord Admiral Seymour had obviously abetted. Parr and Herbert would not allow any criticism of their deceased brother-in-law:

> The Marquis of Northampton then accused me ... when I accused the late Admiral of robbery, wishing to palliate his actions, as he had married his sister, widow of the late King. ... As for the Admiral, I asked him to tell me himself whether he had been blameless

---
1 James 2008b

or not. He did not answer at once, but after a little thought he said: "I don't blame him." And then he began to get exceedingly angry. Then Master Herbert, the King's Master of the Horse, who married another sister of the said Marquis, and who knows no other language but his native English and can neither read nor write, started shouting at the top of his voice. He is also in Warwick's party, and he made it plain. I heard nothing but the words "my Lord Admiral", and saw him make some strange gestures; ... I then noticed they were more embarrassed than before, and finally they said to me that they would communicate the business to Warwick, the Lord Admiral, and would afterwards give me their answer; from which it is clear that the said Warwick has the whip hand of them all, using for his own ends these Marquises and Master Herberts whom no one dares to contradict.[1]

Shortly after Thomas Seymour's execution in March 1549, his seven-months-old daughter had been placed, according to his last wish, in the care of Katherine Brandon, the Dowager Duchess of Suffolk. Although so young, Mary Seymour as a queen's daughter was entitled to a ridiculously expensive household to mark her social rank. All this went "wholly at my charges", as the duchess wrote to her friend, William Cecil, on 27 August 1549, asking him for help to secure aid from the Lord Protector: "I have written to my lady of Somerset at large, that there be some pension allotted unto her according to my lord grace's promise. Now, good Cecil, help at a pinch all that you may help."[2] Alas, this was an inauspicious time to molest the duke, the government being busy suppressing widespread rebellion in England.

It was not until 22 January 1550 that something was moved in Mary Seymour's case. Parliament had reconvened after Somerset's fall and now passed an act which restored her in blood[3] and allowed her any of her father's property that had as yet not passed

---
1 CSP Span 31 January 1550
2 Norton 2011b pp. 240–241
3 James 2008a p. 300

to the crown on his attainder ten months earlier. Such remaining possessions were most unlikely to be substantial, of course.[1] The next and last record of little Mary Seymour occurs on 13 March 1550, when the privy council issued a warrant to the Court of Wards to pay some £438 for "diets, wages, liveries of the household of Mistress Mary Seymour for a year and a half ended at the Feast of the Annunciation of Our Lady next coming".[2] This date would have been 25 March 1550, so was Mary still alive when the warrant was issued or might it have been a document concerning the winding up of her household?[3]

Three years after his attainder and lucky escape from execution, the Duke of Norfolk was still a prisoner in the Tower. His confinement had been gradually eased, and the new administration allowed even visits by his wife and daughter, who were "to have recourse to the late Duke of Norfolk at times and with a train convenient"; he may have enjoyed rather more the "liberty to walk in the garden and gallery", granted in July. In April 1551 he was granted a meeting with his grandson and heir, Lord Thomas Howard, "in the presence of the Lieutenant."[4]

On 30 July 1550 died Thomas Wriothesley, Earl of Southampton, in his London home, it was rumoured by self-administered poison.[5] Suffering from tuberculosis, van der Delft reported, Wriothesley had wished "to be under the earth rather than upon it". Still, he bequeathed his "friend" the Earl of Warwick a gilt cup worth £20 and Lady Warwick another gilt cup worth £10.[6]

*

[1] Porter 2011 p. 342
[2] APC II p. 411; Norton 2011b p. 241
[3] Some biographies of Katherine Parr imply that the final improvement of Mary Seymour's endowment was initiated by her uncle, Protector Somerset, or at least by William Cecil, the Duchess of Suffolk's close friend (Porter 2011 p. 342; Norton 2011b pp. 242). In fact, neither Somerset nor Cecil could possibly have been involved in either parliamentary proceedings or council decisions between October 1549 and February 1550, due to their imprisonment in the Tower.
[4] APC II p. 400; APC III p. 88; APC III p. 254
[5] Adams, Archer, Bernard 2003a p. 136
[6] Rowse 1965 p. 26; Skidmore 2007 p. 154; CSP Span 17 March 1550

The garrisons in Scotland, and since August 1549 renewed hostilities with France, came at a crippling cost. Somerset's war policy had entailed an extraordinary expenditure of about £350,000 p.a. against a regular crown income of £150,000 p.a. It was impossible to continue in this way. John decided to send Lord Paget to France and negotiate a withdrawal of the besieged English garrison at Boulogne, the town that had so valiantly been won in 1544 but was now completely isolated because the French had taken the English rebellions in the previous summer as an opportunity to overrun the Boulonnais. The peace with France was concluded in the Treaty of Boulogne, in March 1550; the high costs of the garrison could thus be saved and French payments of 400,000 crowns or roughly £180,000 were a most welcome immediate cash income.[1] Paget did a good job, as usual, while John was directing affairs from his bed: "My lord of Warrewick lyeth at Grenewhich and is very yll troubled with his sykenes".[2] There was public rejoicing at the peace and bonfires when it was proclaimed on 28 March,[3] although the Habsburg ambassador was naturally disgruntled at any rapprochement between France and England:

> The people are much discontented with the restitution of Boulogne and murmur a good deal against the government of the Earl of Warwick, who keeps himself shut up in his room feigning illness, and will see no one except members of the Council. The other day he made the Earl of Arundel wait two full hours outside his room.[4]

In May 1550, a great ceremonial embassy from France arrived in London to sign the recent treaty. Henry II's ambassador extraordinary was the 31-year-old Gaspard de Coligny, who within two years would follow Claude d'Annebault as Admiral of France.[5]

---

1 Loades 1996 pp. 169–170; Loades 2008a
2 Brigden 1990 p. 125
3 Loades 1996 p. 154
4 CSP Span 17 March 1550
5 Potter 1984 p. 180; CSP Foreign June 1550. Coligny later became leader of

Like with his son's wedding, John seems to have avoided court life, though. The French envoys were entertained by the young Viscount Lisle; he jousted with the Vîdame de Chartres and the young Duke of Suffolk before the king, wearing yellow in "a pastime of ten against ten at the ring" while their counterparts wore blue.[1]

The threat of war with Scotland was also neutralized, England giving up its isolated garrisons in exchange.[2] The Treaty of Norham was signed in June 1551, and a joint commission, one of the first of its kind in history, was installed at Southampton to agree upon the vexed question of the so-called Debatable Lands, or the exact boundary, between the two countries. The English side was represented by the Lord Treasurer, William Paulet, the Scottish side – which was revealing – by the French ambassador in London, Boisdaulphin. It needed more than another year to conclude the issue in August 1552, significantly by French arbitration.[3] Despite the cessation of hostilities, English defences were kept on a high level: nearly £200,000 p.a. were spent on the navy and the garrisons at Calais and on the Scottish border.[4]

In May 1550, John Dudley passed on the office of Lord Admiral to Edward Lord Clinton.[5] He did not lose his interest in maritime affairs, however. Under Henry VIII the English navy had been revolutionized, mainly in military terms, and John, as we have seen, had played a part in this. Now, despite Spanish threats, English voyages to far-off coasts were beginning to take shape.[6] They were all intended to lead southwards, even those to the Arctic, as it was believed that the voyagers would ultimately end up in the Tropic. The reason for this was that gold was believed to

---

    the Huguenots, being famously murdered in the St. Bartholomew's Day Massacre, 1572.
1   Beer 1973 p. 103. The Duke of Suffolk was Katherine Willoughby's 15-year-old son, Henry Brandon, who died of the sweating sickness two months later.
2   Loades 1996 p. 166
3   Merriman 2000 p. 377
4   Loades 1996 p. 209
5   Literary Remains II p. 265. Clinton would go on to serve both Mary (with interruption) and Elizabeth as Lord Admiral until his death in 1585.
6   Loades 1996 pp. 210, 244, 245

occur only in hot countries.[1] John Dudley seems to have struck up a friendship with the veteran explorer Sebastian Cabot, with whom he contemplated even a raid on the coast of Peru.[2] Expeditions to Morocco and the Guinea coast materialized in 1551 and 1552; the voyage to Morocco was sponsored by John Yorke, the merchant and sheriff of London in whose house the Earl and Countess of Warwick loved to stay.[3] A planned voyage to China via the Northeast Passage sailed in May 1553 under Richard Chancellor and Hugh Willoughby – King Edward, in maybe the last high point of his life, watched the departure of the ships from his window.[4] This expedition was "England's first officially sponsored voyage of discovery".[5]

Whether through John's naval career or through people like John Yorke, the whole family became fascinated with mathematics and cosmography; Robert Dudley's love of arithmetics was castigated by his humanist tutor, while John Dudley collected astrolabes and his wife clocks.[6] One of her pieces was set in a little book "that hath the sun, the moon in it etc."; she also possessed a dial with an almanac on one side and a "golden number in the midst".[7]

One of the resident scholars in the Dudley household was the mathematician and astrologer, John Dee, whose ideas were instrumental in the expedition to China.[8] By early 1553, the young magus had been commissioned to write two treatises for Jane

---

1 Mathew 1972 pp. 106–107
2 Beer 1973 p. 193; It may have been John Dudley who convinced Cabot to return to England after 25 years of exile in 1549 (Loades 1996 p. 210).
3 Mathew 1972 p. 108; CSP Span 18 January 1550. See above pp. 78, 85 for the friendship between John Dudley and John Yorke. Van der Delft observed that "The Lord Mayor and the said sheriff are neighbours and friends, and between them govern the town."
4 Loades 1996 pp. 245–247, 238
5 Loades 2008a. Though the quest to find a Northeast passage ended tragically with the deaths of both Chancellor and Willoughby, it inaugurated diplomatic relations between England and Russia and directly led to the foundation of the Muscovy Company in 1555.
6 Chamberlin 1939 p. 55; Haynes 1987 p. 95; Collins 1745 p. 34–35
7 Collins 1745 p. 34
8 Sherman 1995 p. 173

Dudley about heavenly configurations and the tides.[1] As late as 1570 Dee remembered how her son, the younger John Dudley, used to wear round his neck a little book – "his ... counsellor most trusty", with "rules and descriptions arithmetical". Perhaps this book, kept in "a rich case of gold", was the "boke of Arthmetrik in Lattyn" found in his remarkably vast collection of books.[2]

Edward VI was another student of geometry, mathematics, and astronomy. An astrolabe was made for him, significantly bearing the royal arms as well as those of his tutor, John Cheke, and his chief minister, John Dudley. Scores of charts and globes were acquired for Edward, and in 1549 a new world map made by Sebastian Cabot was displayed on a wall at Whitehall Palace.[3]

*

At his coronation the nine-year-old Edward VI was hailed as "a second Josias" by Archbishop Cranmer; when he was 12, the Imperial ambassador claimed that "in the court there is no bishop, and no man of learning so ready to argue in support of the new doctrine as the King ... and this seems to be a source of pride to his courtiers that the King should ... choose for himself who shall preach."[4] As he listened to those sermons he wrote down "every notable sentence, and specially if it touched a king". When he was 11, he composed a treatise in French against the Pope, "the true son of the devil, a bad man, an Antichrist and abominable tyrant". Edward believed firmly in the doctrines of salvation by faith alone and predestination.[5] Still, the sense of his royal supremacy was highly developed and at least as important to him as purely dogmatic aspects.[6]

He found his minister John Dudley most willing to collaborate. John was praised as "that intrepid soldier of Christ" by John Hooper, a preacher committed to reform who impressed the king.

---

1 French 2002 pp. 32–33
2 HMC Second Report p. 102. Mathematicall Preface
3 Hoak 2008
4 Loach 2002 p. 130; Hoak 2008
5 Hoak 2008
6 Loach 2002 pp. 133–134

It was decided that he should become a bishop, but Hooper declined on the grounds of the rather popish ordinal used at the ceremony. He especially took umbrage at the vestments (or "Aaronic habits" as he called them) he would have to wear for the ceremony. This was implied criticism of Cranmer, the Archbishop of Canterbury, but John Dudley and the rest of the council were happy to support Hooper. On 5 August 1550 Edward wrote personally to Cranmer to ask him to drop "certain rites and ceremonies offensive" to Hooper's conscience. The latter, however, found ever more unacceptable details in the consecration ceremony, even publishing a book about it. John Dudley warned him that the king must be obeyed in "indifferent matters", as opposed to theologically important stuff, and he was finally committed to the Fleet prison in January 1551, before accepting his episcopal honour, with all ceremonies performed, in March 1551.[1] Hooper received last minute help from Edward VI, though, when the king spontaneously struck through with his pen all references to saints from the form of the oath.[2]

The use of the moderately Protestant *Book of Common Prayer* had become law in 1549. Edward's half-sister, Mary, was unwilling to give up the mass, though, which she used to have celebrated in great style before her household even in her absence, let alone allow the use of the *Book* in her residences; declining to respect this "late law of your own making ... which in my conscience is not worthy to have the name of law", she in effect chose for herself which law to obey and which not.[3] Somerset was inclined to be lenient with her, which apparently annoyed John Dudley, who pronounced:

> The mass is either of God or of the devil: if of God, it is but right that all our people should be allowed to go to it; but if it is not of God, as we are all taught out of the scriptures, why then should not the voice of this fury be equally proscribed to all?[4]

---

1 Loades 1996 pp. 175–176; Jordan 1970 pp. 294, 296
2 MacCulloch 2001 p. 36
3 Loades 2006 p. 75
4 Original Letters II p. 439

Mary was able to behave like she did knowing that her cousin, the Emperor Charles V, championed her cause, and because the English could not risk to alienate the Habsburgs due to vital trade interests in the Netherlands. Still, as Lord President John took up the issue with her and insisted that she give up public mass in her residences. Her response was to secretly request the emperor's help to escape to the Continent: When Charles indeed sent a ship, she changed her mind in the last minute, though, and stayed in England.

The Council was prepared to concede that she hear mass with three or four ladies in her chamber, but without her household.[1] This was unacceptable to Mary; she pleaded her conscience and maintained that Edward was too young to understand matters of religion, and that he should not "be robbed of freedom by laws and statutes on spiritual matters passed during his minority".[2] She was, in effect, arguing that during a minority the government and parliament had no authority to decide on important issues. Mary had no point, though, for constitutionally the king could not be under age.[3] Increasingly annoyed at this encroachment on his authority, the 13-year-old monarch berated Mary at Christmas (while assuring her that she would never come to harm at his hands).[4] On 28 January 1551 he wrote a long letter to her:

> [I]t appears to us ... that you, our nearest sister, in whom by nature we should place reliance and our highest esteem, wish to break our laws and set them aside deliberately and of your own free will; and moreover sustain and encourage others to commit a like offence. ... My sister, you must learn that your courses were tolerated when our laws were first promulgated, not indeed as a permission to break the

---

1 Loach 2002 p. 130
2 Jordan 1970 p. 259
3 Kantorowicz 1981 pp. 4, 7. A few years after Edward's reign crown jurists would clarify that the king "is not only incapable of *doing* wrong, but even of *thinking* wrong: he can never mean to do an improper thing: in him is no folly or weakness ... no Act which the King does as King, shall be defeated by his Nonage".
4 Jordan 1970 pp. 259–260

same, but so that you might be inclined to obey them, seeing the love and indulgence we displayed towards you. We made a difference between you and our subjects, not that all should follow our ordinances, and you alone disregard them, but in order that you should do out of love for us what the rest do out of duty. ... We now offer to hear all you have to say, you and your partisans, if you are conscientiously opposed to our laws. You shall be permitted to speak frankly, and what you or they have to say shall be listened to, provided you undertake to listen to the answers and debates that shall ensue. ... It is our duty to watch over the welfare of each one of our subjects as each ought to watch over himself. You would be angry to see one of the servants of your household, of those nearest to you, openly disregarding your orders; and so it is with us ... Your near relationship to us, your exalted rank, the conditions of the times, all magnify your offence. ...

We do not know how much of this epistle was composed by Edward's chief minister, however the king also wrote a subscript in his own hand:

> I think of doing what is meet in the matter, and in accordance with the will of God, as my duty binds me to do, and see to it that my laws be loyally carried out and observed. I could not suffer it to ... support some with favour whilst others are justly punished. Truly, sister, I will not say more and worse things, because my duty would compel me to use harsher and angrier words. But this I will say with certain intention, that I will see my laws strictly obeyed, and those who break them shall be watched and denounced.[1]

Edward also suggested a meeting, and on 18 March 1551 the princess met king and council, in the presence of the new Imperial

---
1   CSP Span 28 January 1551

ambassador, Jehan de Scheyfve, who reported the exchanges, though his English was not very good:

> The Council's next move was to try to charge the lady with some disobedience, calling to witness the late King's will, in accordance with which she ought to obey ordinances and submit to the Council's instructions. She replied that she had carefully read the said will, and she was bound to obedience only on the point of her marriage, on which she had not been disobedient. She added that the late King had ordered two masses to be said for him every day, and four obsequies every year, and other ceremonies, which yet remained unobserved on their side. They answered that they felt themselves bound by the will, and obliged to execute its provisions, in so far as they were in no way harmful to the King, their master. She said she knew it well, and was quite confident that the late King had never ordered anything in the least prejudicial to the King, her brother, ... and it was reasonable to suppose that he alone cared more for the good of his kingdom than all the members of his Council put together. Unable to swallow this, the Earl of Warwick spoke the following words: "How now, my Lady? It seems that your Grace is trying to show us in a hateful light to the King, our master, without any cause whatsoever."[1]

Mary then brought up the usual arguments of her conscience and that Edward as a minor could not decide on matters of religion, that "riper age and experience would teach him much more yet", to which Edward retorted that "she also might still have something to learn, for no one was too old for that".[2] The unpleasant encounter ended with Mary urging the king "to take away her life rather than

---

1   CSP Span 6 April 1551
2   Loach 2002 p. 132

the old religion", to which he responded "quickly that he wished for no such sacrifice."[1]

The next round came only two days later when the Imperial ambassador again visited the council and read out a formal threat of war from the emperor, in case the Lady Mary was not allowed her mass in the accustomed way. Fortunately, the emperor was not in a position to go to war,[2] but still, the ministers were apprehensive and, kneeling, tried to make clear to Edward that policy must sometimes go before principle; but Edward would not yield, "neither would agree to it at any king's or kaiser's entreat".[3] Archbishop Cranmer and Bishop Ridley then explained to him that "licence to sin was sin, to suffer and wink at it for a time might be borne", and almost reduced to tears by his councillors, he remained unconvinced. The struggle with Mary and the emperor's ambassador went on for months, until August 1551, when John Dudley told de Scheyfve that Edward now "wished to concern himself with all the affairs of the kingdom", and that he was "as much of age as if he were forty".[4]

At that point John also felt safe to press home to Mary's household that they were not allowed to use "any Masse or other Divine Service than is appointed by the lawes of this realme", as the council ruled on 9 August.[5] For the implementation of this ruling he had even secured the presence of those Catholic lords, the earls of Derby and Arundel. Neither was a council member in summer 1551, and both were made one for one day only.[6] The next step was to send Mary a delegation of the privy council, whom she treated with such a show of contempt and hysterics that they returned empty-handed. The Lord President's reaction was to arrest three or four of her household officers and chaplains. Meanwhile even Charles V had tired of the issue, suggesting that Mary be satisfied with hearing "mass privately in her house, without admitting of any strangers",[7] and indeed some compromise on that

1 CSP Span 6 April 1551
2 Loach 2002 p. 132
3 Literary Remains I p. ccxxviii
4 Loach 2002 pp. 132–133
5 Hoak 1976 p. 68
6 Hoak 1976 pp. 66–69
7 Skidmore 2007 p. 187

line was found: Mary continued her mass in a more private manner, while augmenting her landed property by exchanges with the crown.[1] Relations improved, her servants were set free, and Mary next visited the court in June 1552.[2]

At the time of Somerset's downfall Elizabeth had just turned 16, the age where she could expect to become the head of her own household. With John Dudley in power, she finally received her full share of her father's legacy, £3,000 p.a. in land. The stingy Protector had never seen fit to provide her with the income she was entitled to. In February and March 1550 Elizabeth received lands worth £3,106 p.a. in half a dozen counties.[3] To help her administrate these she appointed William Cecil surveyor of her estates,[4] something his de facto superior, the Earl of Warwick, must have condoned. In fact, Elizabeth was on excellent terms with the Dudleys. In November 1550 Jehan de Scheyfve heard it "from a safe source" that John was going to "cast off his wife" and marry the 17-year-old princess, "with whom he is said to have had several secret and intimate personal communications", John's objective being, of course, the crown.[5] Since de Scheyfve's principal informers belonged to the Lady Mary's circle, it is quite possible that she and her ladies were throwing a little mud at the hated daughter of Anne Boleyn.

*

Richard Morison was the successor of Philip Hoby as the English ambassador at the court of Charles V, and he was a man "in the habit of proclaiming his religion stoutly on every occasion". Unfortunately he did this also before the emperor, who was highly offended by Morison's "persuasive arguments", as Charles surprisingly called them.[6] Ambassador de Scheyfve was instructed to raise the issue with the English government, to tell them "how

---

1 Ives 2009 p. 93
2 Jordan 1970 pp. 263–264
3 Guy 2013 p. 134
4 Guy 2013 p. 137
5 CSP Span 4 November 1550
6 Jordan 1970 p. 142

monstrously their ambassador had forgotten himself to speak in such wise" so that "they might afterwards wish to bring forward excuses":

> After this discourse, Sire, I began to read them your Majesty's letter, which appeared to frighten them sorely. They immediately started to look at one another, as if they knew not what face they had better put upon the matter: so much so that, when I had finished reading the letter, the Duke of Somerset and Earl of Warwick repeated two or three times over that the phrases used by their ambassador to your Majesty were quite new to them. He had, they said, done exceedingly ill, and gone quite beyond his charge. The King and Council had known nothing about it, and were greatly displeased that he should so have forgotten himself.[1]

The heretical regime in England seemed increasingly obnoxious to the emperor, while most of Ambassador de Scheyfve's informants were people with a stake in subverting it – so that, unsurprisingly, there emanated a stream of fanciful reports from that quarter about the country being on the brink of civil war.[2] Encouraged by such reports, and keen on improving her trade interests, Mary of Hungary, the Habsburg regent in the Low Countries, thought it worthwhile to take possession of an English port. From the emperor's viewpoint it would be safest to take over England altogether; if only some young adventurer could be found who would gladly undertake the work of liberation: "It seems that there are three persons who might try their fortune, conquer the country, and marry our cousin ... under colour of taking the king out of the hands of his pernicious governors".[3] – After all, Charles felt responsible for the young King of England,[4] which did not deter him from musing, in October 1551, that "if they had already got

---
1 CSP Span 6 April 1551
2 Loades 1996 pp. 167–168, 212–213
3 Loades 1996 p. 168
4 CSP Span 8 April 1551

rid of the king we could intervene with the pretext of avenging him, or some other excuse easily to be devised."[1]

*

It would seem that John had learnt nothing from Katherine Willoughby's stance on arranged marriages, for Jehan de Scheyfve reported on 1 March 1551 that,

> My Lord of Warwick has been trying his utmost to marry his daughter to the Duke of Suffolk, and my Lord of Somerset has also been endeavouring to obtain the Duke for his. The Duke's widowed mother, however, has refused both matches on the ground that her son is too young, only fifteen or sixteen years old, and in order to avoid his being worked upon she has managed to obtain the King's and Council's leave to take him away from Court for a time.[2]

Mary Dudley decided to take no chances and on 29 March 1551 she married Henry Sidney, in private; on 17 May 1551 she married him once again, this time in public, at her parents' house, Ely Place, London. It was hardly the norm to have two marriage ceremonies, but this was clearly a case of emergency, as Mary herself seems to indicate in a note written into a 15th century psalter that she later used as a calendar for important family dates:

> The marriage of Sir Henry Sidney knight with the Lady Mary Dudley daughter of John, then Earl of Warwick and afterward Duke of Northumberland, was first at Asser the nine-and twenty day of March, in the year of our Lord one thousand, five hundred fifty, and one: and afterward most publicly and honourably solemnized in Ely Place, in Holborne.[3]

---
1 Loades 1996 p. 168
2 CSP Span 1 March 1551
3 Brennan 2006 p. 22. Esher, a stately enough place in possession of the crown, was not in any way related to her or her husband's family. On the other hand,

Clearly, Mary Dudley tricked her father into accepting *her* choice of husband.[1] The fact would have been made a lot easier for him by his son-in-law's friendship with King Edward. Henry Sidney was 22 in 1551, and he is best known today as Edward VI's close companion. Henry's father, Sir William Sidney, had become chamberlain of Prince Edward's household in 1538 and in 1544 advanced to the position of his steward.[2] Henry met the prince during these years and most likely shared lessons with him. In 1547, however, when Edward's new household was assembled on his accession, no posts were reserved for the Sidneys. It was not before John Dudley took over the government in early 1550 that Henry Sidney was appointed a gentleman of the privy chamber. And it was not before several months into his marriage with John's daughter that he became one of the "principal gentlemen" of King Edward, in July 1551, together with Sir John Gates. As such he was one of the now six men charged with the care of the royal person, and at every hour three of them at a time were to be on duty in the king's apartments.[3] Meanwhile, on 17 April 1551, his father-in-law had been created Earl Marshal of England, a state office of little value in perks but supreme in honour. On 15 August 1551 his brother-in-law, Robert, was added as a gentleman to the privy chamber.[4]

Edward VI received a thorough and ingenious humanist training, alternating between a "Latin week" and a "Greek week" throughout 1550 and 1551. French visitors testified to his command of their language and claimed that he spoke Italian and Spanish (he is known to have possessed a popular Spanish book).[5]

---

the description of the second ceremony as "most publicly and honourably solemnized" clearly hints at the first one being a secret affair. Mary's age at her marriage is unknown. She was either born c.1528–1529, or c.1533–1536 (see above pp. 19–20).

1 Adams 2008c first suggested that her marriage may have been "a romantic one". It is intriguing that William Cecil, who would have known about the Dudleys' domestic dramas, not only described Robert Dudley's marriage to Amy Robsart as "*nuptiae carnales*", but later also reminded his own son: "Marry thy daughters in time, lest they marry themselves." (Nares III p. 513).
2 MacCaffrey 2008
3 Jordan 1970 p. 20; Hoak 1976 p. 124; Alford 2002 p. 156
4 Adams 2008b
5 Hoak 2008. Pedro Mexía's *Silva de varia lección* (1540) was a European

With the end of his uncle's regency Edward, who was then 12, started to grow into the role of an adult king.[1] In October 1551, he informed the Lord Chancellor, Richard Rich, who maintained that the signature of eight privy councillors on a document was insufficient, that "the number of councillors does not make our authority". – "It should be a great impediment for me to send to all my council, and I should seem to be in bondage", he angrily recorded in his diary, although he was prepared to forgive: "But by oversight it chanced, and not thinking the more the better."[2]

John Dudley ruled in the king's name, and he took Edward seriously. – "He quickly won Edward VI's admiration, trust, and affection."[3] – Edward had finally acquired a surrogate father.[4] According to a member of the French embassy the secret of Edward's precocious speeches in council meetings lay in the fact that the Earl of Warwick "visited the King secretly at night in the King's Chamber, unseen by anyone, after all were asleep. The next day the young Prince came to his council and proposed matters as if they were his own; consequently, everyone was amazed, thinking that they proceeded from his mind and by his invention."[5] Of course, much more important to the frequently absent Warwick was to have Lord Darcy and Sir John Gates in the privy chamber, together with his son-in-law Henry Sidney.[6]

John behind the scenes also managed Edward's political education: He employed the clerk of the privy council, William Thomas, to secretly send Edward essays on political topics, past his tutors.[7] Thomas, an expert on Italy, introduced Edward to the ideas of Machiavelli. One of his papers cited the maxim that a prince must always maintain a free hand.[8] – "Appointed that I should come to, and sit at, Council, when great matters were in debating, or when I would", the king wrote in his diary on 14

---

    bestseller by 1550 and had been translated into Italian by 1542.
1   Alford 2002 p. 159
2   Hoak 2008; Alford 2002 p. 160; Literary Remains II p. 348
3   Hoak 2008
4   Original Letters II p. 439
5   Hoak 2008
6   For Darcy and Gates see below pp. 115–116.
7   Loades 1996 p. 201
8   Hoak 2008

August 1551. The council also supplied him with agendas of planned business, which Edward then annotated or copied out – for he loved to make lists.[1] From around his 14th birthday on 12 October 1551, Edward's signature on documents no longer needed the council's countersignatures,[2] and he regularly met his own Counsel for the Estate, "to hear debating of things of most importance". The members of this new committee he had chosen himself: councillors, other administrators, judges, and the Earl of Warwick.[3]

John Dudley wanted the king to grow into his authority as smoothly as possible. Disruptive conflicts when Edward took over government could thus be minimized, while his own chances to continue as principal minister would be good, perhaps excellent.[4]

*

After the peace treaty of March 1550 between England and France the talks continued more underhandedly, conducted by a Florentine, Antonio Guidotti. The Habsburgs, naturally, were suspicious, and six months later Charles V's ambassador in France, Simon Renard, updated his master about English-French diplomacy at the court of Henry II and his consort Catherine de Medici (another Florentine):

> Guidotti presented to the Queen a portrait of the King of England … The Queen made a return for the gift by sending Mme. Péronne, governess of the princesses, to the said Guidotti, with a portrait of her eldest daughter, drawn to the life.[5]

Since in 1548 Edward's bride, Mary Stuart, had been whisked out of Scotland into France (under the nose of the English garrisons), any revival of the engagement between Edward and Mary had

---

1 Loades 1996 p. 200–202; Hoak 1976 p. 124
2 Loades 1996 p. 193
3 Alford 2002 pp. 162–168
4 Loades 2004 p. 88
5 CSP Span 21 September 1550

become totally unrealistic; instead, the English government was happy to secure the little princess Elisabeth de Valois (she was only five) for Edward. The proposed marriage needed much negotiating. Jehan de Scheyfve observed in January 1551 that

> The French ambassador is very often, nay nearly every day, at Court, and the Councillors caress him more and more. Though he often negotiates with my Lords, as a rule they meet secretly with Lord Warwick, who keeps his room with the pretext of an illness that has been going on for the last two months. The Italian Antonio Guidotti, who arranged the last peace with France, is also often there. On the day of the Epiphany the said ambassador was summoned to Court and dined with the King and the Lady Elizabeth, and after dinner the King and the Lady Elizabeth were taken to see some bear-baiting and other sports, while the ambassador went to see Lord Warwick, and they too saw the bear-baiting and talked unceasingly all the time.[1]

Simon Renard sent another update from Paris two months later: "I can certify to your Majesty that the proposed marriage of the King of England with the Princess of France is being definitely discussed ... It is also a fact that the Princess, who has had a portrait of the King placed in her chamber, often stands before it, and says to her mother the Queen: 'I have wished good-day to the King of England, my lord.'"[2]

A great embassy to France from England sailed in May and was headed by the Marquess of Northampton. William Parr, boasting an entourage of 62 persons, was accompanied by Viscount Lisle, with a train of only eight servants. The principal purpose of the voyage was to bring the Order of the Garter to Henry II and settle the question of Elisabeth's dowry. As it came, the English demands went down from 1,400,000 crowns to 200,000.[3] John Dudley wrote

---

1 CSP Span January 1551
2 CSP Span 1 March 1551
3 Beer 1973 pp. 113–114

to the English resident ambassador in Paris, John Mason, to ask Henry II to receive Lord Lisle into his service, on Edward's behalf; John was full of hope, elaborating: "As so poor a man may render thanks unto so noble a prince, I pray you execute the office for me because you have advertised me that it has pleased his grace to remember me." – As earlier with the emperor, however, he was unsuccessful in placing his son at a foreign court.[1]

On 20 May the envoys were back, with the treaty, "sealed with the great seal of Fraunce"; a French delegation arrived soon after and was lavishly entertained by the king and the Duke of Somerset.[2] And Antonio Guidotti received his well-deserved reward: a knighthood, cash, and a pension.[3] Finally, in July 1551, the French Maréchal St. André also visited the English court, ostensibly to bestow the Order of St. Michael – the French counterpart of the Order of the Garter – on Edward VI, but chiefly to conclude the marriage agreement. Amid the specially erected "banqueting houses" and pavilions in Hyde Park, Edward had lots of fun playing host:

> After, they dined with me, and talked after dinner, and saw some pastime, and so went home again. ... The same night mons. le marechal St. Andrew supped with me ... The next morning he came to see mine arraying, and saw my bedchamber, and went a hunting with hounds, and saw me shoot, and saw all my guard shoot together. He dined with me, heard me play on the lute, ride, came to me in my study, supped with me, and so departed to Richmond.[4]

Edward, tongue-in-cheek, expressed his sympathy with the truly fat resident French ambassador, who "not finding the delicacies of France in this country", would lose weight – an eternal reproach to the King of England.[5]

---

1   Beer 1973 p. 113
2   Literary Remains II pp. 269–273
3   Loades 1996 p. 156
4   Literary Remains II pp. 331–333
5   Loach 2002 p. 143; Scépeaux I p. 340

In the course of the festivities a marriage settlement was indeed agreed upon (after much haggling over the dowry), and early the next year Edward sent his six-year-old bride a "fair diamond".[1] Richard Morison was to write about John Dudley's negotiations, in 1554, from hindsight and in exile:

> This earle had such a head that he seldom went about any thing, but he conceaved firste three or foure purposes before hand. They thought he was affraide of the emperour; but he had concluded with the Vidam[2] to helpe the French kinge his master into as great an amytie as he coulde with the Kinge and the realme; and to cause our noble Edwarde, of nature no freind to the emperour, to be readie to myslyke him when any safe occasione of fallynge out should be offered, he ment to seeme a freind to the lady Mary, to be taken for imperiall; that so, owinge his frendshipe to France, and winninge creditt with the emperor, he might as time should teach him abuse whetherr of them he listed, and fall in with him that might beste serve his practices.[3]

Whether Morison expected his readers to understand his elaborations or not, his pen created the prevalent picture we have of John Dudley's character. On 25 July 1551, six days after the marriage agreement between Edward VI and Elisabeth de Valois had been signed, John wrote to the Lord Chamberlain, Lord Thomas Darcy. Clearly recognizing Catherine de Medici's powers of intrigue – a decade before she came into the position of regent – he told the story of the miniature of the little Princess and how he had hit upon it in his desk the other day:

> Thes may be to signyfy unto your Lordship that aboute halffe yere or more paste[,] at soche tyme as

---
[1] Loach 2002 p. 108
[2] François de Vendôme, Vîdame de Chartres, a senior representative among the French negotiating team.
[3] Literary Remains I p. ccxxvii

Guydot[1] gave unto the Kinges Majestie a gylt cupp, he also presented unto his highnes a pycteur of the lady Yzabell the Frenche Kynges doughter with whom now the contract between the Kinges highnes and his majestie ys begon to be made[,] and for asmoche as yt might be that the sayde Guydot in that be halffe was but an instrument to others as peradventure to the Frenche quene her own silffe, who as I understand ys the most desyerus woman of the world that her doughter mought be bestowed here to our master, yt wold not do amys therfor in my opinion to shewe the sayde pyctour to the marshall afore the takinge of his leve of the Kinge.

Yt be nether herre nor ther for the matter yet perhapps yt wolde motche satisfy the saide quene whos practys I thinke veryly yt was to send it[,] that the same sholde apere to her not to be rejectyd, wherfor I have thought good to send the saide pycture to you yf the Kinges plesser be so to do, that the same sholde be in a redynes; for the laste day lookinge in a deske of myne I founde yt there and marvelinge a while whose yt shold be[,] yt cam to my remembraunce that at soche tyme as Guydot made the present of yt to his majestie[,] his highnes deliverde it to me and comandyd me to kepe yt, thinkinge yt my dutye to send yt to his highnes with the consideration before rehersed referringe thexecuting therof to his majesties owne apetyt.[2]

*

Lord Darcy was one of two men the Lord President relied on to impart his wishes to his young master, the other being Sir John Gates, the Vice-Chamberlain: "My lorde chamberlein and master vicechamberleyn my speciall frendes … to … sirue my purpos", as

---
1 "Guydot" is Guidotti.
2 HMC Bath II pp. 11–12

John put it.[1] If he needed Edward's signature he ordered Secretary Cecil to take the relevant document – letter, warrant, bill, whatever – to Darcy or Gates. They would then pass on the paper to the king, who would sign it or not.[2] Letters typically went from Cecil to John back to Cecil, who showed them to Darcy and Gates and selective other councillors and to the king: "when you have showed the said letter to the King's Majesty, and if his highness like the matter you may therein work with the rest of my lords", the Lord President explained to Cecil on 27 July 1552.[3] Of course, John generously allowed the likes of Darcy and Cecil to ignore his opinion, or so he promised:

> I do return ... herewith the arguments and collections of Mr. Secretary Cecil, left with me by your Lordship at your late being at Chelsey; which, as I did then partly declare my opinion in some points, seeming to me your Lordship not to mistake the same, hath made me the bolder to scribble a part of my simple mind upon the margin; which, by your wisdoms, when you shall have seen and perused, and not like the same, there is no harm but to strike it out with a pen, for the text remaineth, so as Mr. Secretary can easily find out his own.[4]

The Lord President also managed to effectively control the spending of the king's money by an intricate system of signatures between the council clerks and the secretaries (who were all directly answerable to him).[5]

One of the privy council's duties was to receive foreign ambassadors, who were more likely than others to write down their experiences, showing the council at work: Much of that work was apparently done by shouting, and according to Jehan de Scheyfve the loudest voices were those of "my Lord of Warwick and the two

---

1   Hoak 1976 p. 144
2   Hoak 1976 pp. 143–144
3   Hoak 1976 pp. 307, 113
4   Tytler II p. 160–161
5   Hoak 1976 p. 147

marquesses".[1] François van der Delft also described his experiences: "

> Thereupon they desired me to withdraw into another room, but I might well have imagined myself among them so loudly did they carry on their consultation; nor could I hope that a discussion so heated would be the prelude to a soft answer.[2]

Sometimes, John Dudley tired of all the paperwork, "a mass of matters which I return without having gathered much fruit".[3] He frequently absented himself, which created the problem that his colleagues might decide on particular measures without him: One day, as he was at the baths for his health, the council sent him the draft of a planned proclamation (on food prices), "which the lords have penned according to their opinions and so sent it unto him praying his lordship to peruse it and to amend it as he shall see cause". John however thought, as he wrote Cecil, that the proclamation had been unnecessarily changed without consulting him first, and now he found it odd "that my ... Lord Chancellor hath sought me and travelled the streets on foot only to speak with me who can show him no more than others that were first privy before me." He also wondered that the Lord Chancellor did not at first find him, as "the master of the horse knoweth of my being here for I made him privy to it." In the end he decided that – since he could not leave the baths without stopping that "which is so necessary for my health" – he would give his consent to the council's decisions (in this particular instance the most prominent mover in council happened to be the Duke of Somerset).[4]

*

---

1   de Lisle 2008 pp. 301–302; Hoak 1976 p. 127
2   CSP Span 31 January 1550
3   Wilson 2005 p. 193
4   Heinze 1976 pp. 226–227; Wilson 2005 p. 193. The Lord Chancellor and the Master of the Horse were Richard Rich and William Herbert, respectively.

The English people, as is evident from contemporary broadsheet ballads and alehouse talk, were generally disaffected to the men who ruled in the name of the king. To forestall a repetition of 1549, John Dudley set out to maintain public order by restoring administrative efficiency.[1] Equipped with a new law "for the punishment of unlawful assemblies", he built a united front of landholders and privy council, the government intervening locally at any sign of unrest.[2] His methods were a mixture of old and new. He returned to the ancient practice of granting licences to retain liveried followers, but he also selected lord lieutenants that represented the central government and were to keep ready small bands of cavalry.[3] These measures proved effective and the country was relatively calm for the rest of the reign. In fact, in the summer of 1552 the cavalry bands were disbanded – to save money and because they never had been needed.[4]

The government issued many proclamations against all kinds of disorder. It was observed that the brawling, quarrelling, and fighting in churchyards and even churches was on the increase; the same was true of the bringing of "horses and mules into and through the said churches." All had to stop under pain of imprisonment and the king's displeasure. Persons who shot doves with handguns were to be punished likewise.[5]

Protector Somerset had famously allowed free printing in England – until he thought the better of it and ordered that printers submit any book in English to either Petre, Smith, or Cecil, his closest secretaries who could then allow or stop the sale of it.[6] On 28 April 1551 John Dudley had it proclaimed that to print a book the king's signet letters or a council order – signed by six or more members – were needed. This sort of censorship was necessary because "the prynters do printe abrode what so ever any fond man devisethe be yt never so folishe so sedicious or daungerouse for the

---

1 Hoak 1980 pp. 29–30; Loades 2008a
2 Loades 1996 p. 145; Ives 2009 pp. 111–112, 308
3 Loades 2004 p. 98; Loades 2008a
4 Loades 1996 p. 252; Hoak 1980 p. 42
5 Heinze 1976 p. 244
6 Hoak 1976 p. 195

people to knowe".[7] An alarming case of book reading had occurred in March 1550, when the privy council had ordered Sir John Gates

> to apprehend certeyn light fellows that came out of Suffolk to Wyttam, in Essex, where they drynke all day and looke uppon bookes in the night; texamyn them, take their bookes, and send them [the books] up with their examinacions and put theim in hold.[1]

The Essex fellows lost their books, but they could go free. Examination by torture was part of the system, however, a routine measure that served best "for the boltinge out of the truthe".[2] The Lord President insisted that this was to be "kept very close and secret".[3] His caution referred to the case of one Hawkins, who appears to have forged the Archbishop of Canterbury's signature and sent out seditious bills with the "intent to have stirred a rebellion and commotion." When questioned in the Tower Hawkins refused to name his accomplices and feigned madness. John Dudley announced that

> it should be well done in my opinion that some discreet persons were furtherwith appointed to have the examination of him and either by fair means or foul to cause him to declare his counsellors and supporters.[4]

Not all instances of torture had to do with "political" cases; the council was likewise helping with criminal investigations: The serial robber Reed was threatened with torture; one Willson and one Warren, suspected of murder, had their taste of the rack. As he confided to Cecil, John contemplated ordering torture in similar cases. – The brazen theft of three hawks from one of the Lady Mary's Norfolk parks in January 1553 was taken care of by

---

7 Hoak 1976 p. 195
1 APC II p. 407
2 Hoak 1976 p. 229
3 Hoak 1976 pp. 229–230
4 Skidmore 2007 p. 238; Hoak 1976 p. 229

119

Archbishop Cranmer and the Duke of Suffolk, among others, their lordships ordering "the examination by tortours" of the two culprits.[1]

*

John Dudley's social policy was more practical than Somerset's, which had consisted principally of rhetoric. He likewise strove to alleviate the predicament of the poor.[2] The 1547 "Act for the Punishment of Vagabonds", which had stipulated that any unemployed man found loitering was to be branded and given to the "presentor" as a slave, was abolished as too harsh in 1550.[3] In 1552, John was apparently personally involved in pushing a new poor law through parliament, which provided for weekly parish-based collections for the "provision and relief of the poor". Parishes were to register their needy inhabitants as well as the amounts of money people agreed to give for them; unwilling contributors were to be "induced" by the parson and, if need be, by the bishop.[4] The "idle poor" and "vagabonds" were to be set to work and begging was proscribed as in all previous poor laws. More successful than its predecessors, this act has been described as "effectively laying the foundations of the Elizabethan Poor Law".[5]

The years 1549 through 1551 saw poor harvests and, accordingly, soaring food prices. The government tried to intervene against the "insatiable greediness" of middlemen by searches for hidden corn and by fixing maximum prices for grain, meat, and other victuals.[6] However, the set prices were so unrealistic that farmers stopped to sell their produce at the open market and the regulations had to be rescinded.[7] The regime's agrarian policy, while giving landlords much freedom to enclose common land,

---

1   Hoak 1976 pp. 230, 344
2   Hoak 1980 p. 30; Dawson 1993 p. 247
3   Williams 1998 p. 67; Rathbone 2002
4   Slack 1980 p. 103; Guy 1990 p. 221
5   Slack 1980 p. 103
6   Slack 1980 pp. 105–106
7   Williams 1998 p. 68

also distinguished between different forms of enclosure. Landlords guilty of illegal enclosures were increasingly prosecuted.[1]

The financial legacy of the Protectorate consisted, apart from crippling crown debts, of an unprecedentedly debased coinage.[2] On the second day as Lord President of the Council, John began a process to tackle the problems of the mint. Forming a committee, he set to work with Sir Walter Mildmay and Sir William Herbert, cracking down on peculation by the officers of the mint and other institutions.[3] In 1551 they tried to yield profit and restore confidence in the coin by issuing yet further debased coinage and "crying it down" immediately afterwards. The result was panic and confusion and to get hold of the situation a coin of 92.3% silver content (against 25% silver content in the last debasement) was issued within months. The bad coin prevailed over the good, however, because people had lost confidence.[4] John admitted to Cecil ("scribbled in my bed this morning, at 4 of the clock, the 16th of June 1551") that he found finance a puzzling and disagreeable thing and asked his young City friend, Thomas Gresham, to deal with it.[5]

Gresham and his City colleagues had access to the stock market at Antwerp, which enabled them to "recycle" the king's debt owed to the Fuggers of Augsburg. John and his good friend, the merchant John Yorke, embarked on a scheme to stabilize the pound at the Antwerp exchange. The plan was, as Edward noted in his journal, to "pay all my debts to the sum of £120,000"![6] However, nothing came of it because in the process Yorke was caught in Flanders, *in flagrante delicto*, smuggling £4,000 in bullion out of the country, which was illegal. "For the last few days no one has talked about anything else", the Imperial ambassador in London reported, "and the council have been much exercised about it."[7]

---

1 Dawson 1973 p. 247; Rathbone 2002. The relevant legislation were the "Act for Improvement of Waste Ground" (1550) and the "Act for Tillage and Increase of Corn" (1552).
2 Loades 1996 pp. 169–170; Hoak 1980 p. 30
3 Loades 1996 pp. 162, 227–229
4 Loades 1996 pp. 170–171; Rathbone 2005
5 HMC Salisbury I p. 86–87; Loades 1996 p. 207
6 Loades 2008b pp. 105–106
7 Jordan 1970 p. 458

Later, the council was prepared to rerun such a scheme (minus the illegal smuggling of bullion), this time operated by Thomas Gresham, who finally succeeded in stabilizing the pound sterling at Antwerp.[1]

By late 1552, after the first good harvest in four years, the prices for foodstuffs had dropped.[2] Tax collection practices were in the course of centralization,[3] while the council suggested to adapt the customs rates (which had not been increased since the reign of Henry VII); however, in the face of unrelenting opposition from the City merchants, nothing was done.[4] A favour to the City of London was also the abolition, in 1552, of privileges granted to the Hanseatic League as long ago as the times of Henry VII. While the Hanse was still allowed trade with England, they were at last in no better position than their competitors, the English Merchant Adventurers. Naturally, the Habsburgs, as overlords of most Hanse merchants, were not pleased with this decision, but the improved relations with the City merchants far outweighed this – after all the latter stood as guarantors for the government's borrowings at Antwerp, which in turn were necessary to stabilize the pound.[5] In this way, John Dudley finally succeeded in eliminating the whole of the king's foreign debt. His stated goal of June 1551 – "to have His Majesty out of debt" – had been partly achieved.[6]

---

1 Loades 1996 pp. 211–212
2 Hoak 1980 p. 42
3 Hoak 1980 pp. 41–42; Dawson 1993 p. 246
4 Loades 1996 p. 212
5 Loades 2012 p. 139
6 Hoak 1980 p. 41; Hoak 2008. This still left Mary with £185,000 of domestic crown debts, which is however considerably less than the £300,000 of crown debts (£200,000 domestic) that Mary left to Elizabeth (Loades 1991 pp. 358, 361).

11.
A Fraudulent Scheme

On 11 October 1551, Edward VI made Henry Sidney a knight; on the same day he also dubbed three other knights – Henry Neville, John Cheke, and William Cecil – and made an earl, a marquess, and two dukes: Sir William Herbert became Earl of Pembroke, the Earl of Wiltshire (William Paulet) the Marquess of Wiltshire, and the Marquess of Dorset (Henry Grey) the Duke of Suffolk. Finally, John Dudley, Earl of Warwick, was created Duke of Northumberland. During the ceremony Northumberland was supported right and left by the Duke of Somerset and the Marquess of Northampton, respectively. Sir William Cecil read the patent. There followed a festive dinner, "the trumpets sounding before them" into the hall; "the lords that were newly created sat in their surcoats without mantle or coronet".[1] Surely, the symbolism of the seating order was understood by insiders of the court. On the high table sat the Duke of Suffolk, the Duke of Northumberland, the Marquess of Winchester, and the Earl of Pembroke: The ruling junta lined up in a row. Significantly, "on the other side a little lower sat the Duke of Somerset" with other peers.[2]

Three days later, Edward wrote in his journal, the Duke of Somerset had "sent for the secretary Cicel to tell him he suspected some ill. Mr. Cicel answerid that if he were not gilty he might be of good courage; if he were, he had nothing to say but to lament

---
1 Loades 1996 pp. 180–181
2 Loades 1996 p. 181

him."[1] On 16 October, the Duke of Somerset was arrested after dinner, to which he had appeared late, "Sir Thomas Palmer on the terrace walking there."[2]

The whole drama had been opened on the 7th, when Sir Thomas Palmer brought John Dudley the chain needed for the ceremony on 11 October; the chain "being a very fair one, for every link weighed one ounce", Edward noted. Palmer then said the chain should be delivered to Jarnac the jeweller to prepare it for the great occasion, "whereupon in my lord's privy garden he declared a conspiracy." Back in April, "at St. George's day last", the Duke of Somerset had supposedly planned "to raise the people". But that was not all: "Afterwards a devise was made to call the earl of Warwick to a banquet, with the marquess of Northampton and divers other, and to cut off their heads."[3]

Thus the Duke of Somerset was imprisoned in the Tower a second time; he was joined there by his wife and others in the coming days and weeks: Lord Paget, Lord Grey de Wilton, and the Earl of Arundel. Also arrested were Sir Michael Stanhope, Sir Thomas Arundel, Sir Ralph Vane, and Sir Thomas Palmer himself. Somerset's servants, Sir William Crane and his wife, also went to prison.[4] Crane's testimony was rather damning, as it revealed "how that place wher the nobles shuld have bene bankettid and the heddis striken of was the lord Pagit's house, and how th'earl of Arrondel knew the mattier as wel as he [Somerset]".[5]

*

In late October and early November 1552 the English court was busy over the visit of the Scottish regent and mother of the Scottish

---

[1] Literary Remains II p. 354
[2] Literary Remains II p. 354
[3] Literary Remains II p. 353
[4] Skidmore 2007 pp. 209–210
[5] Literary Remains II p. 361. It is sometimes claimed that Crane's testimony was extracted under torture; however, while indeed on 5 November a warrant was issued for the optional torture of prisoners in connection with gathering evidence against Somerset (APC III p. 407), Crane's interrogation occurred already on 26 October. It seems unlikely that he would have been tortured without a warrant.

queen, Mary of Guise. Edward noted how this came about: "The dowager of Scotland was by tempest driven to land at Portsmouth, and so she sent word she would take the benefit of the safe-conduit, to go by land, and to see me."[1] Edward highly enjoyed such occasions:

> At the gate there [at the Palace of Westminster] received her the Duke of Northumberland great master, and the treasurer and controller and th'earl of Pembroke, to the number of thirty. ... I went to her dinner. She dined under the same cloth of state, at my left hand.[2]

The next day,

> The Duke of Northumberland, the lord treasorour, the lord marquis of Northampton, the lord privy seal, and divers other, went to see her, and to deliver a ring with a diamont ... as a token from me.[3]

The king's cousin, the Lady Jane, was one of the more prominent guests at the banquet, while the Lord Robert Dudley – titled "lord" because he was now a duke's son – stayed in the background.[4] While King Edward found all this perfectly normal, French and Italian visitors were often amused by English court etiquette; they saw dukes and earls kneeling while serving their sovereign at the table ("very strange"[5]), and the king's sister, the Lady Elizabeth, "knelt down before her brother five times before she sat down".[6] While the Lady Elizabeth attended the dinners for Mary of Guise, the Lady Mary had declined to come to court.

✢

---

1 Literary Remains II p. 356
2 Literary Remains II pp. 362–363
3 Literary Remains II p. 363
4 Literary Remains II p. 362; de Lisle 2008 p. 73; Adams 2008b. Jane Grey, Edward's first cousin once removed.
5 Chapman 1958 p. 101
6 Loach 2002 p. 144

Of course an official declaration of the reasons for the arrest of the king's uncle had been prepared quickly for presentation to the French and Imperial ambassadors (the latter being firmly of Somerset's party, after all the duke had always been anti-French), and Jehan de Scheyfve was summoned on 17 October, receiving an introductory lecture by Cecil on how the duke had planned, not just a banquet massacre of councillors, but also to seize the Tower and several other strong places in the realm. De Scheyfve expressed his "great surprise" and said that he

> could not understand what could have driven the Duke to it. At this the Earl of Warwick, recently created Duke of Northumberland, told me that he himself failed to imagine what it could have been; for the Duke had enjoyed the greatest reputation and authority with the Council, and had possessed a huge fortune of 30,000 to 40,000 angels a year. With all due moderation … I replied that greed, cupidity and the lust of power often led men astray, causing disasters in republics and kingdoms. 30,000 angels a year, I added, were enough to live on; and even if the Duke had only enjoyed a fourth part of that sum, it was no reason for attempting such adventures. This answer pleased them greatly … and the Duke of Northumberland went on to say that this evil plot had long been in preparation, and the Council had suspected it.[1]

Indeed, sometime in the late summer of 1551, the Duke of Somerset's brother-in-law, Michael Stanhope, and Edward Wolfe of the king's privy chamber had "laid in wait with bands of men to kill Warwick by the way"; meanwhile, "Warwick at supper would eat nothing, but suddenly in the midst arose and went into the gallery, and there walked."[2] Whatever the exact meaning of these observations, there can be little doubt that Somerset had been contemplating the permanent removal of his de facto successor. The simple truth was that he could not stomach the life of an ex-

---
[1] CSP Span 18 October 1551
[2] Adams; Archer; Bernard 2003b p. 59

protector. Not that he had not been warned by John Dudley to give up hopes of recovering supreme power: Professing his love for the duke, John had talked with Somerset's chancellor Richard Whalley in June 1550, shedding tears in the process.[1]

Somerset, according to a member of the French embassy, had started to intrigue against John even before the grand wedding of their children.[2] He became more and more disgruntled at John's policies – above all the peace with France and Scotland – and surrounded himself with a circle of malcontents. Their favourite topic was "the reformation of the estate of the realm",[3] and they engaged in continuous, if somewhat aimless, plotting. The Earl of Arundel was perhaps the most active member in this circle.[4] He had often been seen at Somerset House, wearing a black cloak, and he freely admitted to having had "talk and communication" with the duke, "and he with me", regarding the "apprehensions" of the Earl of Warwick and the Marquess of Northampton. Somerset confirmed this when he stated that he had "contemplated" John's arrest, saying that he had had no intention to kill his rival, only to have spoken about it. – Arundel, for his part, insisted they had "meant no harm to your bodies".[5] It further transpired that they had planned to arrest Warwick at a banquet before convening parliament in order to "set everything ... right", since "the kingdom had been very badly governed".[6] For Somerset at least, whose own rule had recently ended in total failure, this was a remarkable plan.

Whether he believed his own propaganda or not, Somerset spread it among the masses,[7] who sympathized with him. He used agents to get out the message that John Dudley was the only cause of the economic crisis and bad coinage, and how, if only his, Somerset's, advice had been followed, the people would have been spared much hardship. Despite its utterly devious nature – Somerset in office being responsible for more rounds of

---

1 Tytler II pp. 21–23 (wrongly dated to 1551 by Tytler). Alford 2002 p. 139.
2 Hoak 1976 p. 74
3 Skidmore 2007 p. 214
4 Loades 2004 p. 108
5 Skidmore 2007 p. 214; Hoak 1976 p. 75; Loades 2004 p. 110
6 Hoak 1976 p. 75
7 Hoak 1976 pp. 74–75

debasement than anyone else – his public relations exercise was a success, as the commons began greatly to murmur.[1]

The biggest problem from John Dudley's point of view was that the behaviour of the former Lord Protector threatened the united aristocratic front so vital in a minority regime.[2] Somerset even turned to Catholic peers and the Lady Mary (who was friends with his very Protestant wife) to secure support against John. The Earl of Shrewsbury turned down advances from Somerset's quarter, being a cautious man who had already received a lesson about "the truth of the matter betwixt the earl of Warwick & your lordship": His servant's house had been raided by John Dudley's men, whereat "my closet was broken up and all my books ... tossed together".[3] – Ultimately, Somerset's somewhat vague plan seems to have been to remove his rival with the help of parliament. John accordingly avoided to recall parliament, and a ridiculous battle over antedating and postponing the recall of parliament ensued between the two prominent councillors. Obviously, this could not go on indefinitely, and so John decided to strike first.[4]

There had also developed more personal grievances between the two men. Somerset was miffed by Warwick securing the most honourable – and entirely symbolic – office of Earl Marshal, a position he had held himself while Protector. He probably was also offended by the government denying his mother, the king's grandmother, a state funeral and official mourning at court.[5] After the council decided that to wear morning "profiteth not the dead and harmeth those of little faith", they referred the matter to Edward, who dispensed his uncle from it on the grounds that it had more to do with pomp than edification.[6] Usually understood as a deliberate snub by John Dudley against Somerset, it might also be asked why a grandmother who had never appeared at court and whom Edward had hardly ever set eyes on should come to courtly

---

1 Hoak 1976 p. 74; Skidmore 2007 p. 206
2 Alford 2002 p. 170
3 Skidmore 2007 p. 190
4 Hoak 1976 pp. 75–76. Somerset would use Warwick's absence to antedate the opening of parliament, while Warwick would in turn postpone the date during Somerset's absence.
5 Skidmore 2007 p. 189
6 Loades 2015 pp. 167–168

prominence with her death. After all, Henry VIII had not cared to provide a state funeral for his current queen's, Jane Seymour's, father when the latter died in December 1536; nor, interestingly, had Henry's own grandmother, a Dowager Queen of England, received a state funeral. – Of course, John Dudley may have unnecessarily provoked Somerset's pride; such as depriving him of his separate dining table at court – dining alone in state was the most honourable thing – or pointing out that his old comrade was the king's uncle "on his mother's side" (rather than of the blood royal).[1] But it is as likely that John simply could not afford, in the long term, a rival for power who constantly upstaged him.

Edward Seymour, unfortunately, had forgotten that he had to thank John for his life. As the council's revolt against him took shape in October 1549, no-one in London believed that he would survive his removal from office for long.[2] And now he was, again, the premier peer, a senior member of the privy council, and the wealthiest nobleman in England.[3] This may also help to explain why John felt he finally needed a dukedom. He was undoubtedly the first man in the government, but he lacked the status to go with it. Somerset could always claim precedence; none of the council, not even the Lord President, could tell him "to come or to go", as it was "contrary to usage among lords for a man of lower rank to order one of higher rank to do something".[4] Additionally, John had to advertise his power as well as impress and reward his followers; the huge landed income of a duke was just what he needed.

*

Indeed, back in April 1551, around the feast day of St. George, there had been planned some sort of rising in London, and there had also been found a man with a bloodied dagger near the Earl of Warwick's residence, all of which looked suspiciously like a thwarted assassination plot. Significantly, all the people involved

---

1 Skidmore 2007 p. 189
2 CSP Span 8 October 1549
3 Loades 2012 p. 83; Beer 2009
4 Skidmore 2007 p. 208

were partisans of the Duke of Somerset.[1] As the year 1551 progressed, though, the duke himself seems to have lost interest in all this plotting. As late as August he told his servant Crane to tell the duchess that he "would no further meddle with the apprehension of any of the council and bade her bid M. Stanhope to meddle no more in talk" with Arundel, going as far as to say that "he was sorry he had gone so far".[2] – Even keeping in mind that Palmer's story was fabricated (almost certainly by the Earl of Warwick himself[3]) it is no wonder that John was not impressed by Somerset's – and especially Arundel's – assertions that they had meant no harm to his life.

Somerset's trial was held on 1 December 1551 before his peers; while a handful of members of the peerage were absent, the Duke of Northumberland, the Marquess of Northampton, and the Earl of Pembroke were present. This caused some criticism from Somerset's friends on the jury, rather unusual for the times. – Edward described the principal charge to his friend Barnaby Fitzpatrick:

> Enditement was read, wich were several: some for treason, some for traiterous felony. The lawers redd how Paulmir had confessed that the duke once minded and made him prevy to raise the North; after to cal the duke of Northumberland, the marquis of Northampton, and th'erle of Pembroke to a feast, and so to have slaine them. And to doe this thing (as it was to be thought) he levied men 100 at his house at London.[4]

To the last charge – "having men at his chamber at Greenwich" – Somerset answered that "he meant no harm, because when he could have done harm, he did not."[5] Northumberland then made a sad face, according to an anonymous account, and announced that

---
1 Skidmore 2007 pp. 192–193
2 Skidmore 2007 p. 214; Warnicke 2012 p. 98
3 CSP 27 August 1553
4 Literary Remains I p. 71
5 Literary Remains II pp. 373–373

he did not want the seeking of his life to be construed as treason.[1] Somerset for his part made clear that he "did not determine to kill the duke of Northumberland, the marquis, etc., but spake of it and determined after the contrary"[2] (which meant he had been thinking aloud about their removal and then changed his mind). The trial's conclusion was also reported by Edward:

> So the lordis acquite him of high treason, and condemned him of treason feloniouse, and so he was adjudged to be hangid. He gave thankis to the lordis for there open trial, and cried mercy of the duke of Northumberland, the marquis of Northampton, and th'erle of Pembroke for his ill meaning against them, and made suet for his life, wife and children.[3]

After Somerset's formal conviction, the problem now remained what to do with him. It is usually claimed that John could not wait to see his rival dead; however, 53 days – or nearly seven weeks – between trial and execution is a long time in Tudor political justice and certainly indicative of behind the scenes manoeuvring.

While the court immersed itself in seasonal festivities – supposedly organized by the Duke of Northumberland in order to get Edward's mind off his imprisoned uncle – John had long talks in the Tower with Somerset. We would like to know what they talked; rumours that the disgraced duke would be pardoned and released resulted and his confinement was eased.[4] However, as John wavered in his resolution to execute his erstwhile friend, "the Earl of Pembroke, the Marquis of Northampton and other of Northumberland's supporters considered the conversation so suspicious that the Earl of Pembroke was said to have somewhat fallen out with the Duke".[5] The Duke of Northumberland, even

---

1   Beer 1973 p. 121
2   Literary Remains II p. 373
3   Literary Remains II pp. 373–374
4   CSP Span 27 December 1551
5   CSP Span 27 December 1551

according to the hostile de Scheyfve, was "sorely puzzled at present, and does not know how all this is to end."[1]

John's quarrel with Pembroke and Northampton was soon "smoothed over", and de Scheyfve hinted that Northumberland's reputation and authority were declining "day by day" because he seemed unable "to carry out his designs", meaning Somerset's execution.[2] John needed a show of strength, especially as parliament was to convene on 23 January and he could not risk this to happen with Somerset alive – already people were saying that "the Duke of Somerset shall come forth of the Tower, and the Duke of Northumberland shall go in."[3] On the side of Pembroke and especially Northampton there may also have been an element of revenge in Somerset's death. They may have wished to see avenged their brother-in-law, Thomas Seymour, of whom they would allow no-one to speak ill.[4]

*

On 18 January 1552 the king wrote an execution order for his uncle in his own hand and signed the death warrant.[5] The next day the document was shown in council, and on 22 January Edward VI noted in his diary: "The Duke of Somerset had his head cut off upon Tower Hill between eight and nine o'clock in the morning."[6]

Since Somerset carried considerable popularity with Londoners, a watch and a curfew had been imposed for the occasion; nevertheless huge crowds turned out to hear Somerset's last speech in which he exhorted the people to continue to follow the religion he had promoted while "in authority".[7] The Imperial ambassador reported several rumours; that the Duchess of Somerset could expect the same fate as her husband and that Northumberland had implored the king to pardon Somerset, a tale de Scheyfve could not believe, saying if it was true it had been planted by

---

1   CSP Span 27 December 1551
2   CSP Span 27 December 1551
3   APC III p. 462
4   CSP Span 31 January 1550
5   Jordan 1970 p. 100
6   Literary Remains II p. 390
7   Skidmore 2007 p. 222; CSP Span 12 February 1552; Machyn p. 14

Northumberland himself. He eagerly believed another rumour, though, namely that it had been the French ambassador, present at the council meeting of 18 January, who had talked Edward into executing his uncle.[1]

There was indeed a mysterious French connection; a French mercenary called Berteville had been arrested in October and accused of being Somerset's choice of assassin at the banquet massacre. However, on 1 November he could go free and was even rewarded with money and a house, despite having confessed to the charges. Berteville had been knighted by John at the Battle of Pinkie and days later had rescued him from an ambush, whereby Berteville was "hurt in the buttok" (John organizing a surgeon to tend to his wound).[2] Was he hired by John Dudley? Or by the French embassy, for which he was working as a spy? Even more puzzling, according to King Edward, Somerset, after his trial, also "told certain lords that were in the Tower that he had hired Berteville to kill them".[3]

About a month after Somerset was beheaded there followed the trials and executions of four gentlemen associated with him: Sir Michael Stanhope, Sir Thomas Arundel, Sir Miles Partridge, and Sir Ralph Vane were all first acquitted of treason and then convicted of felony, like their master. John would have had especially few regrets about Vane, who was his neighbour and had once turned up with a private army in a dispute with him over some park.[4]

Court life progressed as usual; it was extravagant, the staff increasing throughout Edward's reign, despite general cuts of expenses during John Dudley's ascendancy. Sir John Cawarden,

---

1 CSP Span 12 February 1552; Hoak 1976 p. 310
2 Literary Remains II pp. 217–218
3 Literary Remains II pp. 374 375. Loades 1996 p. 188; Skidmore 2007 pp. 218–219. Edward repeated this fact in a letter to Barnaby Fitzpatrick, saying that Somerset had "confessid to how he had promised Bartiville to deliver him out of prison if he wold kill the duke of Northumberland." Some historians believe these were blatant lies fed to Edward via Northumberland. However, as Edward listened to more than one voice this would have been a risky thing for John to do.
4 Loades 1996 pp. 167, 190; Jordan 1970 p. 64; Adams, Archer, Bernard 2003a p. 53

the Master of the Revels, was directly answerable to the privy council.[1] For the Christmas season of 1551 the Lord of Misrule was re-introduced at court, having fallen victim to Protestant propriety under Somerset. Like his father, Edward VI was a great music-lover and he personally appeared in masques and plays; the 1551 Christmas festivities had to be frequently adapted according to Edward's wishes, to "his Majesty's pleasure and determination". More rustic entertainments were equally appreciated, the king was fond of tightrope walkers and "tumblers going upon their hands with their feet upward".[2]

The king was also an inveterate huntsman, and it is possible that Northumberland was afraid of Edward having a riding accident.[3] The duke himself introduced a new technique in the hunting of partridges, using his spaniels to catch them with a net.[4] Edward also practised fencing and archery and, of course, was fascinated by tournaments and jousting. His journal is full of result listings. In January 1551 (Somerset staying in the Tower awaiting his fate),

> There was a match run between six gentlemen of a side at tilt.
>
> | Of one side. | Of the other side. |
> |---|---|
> | The earl of Warwick. | The lord Ambrose. |
> | The lord Robert. | The lord Fizwater. |
> | Mr. Sidney. | Sir Francis Knollys. |
> | Mr. Nevill. | Sir Antony Browne. |
> | Mr. Gates. | Sir John Perrot. |
> | Antony Digby. | Mr. Courtney. |
>
> These won by 4 taints.[5]

---

1 Alford 2014 p. 59
2 Loach 2002 pp. 152–153
3 An Italian visitor wrote that hunting gave Edward "an excuse to ride, because his men, out of fear for his life, often seem to keep rather a tight rein on him in this area." (Loach 2002 p. 155).
4 Kolehouse 2005
5 Literary Remains II p. 389

An instructive listing, it clearly shows the Dudley influence at court: Three of John's sons took part in this "match", the younger John, Ambrose, and Robert; but also John's son-in-law Henry Sidney, as well as John Gates, Francis Knollys, and John Perrot of the privy chamber, all three the duke's men. Three days before this sporting event the Imperial ambassador had dined with Edward and his chief minister, the topic being inevitably the Lady Mary's mass and her disobedience:

> The King said he ... would never fail to treat her kindly; upon which he got up to withdraw because of signs the Duke of Northumberland made to him; and he had kept his eye turned towards the Duke all the while. ... I carefully observed the King's face and manners, Sire, and he seems to be a likely lad of quick, ready and well-developed mind; remarkably so for his age. For this very reason he runs great dangers; but if he were well and conscientiously instructed he would become a very noteworthy prince. Northumberland, whom he seems to love and fear, is beginning to grant him a great deal of freedom.[1]

*

Somerset and Northumberland had not just been former friends but had also been related through their children's marriage. The Duchess of Somerset remained a prisoner in the Tower, which appears somewhat unusual; was John afraid of her powers of intrigue? She stayed in the Tower for the better part of two years, the council granting her £100 p.a. to cover her expenses. She was also allowed visits from her mother, who seems to have moved in with her, and was served by two gentlewomen, a number of "the king's servants", and a cook.[2] Her daughter Anne, the young Countess of Warwick, probably had lived with her husband and in-laws ever since her marriage. Now orphaned, she was described by Somerset's evangelical adherents – in a letter to John Calvin, who

---
1 CSP Span 14 January 1552
2 Gentlemen's Magazine XXIII pp. 373–374

was a great fan of the Protector and had hardly realized that Somerset had been an ex-Protector for some time – as having "been married nearly three years to the earl of Warwick, son and heir of the duke of Northumberland, and is happily and honourably settled."[1] Four of her sisters were lodged with Lady Cromwell, the widowed daughter-in-law of Henry VIII's executed minister, while a baby sister was given to another aunt. Anne's two brothers, Edward and Henry, were lodged with William Paulet, the Marquess of Winchester and Lord Treasurer, where they continued with their studies under the same tutors as before. Paulet, meanwhile, was able to pocket £2,400 p.a. out of Somerset's confiscated estate on behalf of the elder boy.[2] The bulk of Somerset's property passed, of course, to the crown; with the exception of a bonus for his eldest son, from his first marriage, whom he had disinherited in a unique parliamentary statute under Henry VIII (with the proviso that he had living sons from his second marriage). Parliament in January 1552 restored John Seymour to his inheritance; he was to receive all that his father had possessed before the Henrician act – which had been contrived through "corrupt and sinister labour by the power of his second wife over him".[3] Unfortunately, John Seymour did not live to enjoy his well-deserved wealth; he died in December 1552.

Edward's last surviving uncle, Sir Henry Seymour, remained untouched by his brother's downfall; he became a major recipient of rewards and served on commissions in his capacity as a country gentleman.[4] Finally, on 30 March 1553, the younger John Dudley was granted his brother-in-law Edward Seymour's wardship, which

---

1 Original Letters I p. 340. There seems to be no evidence for the claim in de Lisle 2008 p. 77 that Anne suffered "a physical collapse" after her father's execution. She did, however, suffer a mental breakdown in later life, falling "into lunacy" in 1566 after the birth of her seventh child to her second husband, Sir Edward Unton (Stevenson 2007). Victorian writers liked to explain her condition with the tragic events of her youth, but it was much more likely a case of postpartum psychosis.
2 Original Letters I pp. 340–342
3 Loades 1996 p. 213; Jordan 1970 p. 337. Thomas Seymour had shared the opinion that Somerset's sons from his first marriage should inherit, which was one of the reasons for the widely reported hatred between him and the Duchess of Somerset (Adams, Archer, Bernard 2003a p. 55).
4 Loades 1996 pp. 226, 277

brought him and his young wife £510 p.a.[1] One of the very few surviving details of his married life is an entry in his wardrobe account for 1551: "a shirt of blackwork that my lady gave my lord for his Lordship's New Year's gift".[2] We do not know Anne's feelings on New Year's Day 1552. Her father-in-law certainly felt some qualms, confessing later that "nothing had pressed so injuriously upon his conscience as the fraudulent scheme against the Duke of Somerset".[3]

---

1   Loades 1996 p. 224
2   HMC Second Report pp. 101–102
3   Hoak 1980 p. 203

12.
Riches upon Riches

The young Earl of Warwick, Master of the Buckhounds, became a Knight of the Garter in 1552. At the ceremony on 23 April he carried the heavy sword of state before King Edward all through Westminster Hall, "unto the chapel" of the palace.[1] Five days later he was appointed Master of the Horse, his brother Robert taking over the Mastership of the Buckhounds. The Master of the Horse was "*the* personal body servant of the monarch once he or she was outside the chamber – whether in the gardens or in the parks; whether on the hunt, playing tennis, in a maze or in festive tents or temporary banqueting halls".[2] Though he did not treat his office as a sinecure, he was clearly in tow with his father, Northumberland simply referring to him as "my son" in his letters.[3] Young Warwick in 1552 still lacked an adequate income of his own, and when he got into financial difficulties it did not occur to him to ask his parents for help:

> I had thought you had had more discretion then to hurt your selffe thorew fantesyes or care, specially for suche things as may be remedyed and holpon. Well ynoghe you must understand that I kno you canot

---
1 Machyn p. 17; Wriothesley II p. 69
2 Murphy 2012
3 Knighton 1992 pp. 238, 239, 287. His next son was "my son Ambrose" or simply "Ambrose".

lyve under great chargyes. And therfor you shold not hyde frome me your debts what so ever yt be for I wolde be lothe but you shold kepe your credyte with all men. And therfore send me worde in any wys of the hole some of your debts, for I and your mother will see theym forthwith payed and what so ever you do spend in the honest servis of our master and for his honour[,] so you do not let wyld and wanton men consume yt, as I have been servid in my dayes, you muste thinke all ys spent as yt shold be, and all that I have must be yours and that you spend before, you may with God's grace helpe yt herafter by good and faithfull servis wherin I trust you will never be found slake[,] and then you may be sure you canot lak serving soche a master as you have toward whome the lyvinge God preserve and restore you to perfyt helth and so with my blessing I comytt you to his tuision. Your loving Father.
Northumberland.

Your lovynge mothere
that wyshes you helthe dayli
Jane Northumberland.[1]

This short letter shows us a remarkably generous father – in money matters, but even more in his confession that he at least had lost his money in the company of "wild and wanton men". He still partook in social life, despite his heavy workload; we are not surprised to meet William Parr:

> My Lord Marquis hath been with me, I thank him; and some good fellows with him: we have been merry. To-morrow he departeth from me by five of the clock in the morning towards my Lord Cobham's, who, as I understand from them this day, is in no little peril of life. Thus I leave, wishing to you [William

---

1 HMC Pepys pp. 1–2

Cecil] the good that your own gentle heart can desire. At Otford, this last of May, at ten in the night.

Your assured faithful friend, Northumberland.[1]

Two days later his mood was less cheerful as tragedy was stalking the Dudley household; only recently John's daughter-in-law, Anne, wife of Ambrose Dudley, had died after giving birth to the only grandchild he would know in his lifetime,[2] and in the night of 1 June 1552 his seven-year-old daughter passed away after a few hours of illness, which he described in an urgent letter to Thomas Darcy and William Cecil the next morning. He wrote to excuse his and his eldest son's absence from court duties on account of the death and the possibility of the disease being infectious.

> I have thought good to signify unto you what moveth me to suspect infection in the disease whereof my daughter died. First, the night before she died, she was as merry as any child could be, and sickened about three in the morning, and was in a sweat, and within a while after she had a desire to the stool; and the indiscreet woman that attended upon her let her rise, and after that, she fell to swooning, and then, with such things as they ministered to her, brought her again to remembrance, and so she seemed for a time to be meetly well revived, and so continued till it was noon, and still in a great sweating; and about twelve of the clock she began to alter again, and so in continual pangs and fits till six of the clock, at what time she left this life. And this morning she was looked upon, and between the shoulders it was very black, and also upon the one side of her cheek; which thing, with the suddenty, and also [that] she could

---

1 Tytler II p. 112. George Brooke, 9th Baron Cobham, William Parr's father-in-law, survived his illness.
2 Anne Whorwood presumably died either in childbirth or from the sweating sickness. Her daughter, probably called Margaret, also died (Adams 2002 p. 328; Adams 2008a; Tytler II p. 114).

brook nothing that was ministered to her from the beginning, moveth me to think that either it must be the sweat or worse, for she had the measles a month or five weeks before, and very well recovered, but a certain hoarseness and a cough remained with her still. This [is] as much as I am able to express, and even thus it was: wherefore I think it not my duty to presume to make my repair to his Majesty's presence till further be seen what may ensue of it.[1]

While noted for its first-hand description of what was probably the sweating sickness, this letter has served as proof of John's supposed wickedness, his "icy heartlessness",[2] or "terrifying heartlessness",[3] being apparent in the description of the corpse of the child. He was clearly in a state of shock, though, unable to talk about his feelings, which nevertheless come through in his anger about the "indiscreet woman that attended upon her" and who "let her rise" (which caused the girl to deteriorate).[4] That he was a loving father also appears from the fact that he, a busy aristocrat

---

1 Tytler II pp. 115–116
2 Chapman 1962 p. 65
3 Weir 2008 p. 93
4 The letter's first editor, Patrick Fraser Tytler, commented in 1839: "It is strange, that not a word of sorrow escapes the lips of the father who saw his little daughter hurried in a few hours from the midst of the joyousness of childhood into the grasp of this fell disease; and yet it would be hard to blame him, for the deepest is often the stillest grief." (Tytler II p. 114). The editors of the *Calendar of the State Papers Domestic*, both in 1856 and in 1992, believed the deceased to be John Dudley's adult daughter-in-law, apparently reading the above letter as a follow-up to one from the previous day, 1 June, to Lord Thomas Darcy and Sir John Gates (printed Tytler II pp. 112–114). That letter mentions the death of Ambrose Dudley's wife; it says nowhere when exactly she died, however, dealing exclusively with property issues, only one of which resulted from her demise. The letter of 2 June, on the other hand, clearly reports a development that has only just occurred; it thus seems unlikely that the "daughter" and "child" of this letter is the same person as "the wife of my son Ambrose" and "this woman" of the previous letter. It is generally different in tone, and the mention of the measles but not her recent accouchement, as well as the careful report of the hourly progress of the disease, suggest that a real child, one "as merry as any child could be", had only just died.

and chief minister, had noticed the child's behaviour as well as her cough in the weeks before.

Apparently, no infection took root in the Dudley household; John still decided on "staying myself and my sons until the full moon next Monday, lest there is another infection in my house." He would then return to court "with my son, Huntingdon, Lord Hastings, and my son Sydney."[1]

Francis Hastings, 2nd Earl of Huntingdon, had been John's ally for years.[2] The earl and his teenage son Henry were regular house guests of the duke, while the younger John Dudley also moved in the earl's household, playing cards or dice with him and giving his servants presents.[3] Henry Sidney, meanwhile, had become his father-in-law's intimate friend, and his father William was granted the manor of Penshurst in Kent. This place, "which the duke oft before required", became disposable in spring 1552, having been the property of the executed Vane, who had been unwilling to part with it (for it had been granted to him for the capture of the Earl of Huntly in the Scottish war).[4] Able to choose from among the crown's wealth of properties – many confiscated from traitors or deprived bishops – John Dudley collected ever more residences. Having returned the crumbling Warwick Castle to the crown in January 1550,[5] by early 1553 he had added to his London residence Ely Place the palatial Durham Place and Syon, as well as the idyllic retreat of Chelsea. Durham Place, where John had feasted with Henry VIII and Anne of Cleves, had posed a bit of a problem; it had been scheduled for the Lady Elizabeth's use and she would not part with it "without conceiving some displeasure before against me, for that I would make labour or means to have the house without first knowing her mind".[6] Fortunately, however, she was now "fully satisfied" with Somerset House on the Strand – the keeper was Robert Dudley.[7]

---

1 Knighton 1992 p. 239
2 Cross 1966 pp. 9, 13
3 Loades 1996 p. 309; Knighton 1992 p. 239; HMC Second Report p. 102
4 Adams, Archer, Bernard 2003a p. 53
5 Loades 1996 p. 295
6 Tytler II p. 162
7 Adams 2008c

Northumberland also acquired the more provincial Knole.[8] And, Lord-Lieutenant of Warwickshire in 1552 and 1553 (jointly with his eldest son), he was at last granted the castle of Kenilworth, the huge medieval royal castle. John immediately started building works, adding new stables.[9] He was a generous master to his labourers, insisting they be paid properly when he heard the contrary.

The Duke of Northumberland's residences were adorned with paintings and maps. The maps celebrated his victories, in Scotland and in Norfolk. Among the paintings there oddly was "a table of the ffryer p", showing Friar William Peto, now in exile, but famous for defending Katherine of Aragon before Henry VIII.[3] Naturally, John Dudley was also a patron of artists and scholars, and in 1552 he was elected Chancellor of Cambridge University (replacing the executed Duke of Somerset). Walter Haddon, the Cambridge Latinist, was very pleased, as he later told John's son, Robert:

> You have certainly inherited a love of scholarship. For your father, although he acknowledged himself uneducated, was yet most devoted to learning. This was certainly apparent in his patronage of me, for, although he received no formal education, he valued highly one able to make a modest display of academic ability.[4]

Young scholars less famous also benefited from the duke's patronage. His servant John Hartforde's son, "handsomely learned", asked for a licence to travel to Paris, Orleans, as well as Padua, and got it.[5] Although he had travelled to Spain, and not to Italy, John Dudley seems to have developed a love for the latter. The adventurer-scholar William Thomas dedicated his *History of Italy* to the Earl of Warwick on 20 September 1549, correctly

---

8 Loades 1996 p. 298
9 Morris 2010 p. 46. The so-called Leicester's Stables and the tiltyard were built by John Dudley, as recent work has shown.
3 Goldring 2014 pp. 289–290
4 Wilson 1981 p. 15
5 Beer 1973 p. 127

sensing where the wind was blowing. Soon, he was a clerk of the privy council and King Edward's de facto tutor in politics. William Thomas was "highly fam'd for his travels through France and Italy", from which he had only just returned, and also published *Principal Rules of the Italian Grammer, with a Dictionarie for the better understandynge of Boccace, Petrarcha, and Dante.*

John Dudley's children Robert and Mary acquired fluency in Italian, being tutored by Michelangelo Florio, a religious refugee from Italy.[1] All these efforts notwithstanding, when the famed astrologer Girolamo Cardano visited Edward's court in August 1552, he not only predicted a long life for the king, but, probably more accurately, described the strange English way of pronouncing Latin and Italian: "they inflected the tongue upon the palate, twisted words in the mouth, and maintained a sort of gnashing with the teeth".[2]

John Dudley, in 1550, also sent the coming architect John Shute abroad, where he was to visit "the most notable places of Italie" in order to "confer with the doinges of the skilful maisters in architecture, and also to view such auncient Monumentes ... as are yet extant".[3] No doubt, John Dudley in due course wished to employ Shute's services for his own building projects, perhaps planning something spectacular, not unlike Somerset House on the Strand. As it came, John Shute on his return presented the drawings he had made, above all in Rome, to the Duke of Northumberland and to King Edward, who was delighted.[4] Shute's travels also resulted in *The First and Chief Groundes of Architecture*, the first vernacular treatise on this topic in England. After it was printed in London in 1563, probably with the help of Robert Dudley, it provided English builders and architects with a sound foundation in Renaissance style.[5]

Meanwhile, Jane, Duchess of Northumberland, had become a great lady at court. She owned a green parrot, a fashionable pet. In

---

1 Haynes 1987 p. 95. Florio also dedicated his translation into Italian of John Ponet's catechism to John Dudley (see below p. 173).
2 Chapman 1958 p. 260
3 Goldring 2014 p. 36
4 Rowse 1971 p. 17
5 Goldring 2014 p. 40

the 1530s, Lady Lisle (the second wife of John's stepfather) had received several birds from a French gentleman:

> Madame, it cannot yet talk, but this is because it hath yet learnt nothing and it is young. As you have one that doth speak it will learn with yours.[1]

While no ambassador found her interesting, Jane still seems to have been influential with her husband, people like Thomas Gresham and Richard Morison (who described Northumberland as "the mastiff himself"[2]) seeking her patronage; she even interceded for the Lady Mary.[3]

*

In early June 1552 the new Duke of Northumberland broke up to an extended progress throughout the north of England. His ducal title had brought him no more than the suspiciously petty reward of £40 p.a. out of the customs of Newcastle,[4] and he was suspected of having his eye on the landed wealth of the former Percy estate and the Palatinate of Durham (whose bishop was in prison). There was also his office of Warden-General of the Scottish Marches (worth £1,333 13s 4d p.a.[5]) that called for an inspection tour; this office he had taken over from Henry Grey, Marquess of Dorset, who characteristically had given up on the "disorders" there.[6] In July 1550, John had decided to build a new fortress at Berwick-upon-Tweed, directly on the Scottish border. The team of experts included his old comrade-in-arms, Sir Thomas Palmer, and they set about constructing a model of a *trace italienne*, or star fort, employing some 1,220 workmen over the next two years in what was then England's largest building site. Alas, many practical problems arose, walls were collapsing and money was

---

1 St. Clare Byrne 1983 p. 249
2 Gammon 1973 p. 177
3 Loades 2008a; Gunn 1999 p. 1267
4 Merriman 2000 p. 353
5 Loades 1996 pp. 222–223
6 Literary Remains II p. 344

disappearing, and John's signature was being forged, unbeknownst to the duke, by the treasurer. In the summer of 1552 it was concluded that only the presence of the Duke of Northumberland could resolve the situation.[1]

The first significant stop was at Burghley, Northamptonshire, at the house of Richard Cecil, William Cecil's father. William had insisted to welcome the mighty duke to his ancestral home, whatever the cost.

> And for your gentle and most friendly request to have me to your father's in my way northwards, I do ... render my hearty thanks unto you, assuring you I will not omit to see him as I go by him, though I do but drink a cup of wine with him at the door; for I will not trouble no friend's house of mine otherwise in this journey, my train is so great, and will be, whether I will or not.[2]

As it turned out, Northumberland stayed more than the quarter of an hour in Burghley; a mini-privy council dispatched several items of business there, most importantly the case of the corrupt official, John Beaumont, through whose sticky fingers had passed a lot of money as receiver-general of the Court of Wards, and who as Master of the Rolls had forged many a document.[3]

Lord Admiral Clinton likewise wished to receive his uncle-by-marriage at his seat Sempringham Priory, in Lincolnshire. Northumberland is first heard of in the north at Carlisle, and only two days later at York, where he acknowledged the "order and quietness".[4] At the end of July he returned to Carlisle stopping at Alnwick, the great former Percy castle, now in his possession.[5] He then went to Newcastle, where he heard John Knox, a truculent preacher to his liking. In the north, where he was popular,[6]

---

1 Merriman 2000 pp. 375–376
2 Tytler II pp. 110–111
3 Beer 1973 p. 131
4 Beer 1973 pp. 133, 134
5 Beer 1973 p. 135; Loades 1996 p. 220
6 CSP Span 9 July 1552

Northumberland saw much disorder and asked the council in London to appoint Lord Wharton, a local magnate, to replace his two deputies who had served so far. Dozens of raiders and murderers came out to the duke, submitting themselves hoping for pardon. Not sure what to do, John first consulted the king and the council, writing to his young son-in-law; he recommended clemency. It also now dawned on him that he would have to stay in the north longer than expected, warning Henry Sidney: "I pray you keep this from my wife."[1]

John returned to the south in late August, meeting Edward and the court on summer progress at Salisbury, before going home to Knole.[2] He was not only responsible for affairs in the north, but also for Irish ones.[3] The Lord Deputy, Sir James Croft, suggested a plantation of loyal Englishmen around the Pale of Dublin (as a buffer against wild Irishmen), but nothing came of the idea until the reign of Mary.[4] At Calais, the other English outpost, there was disorder of another kind. In early 1551 Andrew Dudley had been appointed to the captaincy of the English garrison at Guînes.[5] Incurring large debts "by his service",[6] he became involved in a dispute with the Lord Deputy, Lord Willoughby. John sympathized with his brother, believing Willoughby to have "wilfully proceeded", but he agreed to recall both men to England in January 1552, to be summoned before the privy council and prevent "the renewing of more unquietness between them and their retinues."[7] As it came, to resolve the issue, both men were relieved of their posts. During 1552 Andrew Dudley had also been employed to survey the coastal defenses of Portsmouth and the Isle of Wight and advise on their improvement.[8] This was in preparation of the king's visit, who – a connoisseur of fortification works – stopped by on his progress:

---

1 Beer 1973 p. 135
2 Beer 1973 p. 135; Hoak 1976 p. 317
3 Hoak 1976 p. 130. Among his areas of responsibility on the council was "Things to be considered for Ireland".
4 Sharpe 2002 p. 22; MacCulloch 2002 pp. 94–95
5 Löwe 2004
6 Beer 1973 p. 129
7 Tytler II pp. 103–104
8 Löwe 2004

[W]e went to Portsmouth town, and there viewed not only the town itself, and the haven, but also divers bulwarks ... In viewing of which we find the bulwarks chargeable, massy, well-rampaired; but ill-fashioned, ill-flanked, and set in unmeet places, the town weak in comparison of that it ought to be, too huge great (for within the walls are fair and large closes, and much vacant room), the haven notable great, and standing by nature easy to be fortified. And for the more strength thereof we have devised two strong castles on either side of the haven, at the mouth thereof.[1]

*

After his trip to France to broker the peace with France, Lord Paget had attended government business only sporadically, having too many issues with John's policies. At the same time he was too intelligent to engage in any of the Duke of Somerset's plotting, and although Crane claimed that the supposed banquet to remove the governing clique was to be held at Paget's house, Paget was placed into the Tower on a pretext wholly unrelated to Somerset. It quickly transpired that his life was not in danger. After a couple of months Lady Paget received back all her husband's confiscated property and was allowed to visit him regularly; his confinement was quite relaxed, he was allowed to walk the Tower gardens and pace up and down the palace gallery. Still, he had to stomach a terrible slur to his honour, that of losing his Garter on the grounds that "he was no gentlemen either of his father's side nor mother's side".[2] In June 1552, he was finally charged with peculation in office and allowed his freedom against a fine of £5,000. At first he was to go to the country, alas Lady Paget's "stitch in her side" required the attentions of her London doctor, and so the couple received permission to stay in their suburban residence. In October 1552 the fine was reduced and the case was settled in the following months by the payment of a total of £1,774, before it had been due,

---

1 Literary Remains I p. 81
2 Gammon 1973 p. 181

the government being relieved at this unexpected influx of cash. Finally, in early March 1553, Lord Paget was admitted to the royal presence and allowed to kiss Edward's hand as a sign of his restoration to favour.[1] His coat of arms was also restored, though not his Garter, the vacancy having been filled by Sir Andrew Dudley.

Two months into the reign of Edward VI, on 24 March 1547, Andrew had been given custody of a purse of £1435 9s 6d, and on 3 October 1550 he became keeper of the Palace of Westminster, where he made an inventory of the royal wardrobe and household goods.[2] Now effectively in charge of the privy purse, he was responsible for receiving and paying out the royal cash and looking after "all the jewels … and other things in the palace".[3]

"An inventory of Sir Andrew Dudley's goods remaining at his house at Petty Callyn" after his arrest in 1553 has survived,[4] giving insights into how this well-to-do gentleman bachelor lived. "In his study" Queen Mary's commissioners found "two old hats", and "in a little storehouse over the wardrobe two old swords and one rapier". Andrew's armoury contained a guilt harness and "a great slaughter sword". A very valuable item, the decorated harness would have served as tilting armour rather than in battle. Of riding outfit there was "a pair of stirrups with stirrup leather velvet", a "posting saddle of velvet and a portmanteau of velvet". Six pairs of velvet shoes and "certain boots, buskins, leather shoes and slippers" made an impressive collection of footwear. – Velvet shoes wore off especially quickly; as we have seen, Andrew's nephew John, Earl of Warwick, needed about seven pairs per year.[5]

Sir Andrew's house was roomy: a hall, a parlour, an "outward parlour", his bedchamber, his study, "a little room next to his study, the room next adjoining, the third room next his study", and "the fourth room next his study". Interestingly, this bachelor household also had "a women's chamber" and "the chamber next the women's chamber". Then came "the boy's chamber, the page's chamber", the

---

1   Gammon 1973 pp. 181–184
2   Collins 1745 p. 29; Starkey 1998 pp. 74, 401
3   Beer 1973 p. 128; Loades 1996 p. 250
4   Hayward 2009 pp. 364–365
5   HMC Second Report p. 101

armoury, and "the little house within the armoury". There were two kitchens, "the upper loft", and the wardrobe with "a little storehouse" over it. Outside the main house there was "the little house at the end of the pond". Not all the commissioners found was new and shiny: An old satin gown, "very ill"; a tawny old night-gown lined with marten fur (such a "night-gown" Andrew would not have worn in bed, but when making himself comfortable at home). There were also fabric remnants; of "black friezed velvet", of crimson velvet, of "tawny cloth of gold with works", of "crimson cloth of gold, plain", of "white and crimson cloth tissue". And there was "a little chest containing certain working silk ribbon of divers colours". In one parlour, "upon the bed", clothes were found as if on display: "His Garter robes" and "a black damask gown lined throughout with fine budge" – a present from the king. Also "satin coats all furred", "an old pair of hose of black velvet", and "a black velvet coat all cut", "a gown of black satin coat furred with coney", "a black velvet coat all guarded"; not all was black, though, there was also a green coat.

"In the chamber next the women's chamber" the commissioners found – "a night gown of crimson satin" with gold embroidery and "a pair of hose and a doublet of silk and gold richly wrought of knit work", but also "a plain coat" and "two old black coats of velvet". Last but not least, some jewellery was left behind:

> Item found more in the said Sir Andrew Dudley's study: One very small chain of gold;
> Item one small bracelet of gold;
> Item 30 pairs of aiglets and buttons;
> Item certain broken silver with some outlandish silver coin and some old groats among them;
> Item two little brooches of gold.[1]

Andrew also patronized a company of players, the "lord Andrewe Dudley's players".[2]

*

---
1 Hayward 2009 p. 365
2 Murray II p. 83

The Duke of Northumberland was by now unpopular with large sections of society; all sorts of curious stories were making the rounds, such as that he had his eye on the throne and that he was producing his own coin: one man insisted he had seen a ragged staff on a shilling, while his fellow could only make out a lion.[1] There was still also, nearly 70 years after the Battle of Bosworth, considerable dynastic paranoia surrounding the Tudor monarchy. John thought that the Countess of Sussex, being accused of witchcraft, should "be somewhat better tried and searched; the rather for that she is charged to have spoken and said that one of King Edward's sons should be yet living" – King Edward's sons were, of course, the Princes in the Tower.[2] John Dudley wrote this letter on 30 May 1552, not long after the death of Ambrose Dudley's first wife; his mind therefore may have been already engaged in finding his son a new one. His choice fell on Elizabeth Tailboys, a baroness in her own right with landed possessions in Lincolnshire.[3] She was, however, nearly 10 years older than her husband, as well as a widow.[4] She was also related to Ambrose's mother, and her stepfather was Lord Admiral Clinton,[5] now the husband of John's niece, Ursula Stourton.

John was also making plans for his two youngest sons: Guildford, now some 15 years old, and Henry, even younger. With two of his children, Robert and Mary, having married for love, it was important to secure some really good matches as well. Young Henry's match to Margaret Audley proved the most valuable financially. She was the sole heiress of the Lord Chancellor Thomas Audley, who had died in 1544. About one or two years younger than Harry, she was about 13 in the summer of 1553, by which time the marriage must have been concluded. Lands worth £1,000 p. a. came with it.[6] Guildford's intended bride was the Earl

---

1 APC III p. 462. The ragged staff stood for the earls of Warwick and was part of John Dudley's coat-of-arms. The lion stood for England.
2 Tytler II p. 109. The countess spent five months in the Tower in 1552 (Childs 2006 p. 302).
3 The date of the marriage is unknown, but must have occurred sometime before May 1553.
4 Virgoe 2004
5 Norton 2011a pp. 7, 10
6 Beer 1973 p. 195. The wedding date is unknown, but as the canonic age for

151

of Cumberland's daughter, Margaret Clifford, who by her mother was also a grandniece of Henry VIII, a fact that caused suspicion in some quarters. Elizabeth Huggones, a former servant of the Duchess of Somerset, openly suspected the Duke of Northumberland of hankering after the crown; and the king, she said, was an "unnaturall nephew".

> She tould also the night before at supper for newse that my lord Guilford Dudleye should marrye my lorde of Cumberlandes daughter, and that the Kinges majestie should devise the marriage. 'Have at the Crowne with your leave', she said with a stoute gesture.[1]

Of course she later retracted her statements: "as concerninge these wordes, *'Have at the Crowne with your leave'*, she utterly denieth to have spoken them, or any other like; and deposeth that she never spake nor thought any such matter, nor meant evell of any man, by any of her aforesaid wordes."[2] Mistress Huggones also denied her remarks about King Edward, and even "that she did only impute the death of the duke of Somerset to the duke of Northumberland, and no other man, who she thought was better worthy to die than he". – She utterly denied to have said "these words", although "she then said she thought that those which were the procurers of the duke of Somerset's death, his blood would be required at their hands, even like as the lord admiral's blood was at the duke's hands". It is interesting that, while she was at voicing her opinion about the Duke of Northumberland, she did not impute the death of Thomas Seymour to him, but exclusively to the Duke of Somerset. It is also revealing that while she had served the Duchess of

---

boys to consent lawfully to a marriage was 14, and for girls 12, it would probably have occurred sometime in 1552 or 1553. That is not to say that it could not have been agreed upon considerably earlier. De Lisle 2008 p. 92 sees the match as part of the conspiracy for the crown in 1553, since Margaret Audley was a niece of Henry Grey, Duke of Suffolk; however, if the wedding occurred in proximity to the matches of May 1553 its complete absence in diplomatic correspondence is difficult to explain.

1 Literary Remains I p. clxvii
2 Literary Remains I p. clxviii

Somerset, her husband served Northumberland, which was why she bore "greatest favour and affection to the duke of Northumberland's grace of any other nobleman", after Somerset.[1] She was released in June 1553.[2]

If Northumberland was so keen to marry his sons into royalty, why did he not suggest Ambrose as a husband for Lady Margaret Clifford? Ambrose would have been some seven years older than Margaret while Guildford was almost her age, but Ambrose's brother John, Earl of Warwick, at 19 had also married a girl between five and seven years his junior. The fact remains that Northumberland pursued the "royal" match with Margaret Clifford for his second youngest son at a time he was seeking a new bride for his second eldest. Elizabeth Huggones' opinion notwithstanding, his principal aim in all likelihood was an alliance with one of the great noble houses of the north of England. Edward VI ostensibly wished the union (as Mistress Huggones had said) and the council, on 4 July 1552, wrote in the king's name to the Duke of Northumberland and the Earl of Cumberland that they should "grow to some good end concerning the marriage".[3] It is usually assumed that all this was arranged by Northumberland to press his son's suit against Cumberland's wishes, however in January 1553 the earl appointed commissioners to negotiate a marriage settlement between Margaret and Guildford.[4] Nothing came of it, unfortunately, and Margaret's fiancé (for a few weeks) was to be Sir Andrew Dudley. Andrew sent his best stuffs to the north, for safekeeping with his prospective father-in-law.[5] He reserved items from the royal wardrobe at Westminster for the wedding as well: jewels, silver and gilt cups, a hair-brush, velvet dog-collars, and a pair of pictures of *Diana and Actaeon*.[6] What is clear is that Cumberland by no means was averse to an alliance with the House of Dudley.

---

1 Literary Remains I p. clxvii
2 Skidmore 2007 p. 238
3 Loades 1996 p. 226
4 Hoyle 1992 p. 20
5 Hayward 2009 p. 365
6 HMC Salisbury I pp. 131–132

In September 1551 war once again broke out between France and the emperor. In due course requests for English help arrived from both sides, which in the case of the Empire consisted of a demand for full-scale war, based on the Anglo-Imperial treaty of 1543. However, Charles had rejected to help England keep Boulogne and John was keen to keep his country out of war, anyway.[1] So, the treaties with both France and the Empire were politely ignored. On 10 October 1552 the emperor's ambassador appeared at court to remind Edward's council of the king's supposed duties:

> I first approached the Duke of Northumberland. We talked of several matters, the latest news and other affairs, and I did not fail to mention the demand for assistance, saying that your Majesty felt sure he would support the friendship between the two countries and the cause of their common defence, that had become so necessary now the designs of the King of France had been exposed. That prince appeared to wish to lord it over the whole world, for he showed scant respect for other sovereigns. These and other similar remarks I made in order to incline him favourably towards the alliance.[2]

Northumberland "appeared to be of the same opinion," assuring de Scheyfve that the council, and the king, were wholly inclined to Anglo-Imperial friendship. John managed to say that "[f]or his own part, he had always done his best to further it; and he said in so many words that anyone who did otherwise would be no faithful servant to the King." But it was also true, he told de Scheyfve, "speaking quite frankly and by way of conversation", that Charles "seemed not to care much for" King Edward. Since the death of Henry VIII no special embassy from the emperor had turned up in England: "The Duke went so far as to appear to imply that it would have been at least suitable to send someone to make

---

1   Loades 1996 pp. 203–207; Loades 2011 pp. 301–302; Beer 1973 p. 138
2   CSP Span 10 October 1552

the demand for aid." John went on listing all the instances where the emperor had let down the English in recent years, until the ambassador told him that "now was the time to cease discussion" and concentrate on the French menace. "At that the Duke laughed", taking the ambassador's arm.[1]

Northumberland indeed now believed, he assured Cecil, that the emperor had shown "more good will" than for a very long time. The French ambassador, meanwhile, made two attempts to contact the duke privately in Chelsea; John was ill, however, diplomatically or otherwise, and referred him to the council.[2] To Darcy and the secretaries Cecil and Petre John explained how he was forced, due to circumstances, to be "affectionate" with France, "our ancient enemy".[3]

Meanwhile, a storm in the teacup had been going on over the issue of France. Thomas Stukeley was an English mercenary in the services of the French crown, claiming a special relationship with both the French king and his chief minister, Montmorency. In September 1552 he turned up in England with a letter of recommendation from Henry II to Edward VI. Then he revealed supposed French plans for the capture of Calais and for an invasion of England, the furtherance of which, he claimed, had been the object of his mission. Though he earned disbelief from the privy council, there was also alarm – but when the English ambassador in Paris, Sir William Pickering, was informed of Stukeley's story, he wrote back that neither Henry II nor Montmorency were inclined to trust the English adventurer. Northumberland decided to clap him in the Tower and apologize to the French king and ambassador.[4] Sir William Pickering, meanwhile, like all ambassadors, complained about the lack of funds, he "had not 20 crowns left" in October 1552; and yet John had supplied him with "silver candlesticks" and other household stuff.[5]

---

1 CSP Span 10 October 1552
2 Beer 1973 pp. 139, 212
3 Beer 1973 p. 139
4 Loades 1996 pp. 204–205. Thomas Stukeley remained in the Tower until August 1553, when he was released by Queen Mary; he was imprisoned for debt only days later.
5 Beer 1973 pp. 110–111

13. Obstinate Doctors

As Edward VI was drawn to the more radical elements of Protestantism, John Dudley made sure to appeal to the king's religious taste (which apparently was also his own). Even more than Somerset he became a chief backer of radical Protestants among the clergy, making people like John Hooper and John Ponet into bishops.[1] And so the English Reformation went on apace, despite its widespread unpopularity.[2] In 1552 a revised edition of the *Book of Common Prayer* appeared, rejecting the doctrine of transubstantiation, and the Forty-two Articles, issued in June 1553, proclaimed justification by faith alone and denied the existence of purgatory. Despite these being cherished projects of Archbishop Thomas Cranmer, the primate was displeased with the way the government handled the publication of the Book and the Articles.[3] By 1552 the relationship between Cranmer and Northumberland was icy.

At the heart of John Dudley's problems with the episcopate lay the issue of the church's wealth, from the confiscation of which the government and its officials had profited ever since the Dissolution of the Monasteries under Henry VIII. The most radical preachers believed that bishops, if needed at all, should be "unlorded".[4] This

---

1 Jordan and Gleason 1975 pp. 4
2 MacCulloch 2001 p. 56
3 MacCulloch 2001 p. 101; Loades 1996 p. 254
4 Loades 1996 p. 176

attitude was appealing to John, as it conveniently allowed him to use church property to fill up the Exchequer or distribute rewards. When new bishops were appointed – typically to the sees of deprived conservative incumbents – they often had to surrender substantial land holdings to the crown and were left with a much reduced income.[1] The dire situation of crown finances made the council resort to a further wave of church expropriation in 1552 and 1553, targeting chantry lands and church plate.[2] Still, John's provisions for reorganized dioceses reveal his concern that the preaching of God's word should not be hampered by a lack funds.[3] The confiscation of church property, as well as the lay government's direction of church affairs, aroused the clerics' disapproval, be they reformed or conservative.[4] Among them, the duke almost became a *bête noire,* and the dislike was mutual. Especially the deprivations of the staunchly conservative bishops, Steven Gardiner of Winchester and Cuthbert Tunstall of Durham, were drawn-out affairs. Both men spent the better part of Edward VI's reign in prison; like the Lady Mary they believed they did not have to take a minority government's religious legislation seriously.[5] John grilled both men personally in the Tower during 1551, and both had a personal history with him: John had hit Gardiner in the face in the presence of Henry VIII and had been advised by Tunstall as a beginner in northern affairs. After Tunstall was finally an ex-bishop in October 1552, Northumberland for nearly half a year pleaded in vain for the appointment of a new bishop:

> And then for the North, if his Majesty make the Dean of Durham Bishop of that see, and appoint him one thousand marks more to that which he hath in his deanery, and the same houses which he now hath, as well in the city as in the country, will serve him right honourably, so may his Majesty receive both the

---

1 Loades 1996 pp. 176–177; Heal 1980 pp. 141–142
2 MacCulloch 2001 p. 54
3 Heal 1980 pp. 145–146, 149
4 MacCulloch 2001 p. 55; Heal 1980 p. 147
5 They had behaved rather differently under Henry VIII.

castle, which hath a princely site, and the other stately houses which the Bishop had in the country.[1]

The candidate, Robert Horne, refused the position – for though his own income would increase considerably, the see's income would be too much diminished! The duke at first was impressed by so much stature, thinking that such a man was just the right man for the job,[2] but – as "this old year past was not happy for old Durham to receive a new bishop"[3] – his mood turned definitely sour in January 1553:

> And what order was lately taken with the Dean of Durham I neither yet did hear nor have been made privy to it; and where he is, and how he is employed … whether he be gone home, or whether he remain here, I know not; but wheresoever he be, I have been much deceived by him, for he is undoubtedly not only a greedy, covetous man, but also a malicious.[4]

Another candidate could apparently not be found, and the issue still rankled:

> [F]or the love of God, let not the See be so long destitute of some grave and good man; yea, rather a stout honest man that knoweth his duty to God and to his Sovereign Lord, than one of these new obstinate doctors without humanity or honest conditions. These men, for the most part, that the King's Majesty hath of late preferred, be so sotted of their wives and children that they forget both their poor neighbours and all other things which to their calling appertaineth; and so will they do so long as his Majesty shall suffer them

---

1 Tytler II pp. 142–143
2 Beer 1973 p. 142
3 Tytler II p. 152
4 Tytler II pp. 152–153

to have so great possessions to maintain their idle lives. Beseeching God that it may be amended.[1]

It is highly revealing that Northumberland proved unable to press his point until parliament resolved the issue by splitting up the diocese in spring 1553; and the two new sees still remained vacant at the close of Edward's reign![2] The break-up and reorganization of the prince bishopric of Durham has always been interpreted, from John Foxe the martyrologist onwards, as the Duke of Northumberland's attempt to create himself a county palatine of his own, fitting his ducal title. If he entertained such hopes the only gain he made out of it was a meagre £50 p.a. from the stewardship of the newly created "King's County Palatine"; for, as it turned out, Durham's entire revenue was allotted to the two successor bishoprics and the nearby border garrison of Norham Castle.[3]

*

In Northumberland's train on his return to the capital, in August 1552, had travelled John Knox, who had impressed the duke when preaching to the people of Newcastle. John Dudley made him a court preacher and thought he would make an excellent bishop – "I would to God it might please the King's Majesty to appoint Mr. Knocks to the office of Rochester". He hoped that Knox would be "a whetstone, to quicken and sharp the Bishop of Canterbury, whereof he hath need".[4] Knox, soon known as "the Duke's preacher",[5] indeed made life more difficult for Cranmer by taking offence at kneeling at communion, which he thought was idolatry: "The Duke of Northumberland has fetched hither a new Scots apostle from Newcastle, who has already begun to pick holes in the new and universal reformation", the Imperial ambassador was pleased to report.[6] In the end Cranmer grudgingly conceded a so-

---

1 Tytler II p. 153
2 Beer 1973 p. 142; Loades 1996 p. 234
3 Loades 1996 pp. 198, 302
4 Tytler II p. 142
5 MacCulloch 1996 pp. 525–526
6 CSP Span 20 November 1552

called black rubric to be included in the new edition of the *Book of Common Prayer* – it declared that no adoration of the host was intended by kneeling at communion. However, if Northumberland thought he had found a manageable cleric he was much deceived. Knox refused to collaborate in everything else and rather joined fellow reformers in a concerted preaching campaign against covetous men in high places.[1] He had even declined the bishopric, an emergency Secretary Cecil thought warranted an audience with the duke:

> Master Knox being here to speak with me, saying that he was so willed by you, I do return him again, because I love not to have to do with men which be neither grateful nor pleasable. I assure you I mind to have no more to do with him but to wish him well.[2]

Knox had also questioned John's faith, to his very face: "you might see in his letter, that he cannot tell whether I be a dissembler in religion or not". John would not put up with this: "I have for twenty years stand [stood] to one kind of religion, in the same which I do now profess; and have, I thank the Lord, past no small dangers for it."

Meanwhile, Knox had returned to his flock at Newcastle, where on Christmas Day he provocatively preached about secret Catholics at court and the threat of a Catholic revival should the king come to harm. His audience became nervous and Lord Wharton, Deputy Warden of the Scottish Marches, sent Knox to London to be examined on suspicion of treason.[3] With Knox arrived many letters, from Lord Wharton, from the mayor of Newcastle, and from Knox himself; having perused them at Chelsea, John sent them back to Cecil, with instructions. Only one letter had impressed him:

> Herewith I do return unto you ... also one letter from poor Knox, by the which you may perceive what

---

1 Ives 2009 p. 116
2 Tytler II p. 148
3 Dawson 2015 pp. 62–63

perplexity the poor soul remaineth in at this present; the which, in my poor opinion, should not do amiss to be remembered to the rest of my Lords, that some order might be taken by their wisdoms for his recomfort.

After all, Edward had come to like John Knox:

> I think it very expedient that his Highness' pleasure should be known, as well to the Lord Wharton as to those of Newcastle, that his Highness hath the poor man and his doings in gracious favour; ... for that it seemeth to me that the Lord Wharton himself is not altogether without suspicion how the said Knox's doings hath been here taken, wherefore I pray you that something may be done whereby the King's Majesty's pleasure ... may be indelayedly certified to the said Lord Wharton, ... with commandment that no man shall be so hardy to vex him or trouble him ... for that his Majesty mindeth to employ the man and his talent from time to time in those parts, and elsewhere ... And that something might be written to the Mayor for his greedy accusation of the poor man, wherein he hath, in my poor opinion, uttered his malicious stomach towards the King's proceedings if he might see a time to serve his purpose.[1]

Was Knox being prophetic? Did Lord Wharton, did the mayor of Newcastle, did Northumberland know something in the early days of 1553? The duke was no stranger to melancholy, the malady of princes. Some complaints were real enough and have been diagnosed as some form of stomach ailment, possibly an ulcer. Doctors tried to stop his "inward bleeding", and to "restore corrupted blood" as well as "the bloody flux from the lungs".[2] A French diplomat and eyewitness wrote shortly after John's death

---

1 Tytler II pp. 158–160
2 Skidmore 2007 pp. 236–237

that he had suffered from instances of severe pain, and that one of his arms had been rendered useless, probably by an injury.[1]

In October 1552 the "falling of the uvula" troubled him so much that he was "forced to keep my chamber for it is now a fortnight since it began to fall and continueth worse and worse so that I can scarcely eat any meat for it".[2] By December and January he was obsessed with "cure and medicine", suffering from what may have been a heavy cold: "my health daily worsens, neither close keeping, furs nor clothing can bring any natural heat to my head and I have no hope of recovery." – "I fear to be sick as I burn hot as fire; so did I yesterday ... having great pain in the nether part of my belly. But feeling no such grief now, the heat is nevertheless fervently upon me."[3]

Thus in the autumn and winter of 1552/1553 John Dudley experienced a long time of illness and melancholy, William Cecil serving as de facto therapist. While the duke never failed to admonish his fellow royal servants to work for the common good, "and to despise this flattering of ourselves with heaping of riches upon riches, honours upon honours, building upon building",[4] he keenly felt his unpopularity and Edmund Dudley came to mind; even though it had not been safe to name any of his grandsons after him, Edmund was unforgotten:

> And, for my own part, if I should have past more upon the speech of the people than upon the service of my master, or gone about to seek favour of them without respect to his Highness' surety, I needed not to have had so much obloquy of some kind of men; but the living God, that knoweth the hearts of all men, shall be my judge at the last day with what zeal, faith, and truth I serve my master. And though my poor father, who, after his master was gone, suffered death for doing his master's commandments, who was the wisest prince of the world living in those days, and

---

1 Ives 2009 pp. 311, 125
2 Skidmore 2007 p. 236
3 Ives 2009 pp. 124–125
4 Hoak 1980 p. 46

> yet could not his commandment be my father's [dis]charge after he was departed this life; so, for my part, with all earnestness and duty I will serve without fear, seeking nothing but the true glory of God and his Highness' surety: so shall I most please God and have my conscience upright, and then not fear what man doth to me.[1]

Clearly, in the early days of 1553 the Duke of Northumberland's mood was not as cheerful as the season required. Shut up at Chelsea – while the court revelled elsewhere – he felt misunderstood and weary of life: "Whosoever" thought that he absented himself from court for other reasons than "lack of sufficient health, he judgeth me wrong". An Italian proverb came to his mind ("though it become me not to say of myself, yet the saying is true"), that "of a faithful servant shall become a perpetual ass." – "So, though I were able to bear the burden, I trust my Lords do not mind so to use me once". Incredibly, he had also managed to live beyond his means – "so long have I passed forth this matter in silence and credit, that shame almost compelleth me to hide me." It was "high time" he found "a way to live of that which God and his Highness hath sent me", and keep away his creditors, "the multitude of cravers ... that hangeth now daily at my gate for money".

> What comfort think you may I have, that seeth myself in this case after my long travail and troublesome life, and towards the end of my days? And yet, so long as health would give me leave, I did as seldom fail mine attendance as any others did; yea, and with such health as, when others went to their sups and pastimes after their travail, I went to bed with a careful heart and a weary body; and yet abroad no man scarcely had any good opinion of me. And now, by extreme sickness and otherwise constrained to seek some health and quietness, I am not without a new evil imagination of men. What should I wish any longer

---
1 Tytler II p. 150

this life, that seeth such frailty in it? Surely, but for a few children which God hath sent me, which also helpeth to pluck me on my knees, I have no great cause to desire to tarry much longer here. And thus, to satisfy you and others whom I take for my friends, I have entered into the bottom of my care, which I cannot do without sorrow: but if God would be so merciful to mankind as to take from them their wicked imaginations, and leave them with a simple judgment, men should here live angels' lives; which may not be, for the fall of Adam our forefather procured this continual plague, that the one should be affliction to the other while we be in this circle, out of which God grant us all his grace to depart in his mercy. And so I leave, wishing the good unto you that your own self can desire. ...

To my very loving friend,
Sir Wm. Cycill, Knight[1]

---

1 Tytler II pp. 154–155

14.
The King's Will

On 28 December 1552 the Duke of Northumberland imparted his latest thoughts on English diplomacy to William Cecil. King Edward had just okayed the council's suggestion "to employ ministers abroad for the public weal of Christendom", that is to send envoys to Europe to offer English assistance in negotiating a peace between the Empire and France. Cecil was to tell Edward that he was to "be better served if those sent have grace and wit to note what they see and hear". Those appointed by the council were Sir Andrew Dudley ("my brother") and Sir Henry Sidney ("my son"), and it had not yet been decided who was to go to the emperor and who to the King of France; however, Northumberland thought that his son-in-law Sidney had "more means to express his mind in the Italian tongue than in the French" and so perhaps he should be the one to meet Charles V (whose first language, incidentally, was French).[1] Ignoring the duke's suggestion, the council sent Henry Sidney to France and Andrew Dudley to the Low Countries, where the emperor was staying. For the last few years John Dudley had balanced successfully on a tightrope between the two great powers, keeping England neutral. Under these circumstances a general peace was welcome,[2] especially as the negotiations would augment Edward's prestige.

On 1 January 1553 Sir Andrew Dudley called on Jehan de Scheyfve to pay his respects and announce his mission:

> He declared to me of his own accord that his charge was a very important one, but did not make himself

---
1 Beer 1973 p. 139; Knighton 1992 p. 283
2 Loades 1996 pp. 241–242

more plain; he thanked me ... and, after some more conversation, departed.[1]

Dudley and Sidney were chosen for their known personal closeness to the king rather than for any particular skills,[2] yet the more convincingly they could represent the peace initiative as Edward's personal agenda. Northumberland also suggested that in due course they could be joined by "more experienced" diplomats and that the journey could also serve for their "learning and education".[3] So, Andrew Dudley once again travelled to Brussels, where he was received by Mary of Hungary on 8 January. One of the letters carried by him may have been an address from the emperor's cousin, the Lady Mary, whom Northumberland had asked to emphasize England's goodwill towards the Empire.[4] Impatient to see the emperor himself, Andrew tried to intercept him on his way to Flanders. Sir Richard Morison, still resident ambassador with Charles V, knew nothing of this until he met Andrew at Trier, on the Moselle. The ailing ruler was averse to be molested by diplomats while journeying, but Morison managed to arrange an interview at Luxembourg in which Charles referred them to a later occasion.[5]

Morison and Dudley went back to Brussels, where during February they were busy hosting their Imperial colleagues, including Diego de Mendoza, godfather to Guildford Dudley:

> On the 9th Morysine invited Mons. de Rie to dine with Dudley at his lodgings, where he should meet Don Diego di Mendoza ... and others. ... After dinner De Rie accepted an invitation from Dudley to dine with him on the following day, and to bring his guest with him as he had done to Morysine. The same evening Mons. de Courriers came to town, and he also gladly came to dine at Dudley's.

---

1   CSP Span 4 January 1553
2   Loades 1996 p. 242
3   Knighton 1992 p. 284
4   Beer 1973 p. 140
5   Jordan 1970 p. 175

The Duke of Northumberland also received a letter with the news that "Don Diego has promised to write to your Grace. I think my Lord Guildford, your son and his godson, shall have a fair jennet from him."[1] At last, Charles V was ready to meet the English envoys,

> for on Friday the 10th instant he sent a gentleman of his chamber to Dudley to tell him that the Emperor would speak with him on the morrow, as accordingly at three o'clock of the Saturday he did. The Court was very well furnished with noblemen, all of them very glad to embrace the Ambassadors, and glad to talk well of England. The Emperor came forth without staff or any to lead him, his chair being set on the farther end of the chamber that they might see he could go so far without any stay. In the conversation which ensued between his Majesty and Dudley, the former said that until particularities were known from his enemy how could he will the King of England to work in the matter of peace? What answer could he give? All the world knew he began not the wars; they knew France took his subjects' ships and goods, had invaded the empire, hired men to rebellion, taken from the empire things belonging to it, and from himself part of his inheritance. For himself, he always loved peace and wished the quietness of Christendom, and if he might have such a peace ... his will was good, and he would be glad to have a peace ... But he knew, if peace were made, the French King would no longer keep it ... than he thought it his best.[2]

After Charles had stressed a few more times that he was amenable to a reasonable agreement, Andrew Dudley's great moment arrived:

> When about to take leave, and offering to kiss his hand, the Emperor cast his arm about Dudley's neck,

---
[1] Higginbotham 2011a
[2] CSP Foreign 12 February 1553

with great show of accepting his coming, of liking his message, and of allowing his behaviour in the doing thereof.

Dudley and Morison noted that the chamber had been hung with tapestries depicting the emperor's victories.

> De Rie and others accompanied them home ... They had scarcely arrived at home when Don Diego, who had called during their absence, returned to desire Dudley not to fail him to-morrow at dinner. De Rie promised by the way, that he would not leave Dudley so long as he could enjoy him, and when he could no more, his trust was they should meet one day again.[1]

On taking his leave, Dudley alongside his resident colleagues, Morison and Chamberlain, received "very gentle entertainment" from the regent; Morison was as sorry to stay as Dudley was "glad to be gone".[2] Back in England he delivered a gracious letter to King Edward from the emperor and elicited the close interest of the Imperial ambassador, who in his turn informed Charles V:

> Sire: I received your Majesty's letters of the 13th through Dudley, who arrived in this town on the 18th of the month and had audience of the King and my lords of the Council the following day, and came to see me the same afternoon. ... He declared that your Majesty had done him great honour, and bestowed a present on him. ... He declared that he had perceived most clearly that your Majesty indeed loved the King, his master. I assured him such was the truth, and that your Majesty had always held him as his son, and proved it in the past, in contrast to the course adopted by certain others.[3] As we had entertained one another at some length with these professions of mutual

---

1 CSP Foreign 12 February 1553
2 CSP Foreign 12 February 1553
3 France.

love, ... and never a word had he said about the letter from your Majesty to the King, or his negotiation, I made bold at last to question him if he had accomplished his mission to your Majesty. He replied that he had made his report to the King and my lords of the Council on what your Majesty had declared to him, and did not enlarge beyond this, which he did, in my opinion, rather to safeguard his reputation than for any other reason. Therefore I thought it well to say no more at the time and let the matter drop there. ... I can assure your Majesty that the Court and the town are full of the honours and welcome given to the said Dudley, and that all seem pleased about it, especially at the good understanding between their Majesties; and some go so far as to say that under colour of the said embassy a closer alliance may be about to be negotiated. The matter has given some umbrage to the French ambassador. To sum up, Sire, and reverting to the question of friendships, Dudley said to me that the friendship with France would never prove to be a real one, that the English had never thought much of the French, and he believed that if your Majesty wished to employ Englishmen, you would get a good number together. I replied that they had proved their zeal in your Majesty's service, and after a few more words of no importance, Sire, he took his leave.[1]

In early April follow-up missions were sent to both Brussels and Paris. Jehan de Scheyfve also had an audience, with the Duke of Northumberland, who opined that "if the King of France were inclined to make peace, his Imperial Majesty ought to forgive what had happened". When de Scheyfve insisted that "by all appearances the King of France was not seeking peace" and was "was making a brave show of warlike preparations", John Dudley "answered, smiling, that the Emperor was also making great preparations, but he did not explain himself further."[2] Henry

---

1 CSP Span 21 February 1553
2 CSP Span 17 March 1553

Sidney had also returned to England, with promising signs from the King of France;[1] alas, all these niceties were ended in the first week of June by the warring parties, the benefits from continued hostilities turning out more advantageous to them.[2]

In February 1553, the Lady Mary came to London with a great retinue. She was welcomed at the outskirts by the young Earl of Warwick at the head of 100 lords and gentlemen of the king's household. Three days later she visited Edward, who was sick, in Westminster. In her entourage rode, among many others, "the duchesses of Suffolk and Northumberland", and at the gate of Whitehall Palace "my lord of Suffolk and my lord of Northumberland" were waiting on her. She was treated "as if she had been Queen of England" and the king "received her very kindly and graciously, and entertained her with small talk, making no mention of matters of religion."[3] There may have been talks concerning the question of her marriage, though. Ambassador de Scheyfve had noticed that the French and Venetian ambassadors "had recently held unusually frequent interviews with the Duke of Northumberland" and did his "utmost to ascertain what his business with them might be." As it turned out, Mary had a suitor in Ercole d'Este, the son of Lucrezia Borgia and heir to the Duchy of Ferrara, who was "at present in France". Mary, for her part, told de Scheyfve that she was not aware of any such plans and certainly would not be married off.[4]

*

On 1 March 1553 King Edward VI opened Parliament. Not in the usual way (he was too ill for that), but in a low-key ceremony in Whitehall Palace. On the last day of the month the king performed the closing in the accustomed form again, for his health was better, and on 11 April he travelled to Greenwich to take the air.[5]

---

1 CSP Span 31 March 1553
2 Loades 1996 p. 244
3 CSP Span 17 February 1553
4 CSP Span 17 February 1553
5 Loades 1996 p. 237

At his retreat in Chelsea Northumberland had been brooding over the issue of parliament, especially how to incline members to grant a subsidy:

> I am of opinion that we need not to be so ceremonious as to imagine the objects of every froward person, but rather to burden their minds and hearts with the King's Majesty's extreme debts and necessity, grown and risen by such occasions and means as cannot be denied by no man.[1]

Some of these causes John had recently detailed in a letter to the council: The king's "great debt" had been "partly left and augmented by the late Duke of Somerset", and to make matters worse, "his Highness, left by his father in peace with all princes, was suddenly, by that man's unskilful protectorship and less expertise in government, plunged into wars".[2]

Despite his privileged access to the king, as Master of the Horse, the younger John Dudley is never mentioned as one of the persons influential with Edward, nor seems his father to have been able to use him otherwise to promote his policies. This became clear when Northumberland proposed to bring "in by writ some heirs-apparent into the parliament-house, whereby they may the better be able to serve his Majesty and the realm hereafter."[3] Indeed, young Warwick was summoned to attend the Lords in March 1553, but he left no mark on proceedings and it is unclear whether he was allowed to participate in debates at all.[4]

De Scheyfve had heard that Edward was to be declared of age in this parliament, giving him "full powers" and "absolute authority"; however, nothing of the kind seems to have been broached.[5] A lot of business was done, though. A subsidy was

---

1 Tytler II p. 161
2 Knighton 1992 p. 283
3 Tytler II p. 163. Listing examples from recent history for his proposal, he speaks of Anne Boleyn as "Queen Anne" (Knighton 1992 p. 289). It is interesting to compare this with Edward VI, who allegedly called her simply "Anne Boleyn" in June 1553 (see below p. 182).
4 Loades 1996 p. 236
5 CSP Span 21 February 1553

passed without difficulty and more church matters were dealt with. During this parliament Northumberland once and for all wrecked the reform of canon law. If Cranmer's project had succeeded the crown would no longer have been able to seize church lands, which was certainly not a thing John Dudley would nod through. Also, legally the church would have basically turned into a state within the state with great powers over laymen. The death penalty was to be imposed for adultery, and the church would have meddled even more than before in matters like marriage, the bastardy of children, and wills. Cranmer had also planned a form of inquisition, where the "heretics" were to be burned between 16 days of conviction, unless they publicly abjured their erroneous beliefs.[1]

John would have none of that. At a meeting of the House of Lords, he "openly and before all" attacked the primate and his brethren, warning them not to question the king's policy – and especially not the confiscation of church lands, which some had denounced as heretical:

> Let the bishops henceforth take care that the like should not occur again, and let them forbear calling into question in their sermons the acts of the Prince and his ministers, else they should suffer with the evil preachers.[2]

When Archbishop Cranmer maintained that all reforms talked of were "aimed at correcting and showing up vices and abuses. The Duke of Northumberland replied that there were vices enough to denounce; that the fruits of their lives seemed meagre enough."[3] – Despite his quarrels with the bishops, John was happy to help them as long as he had not to deal directly with Cranmer; John Ponet obtained Northumberland's help in producing a schoolchildren's

---

1   Jordan 1970 pp. 360, 361; MacCulloch 1996 pp. 533–534; Ives 2009 pp. 115–116. "Had the duke of Northumberland not quarrelled with Cranmer, a type of Protestant Inquisition would have been in place when Mary came to the throne." (Edwards 2011 p. 257).
2   CSP Span 10 April 1553
3   CSP Span 10 April 1553

catechism in Latin and English, which also resulted in a Latin dedication to the duke.[1] As late as June 1553 he backed the privy council's invitation of Philip Melanchthon from Wittenberg to become Regius Professor of Divinity at Cambridge University. But for the king's death, Melanchthon would have come to England – his high travel costs had already been granted by Edward's government.[2]

*

Historians have disagreed considerably on deciding when exactly the Duke of Northumberland's plot to plant his son Guildford on the English throne – by marrying him to Lady Jane Grey – came into being. Traditionally this happened quite early, sometime in 1552, so as to give the duke enough time for his nefarious enterprise. It has been observed that he did not have enough time,[3] though, so that in recent decades (i.e. from 1970 onwards) the date has wandered to early 1553, or to the spring, or even to the early summer of that fateful year. In parallel it has also been debated whether there was even a plot at all, or whether the attempted change in the succession was rather instituted according to the wishes of the adolescent king. Most historians now believe that Edward VI and his chief minister plotted together.

Tradition has it that Edward was a sickly child and suffered from a weak constitution, but his health seems to have been normally robust. However, at Christmas 1552 he caught a cold, and in early February 1553 he was suffering from a high fever which alarmed the authorities enough to summon the Lady Mary, his half-sister, to London. As we have seen, on arrival she was obsequiously honoured in recognition of the fact that she was the heir apparent. Edward never fully recovered his health, but it was not at all clear from the outset of his illness that he would be dead within a few months. There were intermittent signs of hope until in late May his condition worsened dramatically. Henry VIII had buttressed his changes to the succession of the crown by acts of

---

[1] Alford 2002 p. 139
[2] Loades 1996 p. 254; MacCulloch 2001 p. 170
[3] Loades 2008a

parliament, and according to English legal thinking this set a precedent that any further changes would also need to be sanctioned by parliament to be lawful. Aware of this, Edward VI on 19 June 1553 personally stipulated that his will should be ratified by that body. The next day the writs were sent out for the assembly to meet on 18 September. Tantalizingly, Edward VI had opened a parliament on 1 March 1553, only to close it on 31 March. Oddly enough, the government had *dissolved* the parliament instead of simply *proroguing* it, which would have dispensed with the need of new elections for the next session of parliament; this indicates that on 31 March Northumberland had no idea that he would be in need of one in the foreseeable future. As it came, the parliament called in June for September really came together in October 1553, to inaugurate the reign of Queen Mary. Is it conceivable that John Dudley would have disbanded the one institution that could have sanctioned his alleged plans for the crown, the business unfinished? It has been argued that he would not have dared to broach the subject of the succession in parliament;[1] however this seems unconvincing in the light of his bold later doings, and he had already decided to call parliament in the first place in spite of misgivings over asking them for a subsidy. While, as was usual, the subsidy was the chief purpose there were also other tough questions handled with great efficiency,[2] and a mid-Tudor parliament could not seriously have denied its sovereign anything if demanded by him in person (as Edward, though in bad health, could certainly have done). It is likely therefore that in March 1553 the government – or Northumberland and his cronies – were not yet aware of Edward's plans for the succession or even his hopeless case.[3]

---

1 de Lisle 2008 p. 87
2 Loades 1996 pp. 231–232, 236–237
3 Loades 2004 p. 64. It is sometimes claimed that the Venetian ambassador had an audience with the king in March, in which he found him to be clearly dying (Chapman 1958 p. 269; Hoak 2008; de Lisle 2008 p. 87). However, in the *relazione* or diplomatic report out of which this detail seems to have been evoked there is no mention of any audience or of a moribund Edward (CSP Venetian 18 August 1554), and anyway the ambassador writing on 17 March that Edward was – possibly – mortally ill was the Imperial, not the Venetian. The Habsburg ambassador, of course, had no audience with Edward and also

What was the nature of Edward's illness? His symptoms were those of a lung disease, either tuberculosis or a form of pulmonary infection caused by a severe cold in February 1553. According to his doctors (and de Scheyfve's spy in the sick room), Edward suffered from "a suppurating tumor on the lung" and ejected foul matter with a strong stench. Suffering from an array of painful symptoms – some of which were treated with opiates[1] – he may have died from general septicaemia and kidney failure. Against the traditional diagnosis of tuberculosis has been cited the apparent absence of significant amounts of coughed-up blood.[2] Still, most authorities believe the king was a victim of tuberculosis, a disease impossible to diagnose in the 16th century until a very late stage, which partly explains the wishful thinking prevalent among Edward's councillors; for example, on 7 May Secretary Petre and the Duke of Northumberland both wrote independently to Secretary Cecil, hopeful of the king's recovery and citing the royal physicians.[3] John started with his usual complaints, about "the forgetfulness of others", of course not having in mind Cecil, who was ill at home taking a leave out of the duke's book.

> I have receyved soche lettres as came in your packytt, the which I hartelie thank you, wishing yt might have byn so, as your helthe wolde have permytted you to have delivered them your silffe. Yt was styll sayde here, that you had but a grudginge of an ague; but now we heare the contrary, and that you have byn thies thre or four fytts grevously handelyd: for which I am right sorye, trusting to God the worst ys past. Whereof I wolde be as gladde as any man, both for your own compforte, as also for the advauncement of the King's waightie affayres. Your companyon doth beare out the burdeyn with as moche payne as any man can do, so moche ys his good wil towardes the service of his

---

    had a natural interest in believing that the king's days were numbered (CSP Span 17 March 1553; Loades 2004 pp. 120–121).
1   Skidmore 2007 p. 250
2   Loach 2002 pp. 161–162
3   Loades 1996 pp. 237–238

master and his countrie, that of a great deale of payne he maketh litle appearance. Others we have, whos sorte you are wel acquaynted withal, that nether ernest zeale, or consideration of tyme, can skarcely awake them out of theyr wonted dreames, and smothelie wynketh al care from theyr harts, how urgent or wayghtie soever our causes ar. Which thinge I can so yvel beare, as indeed of late, but for my duty to the state, my harte colde skarsly endure the mannour of yt, specially in thies mooste careful dayes. Well, I do herewith too much trouble you, and receyvyth no plessir with so often remeinbring [remembering] the forgetfulness (or, I sholde say, the carelesnes) of others.

But now I wil recompfort you with the joyful compfort, Which our physicians hath thies two or three mornings revyved my spiritts withal; which ys, that our soveraine Lord doth begin very joyfully to encrese and amende, they havyng no doubt of the thorro recoverye of his Highnes, the rather becaus his Majestie is fully bent to follow theyr counsil and advyce: and thus with my hartie commendations, I wish you perfytt helthe.[1]

During March and April Northumberland informed Mary of Edward's condition and her title of princess was restored to her, with her full arms.[2] It was also mooted that she might marry Prince Philip, the emperor's son and heir.[3] – On 24 April King Edward granted wedding apparel to his first cousin once removed, Lady Jane Grey, and her bridegroom Lord Guildford Dudley. Sir Andrew Dudley was to release cloth of silver and gold and velvet for the

---

1 Strype Memorials II Pt. 1 pp. 505–506
2 CSP Span 10 April 1553; CSP Span 28 April 1553. Mary had lost these honours with Henry VIII's 1534 succession act, which had also declared her a bastard.
3 CSP Span 28 April 1553

marriage of his nephew from the royal wardrobe.[1] The festivities were scheduled for 25 May.[2] On 20 May, Northumberland wrote to Sir Thomas Cawarden, Master of the King's Revels, to organize "a couple of fayre maskes, oon of men and another of women" for Thursday next.[3] It was a triple wedding: Jane married Guildford, her sister Katherine married the Earl of Pembroke's son, Lord Herbert, and Guildford's sister Katherine, who was about 10 years old, was matched with the son of the Earl of Huntingdon, Lord Hastings.[4] According to William Cecil, the Marchioness of Northampton had been "the greatest doer" in the match-making.[5] King Edward heartily approved of the marriages and sent Lady Jane jewels to wear on the occasion, but he was too ill to attend in case he would have wanted to. The French and Venetian ambassadors attended the festivities which lasted for two days and were "celebrated with great magnificence and feasting at the duke of Northumberland's house in town",[6] Durham Place. Unfortunately, one of the bridegrooms and some of the guests suffered an attack of food poisoning: Guildford, one of his brothers, Lord Admiral Clinton, "and other lords and ladies ... fell very ill after eating some salad". – "It seems the mistake was made by a cook, who plucked one leaf for another."[7]

John had not attended the wedding (as usual); "during the Whitsuntide holidays, M. de L'Aubespine, First Secretary to the King of France" had arrived in London, "in a coach drawn by four horses." He visited the court on 28 May, where he was "very honourably received and entertained" and "almost all the members

---

1   Strype Memorials II Pt. 2 p. 256
2   de Lisle 2008 p. 304; Ives 2009 p. 321; CSP Span 30 May 1553. The date is often given as 21 May 1553; however, John Dudley's letter of the 20th implies it occurred on the 25th, which is confirmed by the Imperial ambassador.
3   Feuillerat p. 306
4   Katherine Dudley's marriage was not yet fully binding, as she was still under 12 years old, the legal age of consent (Adams 1995 pp. 43–44). There was also a betrothal: Jane Grey's youngest sister, Mary, about eight years old, was promised to Arthur Grey, the heir of Lord Grey de Wilton (Doran 2008).
5   Strype Annals IV p. 485
6   Ives 2009 p. 185
7   CSP Span 12 June 1553

of the Council were present, even the Duke of Northumberland, who had been absent from Court for a few days."[1]

Edward was too ill to see the visitors, though, and so the council suggested a fake audience after dinner, when the French dignitaries were led into the king's presence chamber, Edward staying in his bedchamber. L'Aubespine and Boisdaulphin offered the French king's sympathy and support, saying "in so many words that the Duke's cause should also be the King's" (so the Imperial ambassador found out). Taking the hint, Northumberland replied that there was little hope for Edward – *peu d'espérance* – and asked them what they would do in his place.[2]

*

That Edward's condition was worsening and that he was on the brink of death was now common knowledge; and Jehan de Scheyfve had convinced himself that John Dudley was engaged in "some mighty plot" to settle the crown on his own head. The only question was how to achieve that: "Some folk say the Duke of Northumberland might try to find means of getting rid of his present wife, and ally himself with the Princess, though this seems unlikely enough."[3] Four days later he was still in the dark: "No one is able to find out exactly what Northumberland is planning to do." – But it seemed clear that the duke was "determined to stay at Court until things have reached some settlement." John had even stopped his treatment.[4] Instead, he was interfering with the king's; de Scheyfve had heard that "some folk believe him to possess certain knowledge as to when the King is to expire, and that he has been guilty of harming his Majesty's person. Ever since he got rid of the Duke of Somerset – or even before that – he has been seeking to devise means of removing the King and aspiring to the Crown, for he knows that if the King were to come of age matters might change".[5]

---

1   CSP Span 30 May 1553
2   Vertot II p. 6; CSP Span 11 June 1553
3   CSP Span 11 June 1553. The princess in question was Mary.
4   CSP Span 15 June 1553
5   CSP Span 11 June 1553

There was also talk, again, that to make himself king he "he might find it expedient to get rid of his own wife" – and marry the Lady Elizabeth.[1] – The younger John Dudley was perhaps the more plausible candidate: "Some say that the Lady Elizabeth, sister to the King, is to come to town shortly; and that the Earl of Warwick, the Duke of Northumberland's eldest son, wishes to put away his wife, daughter of the late Duke of Somerset, and marry the said Elizabeth." The suggestion of Warwick's divorce from his wife had surfaced "already a year ago."[2] The issue was certainly worth considering: Whether Warwick had consummated his marriage with Anne is impossible to know, but given her young age it would have been entirely plausible if Northumberland and Warwick had pursued an annulment on the grounds of non-consummation. The idea seems never to have been seriously entertained, though, and it was probably just another piece of gossip. De Scheyfve also believed it might have led to frictions between the dukes of Northumberland and Suffolk, now closely related through the marriage of their children.[3]

John Dudley and Henry Grey were in fact also second cousins once removed, John's mother having been born Elizabeth Grey.[4] Jane Grey and Guildford Dudley were thus third cousins once removed, and, if they had been Catholics, would have needed a papal dispensation to marry. This family relationship may have been conducive to their fathers' friendship, which, as we have seen, predated the two men's political alliance from late 1549 onwards. Henry Grey, for unknown reasons, was not highly regarded by Henry VIII, and he was equally unsuccessful under Protector Somerset. His career as a whole suggests that he may have been a somewhat ineffectual man. He was a keen Protestant, but now it was his daughters who made him an important player. For at some point Edward had written a document – which he now brought to his councillors' attention.[5]

---

1 CSP Span 30 May 1553; CSP Span 11 June 1553; CSP Span 15 June 1553
2 CSP Span 30 May 1553; CSP Span 5 May 1553
3 CSP Span 30 May 1553
4 See Table 4.
5 Loades 2004 pp. 120–121

My Devise for the Succession

> 1. For lack of issue male of my body to ... the Lady Frances' heirs male, for lack of such issue to the Lady Jane's heirs male, to the Lady Katherine's heirs male, to the Lady Mary's heirs male, to the heirs male of the daughters which she [the Lady Frances] shall have hereafter. Then to the Lady Margaret's heirs male. For lack of such issue, to the heirs male of the Lady Jane's daughters. To the heirs male of the Lady Katherine's daughters, and so forth till you come to the Lady Margaret's daughters' heirs male.[1]

The Lady Frances, now Duchess of Suffolk, was Lady Jane Grey's mother; her own mother had been Henry VIII's younger sister, Mary. The ladies Katherine and Mary were Jane's younger sisters, while Lady Margaret was Jane's cousin, the daughter of Eleanor Clifford *née* Brandon, the Lady Frances' younger sister. The whole point of Edward's paper was male succession, and the rest of his "devise" dealt with possible scenarios concerning his hypothetical male heir: "2. If after my death the heir male be ... 18 year old, then he to have the whole rule and governance". – Edward clearly envisaged the possibility of himself having adult children, as well as that Lady Jane's and her sisters' daughters had male heirs. Obviously, at the time Edward wrote the draft, he did not expect to die any time soon; it was pure speculation, one of his countless agendas and school exercises.[2] The next points consisted of detailed stipulations should his male heir be still a minor: there were to be several forms of regency councils, depending on whether the heir was below or above 14 years of age – and the councils were to be both advisory and controlling boards to several classes of female regents.[3] Point 5 is nothing short of breathtaking:

> If I died without issue, and there were none heir male, then the Lady Frances to be governess regent. For

---

1 Chronicle of Queen Jane p. 89
2 Loades 2004 pp. 68–69
3 Alford 2002 pp. 172–173

lack of her, her eldest daughters and for lack of them the Lady Margaret to be governess ... till some heir male be born, and then the mother of that child to be governess.[1]

That is to say in the case there should be no male heir available, the country should have *no monarch at all* until a royal male baby be born, a notion as impractical as absurd. Edward's document seems not altogether untypical for a teenager, but it is unthinkable that any grown-up politician should have had any share in its conception.[2] It would be quite like such a politician though to suggest the small but significant changes, which only made the document feasible in practice: *"*To the Lady Frances' heirs male, *if she have any* such issue *before my death,* to the Lady Jane *and her* heirs male.*"* The words in italics Edward simply inserted above his original text, thus writing Jane herself into the royal succession.[3]

Of course all this ignored Henry VIII's 1544 Third Succession Act, which had put Henry's two daughters Mary and Elizabeth back into the succession after Edward, while still declaring them as illegitimate. However, Edward's scheme implicitly retained Henry's exclusion of the Scottish branch of his dynasty, as well as the barring of the Lady Frances herself from the throne, two points stipulated in his father's arrangement.[4]

To what extent Edward's "devise", or rather its last amendment, was influenced by others remains unclear. John Dudley was the obvious suspect, but other people were also believed to have pushed the king to disinherit his sisters: Sir John Gates, Edward's tutor, John Cheke, and Bishop Thomas Goodrich, all keen Protestants, were mentioned.[5] Not that the king needed much pushing, though: It is entirely possible that Edward himself came up with the idea of appointing Jane – whom he liked – as his heir.[6]

---

1 Chronicle of Queen Jane p. 89
2 Loades 1996 p. 233; MacCulloch 2001 p. 41; Ives 2009 p. 141
3 Alford 2002 p. 172
4 Ives 2009 pp. 35, 39–40; de Lisle 2008 pp. 24, 95
5 Loach 2002 pp. 163–164; Ives 2009 p. 150; Hoak 2015 pp. 19–20
6 Loades 2008a; Hoak 2008; Alford 2002 p. 172

He personally supervised the copying of his will, summoning lawyers to his bedside to give them a speech: He declared that he feared the country would plunge into civil war on his death if his sister Mary succeeded; therefore "my resolve is to disown and disinherit her together with her sister Elizabeth, as though she were a bastard and sprung from an illegitimate bed." – While Mary was the daughter of "Katherine the Spaniard, who ... had been espoused to Arthur, my father's elder brother", it was "the fate of Elizabeth ... to have Anne Boleyn for a mother." Also, if Mary were to come to the throne she would most certainly marry a foreign prince and "it would be all over for the religion whose fair foundation we have laid" – wherefore it was better that "our most dear cousin Jane" should inherit the crown. Edward "most eagerly desired" his crown lawyers to "perfectly" draw up his last will, and also said nice things about Guildford Dudley.[1] The judges, among them Sir Edward Montagu, Chief Justice of the Court of Common Pleas, found "divers faults" in Edward's ideas and the next day concluded the king's wishes were treasonable. So they told the Earl of Huntingdon and Lord Admiral Clinton; one of the lords slipped out of the room to tell Northumberland, who "cometh into the Council Chamber ... being in a great rage and fury, trembling for anger, and amongst his rageous talk called the said Sir Edward, 'Traitor'", shouting that he would fight the chief justice in his shirt. Montague's colleague, Mr. Bromley, was afraid that "the duke would have stricken one of them."[2] The next day, 15 June, Edward, "with sharp words and angry countenance", harangued the judges again.[3] So Sir Edward Montagu remembered in his petition to Queen Mary; he also recalled that, in Edward's chamber, the lords declared it would be open treason to disobey their sovereign's explicit command.[4]

The letters patent of 21 June 1553, which resulted from the king's last meeting with the lawyers, were signed by 102 peers of the realm, London aldermen, bishops, archbishops, judges, and councillors, among them the Duke of Northumberland, the Earl of

---

1 MacCulloch 1984 pp. 247–248
2 Fuller IV p. 140
3 Ives 2009 p. 148
4 HMC Montague p. 4

Warwick, Sir William Cecil, and Sir Edward Montague.[1] The document retained many of the more bizarre elements of Edward's "devise", referring to Henry VIII's annulled marriages in sober legalese and even discussing the 1544 succession act. The king's preoccupation with male inheritance also implied that the document benefited the Greys more than the Dudleys: If Jane and Guildford had only daughters, Jane's sister Katherine was to inherit the crown after her;[2] if Guildford died young, Jane could take another husband; if Jane died young without leaving a son, Guildford would lose his position of influence. It also cut Lady Margaret Clifford, now "at the king's request" Andrew Dudley's fiancée,[3] out of her place in the succession: Only her heirs male should be able to ascend the throne.[4] Clauses like these show that Edward was still directing affairs – it would have been absurd for John Dudley to mastermind or even insist on them.

Archbishop Cranmer had qualms about Edward's wishes, trying to dissuade the king, so he later said, but was prevailed upon by Edward in person "and other[s] of the council", though not Northumberland, who was not present: "For the duke never opened his mouth to me, to move me any such matter."[5] Part of Cranmer's problem was the oath to uphold Henry VIII's will, to which "the councel answeryd that they had consciences as well as he". –

> [A]nd then the king told him that the judges had enformed hyme that he might lefully bequethe the crown to lady Jane and his subjectes receyve her as quene, notwithstanding theyr former othe to kyng Henry's wyll. Then the seyd archbushop desired the kyng that he myght first speake with the judges, which the king jently graunted him. Then he spake with so many of the judges as were that tyme at the court ... who all agreed in one that he might lefully subscrybe to the kynges wyll by the lawes of the realme;

---

1 Chronicle of Queen Jane pp. 99–100
2 Alford 2002 p. 172; Chronicle of Queen Jane p. 95
3 Stopes 1918 p. 250
4 Chronicle of Queen Jane p. 95; Ives 2009 p. 147
5 Cranmer p. 444

wherupon he, returning to the kynge, by his commandment graunted to set his hand therto.[1]

Foreseeing that support for his plans could become rather lukewarm after his death, Edward also demanded of the most important officials and noblemen that they enter a sworn bond to upheld "his majesty's own devise". This document was signed by 24 people, including Northumberland and Warwick, Cranmer and Cecil, and Judge Montague.[2]

It has sometimes been claimed that Edward could not have written a legal will (even a "private" one) because he was under age. In law, however, the English king had two bodies, a body natural and a body politic; while the body politic was not subject to the imperfections of the body natural (such as minority), even when "in his Body natural, and not in his Body politic, ... the King is not void of Prerogative in regard to Things which he had in his Body natural. ... [Because] the Body natural and the Body politic are not distinct, but united and as one Body."[3] It could thus be argued that Edward – because he was a king – was able to formulate a last will. And that is just what he did. It survives only in minutes taken by Secretary Petre, to be co-ordinated with the arrangements of the letters patent and made ready for the lawyers. Edward's stipulations are interesting:

> First, thatt during the yong yeres of any my heyre or successour, my executours shall nott agree to enter into any warres, except uppon occasion of invasion to be made by enemyes: nor, to the best of ther powers, shall suffer any quarell to be onjustly pyked by our subjectes wherof any warre may ensue.
>
> Seconde, our sayd executours shall nott suffer any peece of relligion to be altred, And they shall diligently travayle to cause godly ecclesiasticall lawes to be made and sett forthe: suche as may bee agreable

---

1 Narratives pp. 225–226
2 Chronicle of Queen Jane pp. 90–91
3 Kantorowicz 1981 pp. 11, 12

with the reformation of relligion now receyved within our realme ...

Fyftly, my will is, that my sistars Mary and Elizabeth shall follow th'advise of my executours ... in ther mariages, And if they so doo, and will be bownde to lyve in quiett order, according to our appoyntment, and as by our sayd executors shall bee appoynted, we will, thatt they, and eythar of them, shall have of our gift one thousande powndes yerly, by way of annuite owt of our cofers. And if they doo marry ... then we will thatt eythar of them shall have towardes ther mariages, of our gift, ten thowsande powndes, over and above the money for ther mariages given by our father's bequest.[1]

From this it clearly appears that Edward expected his sisters to abide by his provisions, in the interests of the country's peace.

*

On 27 June 1553 the members of the privy council of England swore themselves to secrecy about their forthcoming proceedings, banning the council clerks from their presence. The secret matter in hand was the succession of the Lady Jane to the crown.[2] The date of 27 June is noteworthy, as it seems a very late date to start plotting in earnest. John Dudley's pursuit of a European peace had lasted from December 1552 until late May 1553, and it is significant that it was the Continental powers that ended the diplomatic initiatives. Was Northumberland planning to exclude Mary from the succession all these months? Is it conceivable that he would have risked to offend the emperor, Mary's great protector, so much and at the same time give him a free hand against England through a peace with France?[3]

---

1 Chronicle of Queen Jane p. 101
2 Hoak 1976 pp. 10, 277
3 Jordan 1970 p. 177; Loades 1996 pp. 241–244

Meanwhile, more mundane business had been going on as well: On 13 March 1553 the privy council busied itself with granting a licence for the export of 200,000 pairs of old shoes.[1] During May 1553 the English government tried to get hold of a man known by the name of Black Will, "who of long time has been a notable murderer and one of the most wretched and vile persons that lives". Will had reached Flanders – Habsburg territory – where English agents finally succeeded in hunting him down after more than two years. A flurry of diplomatic activity ensued, and ambassador Philip Hoby received instructions how to achieve Black Will's extradition. Hoby reported success on 19 May, writing that "Black Will is to be delivered up, it being a pity so abominable a murderer should escape unpunished"; but in the end the regent did not quite comply with the English government's wishes. However, Black Will did not escape punishment, for, after committing several further murders, he was executed in Flanders.[2]

To France, meanwhile, the notion of the emperor's cousin on the English throne was extremely disagreeable; Henry II's new ambassador, Antoine de Noailles, had several talks with Northumberland and the council, indicating support for any schemes to remove Mary from the succession. On 15 June Henry II personally wrote a letter "à mon cousin le duc de Northomberland"; the contents, alas, consisted chiefly of a demand to extradite a French nobleman and his wife, who, accused of crimes against the state, had escaped from prison and found refuge in England.[3] On 24 June de Scheyfve wrote: "I hear that Northumberland and Suffolk, accompanied by only one servant, went to visit the French ambassador two nights ago, and were held up and made to give their names by the watch."[4] John tried again on the 26th, and this time had himself rowed up the Thames alone to make the secret visit.[5] Noailles found him less "close-lipped" as he used to be, ensuring the ambassador that "they had provided so well against the Lady Mary's ever attaining the succession" that

---

1 Hoak 1976 p. 220
2 Bellamy 2005 p. 124; CSP Foreign 19 May 1553
3 Vertot II pp. 36, 30
4 CSP Span 24 June 1553
5 Loach 2002 p. 166

France need not to worry. Then, to sound out the duke further, Noailles "did not forget to tell" Northumberland "how pleased" the King of France would be if the crown – *"tel chapeau"* – "should fall to him himself". John "very humbly" thanked "your Majesty", but said he was "too unworthy of such an estate and that he would consider himself unfortunate to think of it".[1]

*

Money is probably the best evidence for the existence of a conspiracy in 1553. The "cash flow" does not only tell us whether there was a plot, but also when it took place. In May, but mostly in June 1553, a lot of property changed hands in England: To put his daughter-in-law, Lady Jane Grey, on the English throne, John needed to buy support. The greatest plums went to the Princess Mary, by law the heir to the throne. Not every royal grant in 1553 was a bribe, though. Many beneficiaries indeed seem to have profited from death bed largesse rather than needing to be bought. Henry Gates, brother of Sir John Gates and granted lands worth £102 12s 7d p.a., was unlikely to disagree with the accession of Jane Grey. John Gates, deemed a fanatical Protestant, was later even suspected of coming up with the plan to make her queen. Several beneficiaries were personally close to Edward, while not being powerful figures themselves. One of the earlier grants, lands worth £100 p.a., was made on 22 May 1553, to John Cheke, the king's beloved tutor. Others who received grants were Sir Henry Sidney and Thomas Wroth of the privy chamber, the friends in whose arms Edward died only days later. None of these men had to be bought. Sidney and Wroth worked closely with Northumberland, and Cheke, another keen Protestant, as we have seen was reported to be one of those planting Mary's demotion into Edward's head.

The most important and most difficult people to buy were the noblemen. The Earl of Shrewsbury was a great provincial magnate, something between cool and hostile towards the Edwardian regime and keeping aloof from involvement in central government. On 26 June he received the mansion of Coldharbour, London, and lands

---
1 Harbison 1940 pp. 43, 38

worth £66 13s 1½d p.a.[1] – He had already shown his support by helping John to "handle" one of the reluctant judges.[2] More difficult, and as it turned out, impossible, to win was the grand Earl of Arundel. Other than Somerset he had kept his head, but he was fined, on his release from the Tower in December 1552, with £4,000 to be paid in yearly instalments of £666. On 10 May 1553 the amount was reduced to £3,221.[3] A common enough procedure, as such fines were virtually never paid in full; however, the date also indicates that any plots for the succession were not yet in the making. Interestingly, Arundel's fine was remitted on 1 July. Only on 21 June 1553, the day he and so many others signed Edward's "devise", was Arundel restored to the privy council.[4] Due to his marriages, the earl was related to Jane and technically her uncle; on the other hand he was likely to welcome Mary's accession, if only for personal reasons.

The other noblemen receiving grants were not enemies of the regime, but allies. John Russell, Earl of Bedford, may have been not particularly committed, but he too was a Protestant, and John Dudley had already rewarded his support (with an earldom) on an earlier occasion. Henry Neville, Earl of Westmorland, 29 years old, could almost be called the Duke of Northumberland's *protégé*. An incorrigible gambler, he was always in debt. His ancient name notwithstanding, he owed his position of power in the north to the duke's regime, in whose interest he worked. The Earl of Pembroke and the Earl of Huntingdon were of course allies, almost cronies, and Huntingdon also a recently acquired relative, his son having just wed John's daughter. Of the remaining peers, lords Clinton and De La Warr were relatives, too; De La Warr was the Duchess of Northumberland's uncle, Clinton the duke's nephew. Lord Darcy, on the other hand, was one of those men Northumberland called "my special friends". Another friend, the London financier Thomas Gresham, received his generous grant of lands worth £201 14s 9½d p.a. on 1 July 1553, days before the king's death; it is always a

---

1   Skidmore 2007 p. 327
2   Fuller IV p. 143
3   Lock 2004; Ives 2009 p. 94; Loades 1996 p. 262
4   Ives 2009 pp. 161–162

good thing to have warm relations with money people, and Gresham had been very useful before.

The most intriguing group of grants are those given to Princess Mary and her circle. Mary received the substantial Framlingham Castle and Park in mid-May and Hertford Castle as late as 6 June.[1] In the same month she also received lands worth £604 17s 1¾d p.a. in exchange for lands near the Essex coast, and a diamond and pearl pendant from Edward VI.[2] As late as 19 June – the day public prayers started to be held for Edward's recovery – her best friend and lady-in-waiting, Susan Clarencius, was allowed to buy more lands in Essex.[3] Framlingham Castle in Suffolk (which she would use as her fortified headquarters within a few weeks) was the most generous gift Mary ever received from her brother. It came as the last step in an exchange of lands talked of since December 1552, but the point in time is still highly significant. Added to this came the considerable lands, and another functioning castle, received in Hertfordshire on 6 June. How plausible is it that Northumberland would have transacted this deal with Mary when at the same time he was plotting her overthrow? Or was it actually a deal of another nature? It has been argued that the Edwardian government sought to buy even the king's sisters. That the grants of Framlingham and Hertford Castle to Mary and some other benefits to Elizabeth (as hinted at by William Camden) were part of a deal to accept their brother's ideas for the succession.[4] We must remember that Mary actually took possession of her new strongholds and that Framlingham especially proved to be crucial in her forthcoming struggle, for the crown and against Northumberland and his troops. Had she duped the duke? That Susan Clarencius was favoured as late as 19 June only supports this impression. Whatever the answer, it seems inconceivable that Northumberland would have let Mary have a place like Framlingham – in her home turf East Anglia – if he had anticipated to fight against her in the near future. It would have been strategic suicide.

---

1 Skidmore 2007 p. 264; McIntosh 2008 ch. 4; MacCulloch 1995 p. 538
2 Skidmore 2007 pp. 264; 329
3 MacCulloch 1995 p. 538; Ives 2009 p. 186
4 McIntosh 2008 ch. 4

All the time, the council had also been busy with more normal business, like issuing town charters and levying money from people who thought they could produce their own with impunity: On 27 May 1553 Richard Edon had to agree to pay the king "the summe of two hundreth poundes of good and lawfull monney of England", as well as to abstain "from hence forth" to "use the feat of Alchemie".[1] And on 28 June a place called Stratford-upon-Avon received a royal charter incorporating the town as a royal borough. This meant it became independent from its lord, John Dudley, who had "acquired" the manorial rights in 1549 from the Bishop of Worcester, Nicholas Heath, then in trouble over his conservative stance.[2]

The ambassadors were still fretting over what "the duke" was up to. De Scheyfve did not rule out that Northumberland and Suffolk "might rule as governors or joint-protectors" in order "to exclude the Princess", which he thought was the main point.[3] Noailles, meanwhile, was nervous that the emperor could offer Mary to Northumberland as a bride for his son, the Earl of Warwick, whose marriage to Anne Seymour could be dissolved.[4] This, he feared, was not unlikely as the two dukes were now at loggerheads; Suffolk, Noailles believed, hated Northumberland for favouring his daughter, Jane, over his wife, Frances, as queen; Noailles even feared that Suffolk could turn to the emperor to revenge himself on Northumberland.[5]

---

1 APC IV p. 279
2 Honan 2000 p. 5; Ackroyd 2006 p. 13
3 CSP Span 15 June 1553
4 Harbison 1940 p. 44
5 Harbison 1940 pp. 44–45

15.

Jane the Queen

Edward VI died in the evening of 6 July 1553, in the arms of his favourite courtiers Henry Sidney and Thomas Wroth. In his last moments he told Sidney that he had "elected" the Lady Jane "not out of spleen unto his sister for her religion, but out of pure love to his subjects, that he desired they might live and die in the Lord, as he did."[1] For the king's treatment in his last weeks Northumberland had called in the services of his own physician, as well as a female quack and an Oxford professor.[2]

Hours after Edward's death Antoine de Noailles turned up at court (having heard rumours that the king was no more) and presented another missive from Henry II. The ambassador promised the French king's support for the council's moves, but he had chiefly come to warn them against the emperor's wicked plans: "I could easily see in their faces the great satisfaction and joy ... in hearing such offers presented on behalf of such a great prince". – "They remained silent ... because of the pleasure they had received". On leaving, Northumberland took Noailles' hand and "then suddenly" turned and asked if he could have anything in writing of what the ambassador had read to them. Of course, Noailles was far too intelligent for that, and "so I prayed him to withdraw his request, saying that these offers and many larger ones

---

1 Literary Remains I p. ccliv
2 Beer 1973 p. 150. A whole tradition of horror stories has grown around John Dudley bringing in a woman healer, one of them being that Edward was administered arsenic to prolong his life. There is no contemporary or near-contemporary source which mentions this substance, however, although it may have been applied as standard medication. It would rather have been applied by the academic doctors, though, as the woman would almost certainly have been a herbalist (arsenic being a mineral).

were addressed expressly to him and that I would discharge myself of them whenever it should please him." John was content with this and left, "carrying the conversation no further". After consulting with the other lords he returned and thanked the King of France "for all the honest, great, and generous offers".[1] – The council's ensuing letter to England's ambassador in France was less optimistic.[2]

The morning after the king's death John sent his son, Robert, into Hertfordshire with 300 men to capture Mary.[3] Apparently, he did this reluctantly and John Gates had to remind him: "But, sir, will you suffer the Lady Mary escape, and not secure her person?"[4] – On 8 July the London magistrate was sworn to Queen Jane, and on 9 July John's daughter Mary Sidney brought her sister-in-law Jane to Syon House, now another residence of the Duke of Northumberland. The two young women arrived by boat. After a while, Northumberland and Northampton, as well as the earls of Huntingdon, Arundel, and Pembroke appeared. First Huntingdon and Pembroke knelt and spoke to Jane, saying, as she remembered, unwonted flatteries; then Northumberland explained to her that the king had died and that she was now queen, Edward having left her the kingdom. Jane was at first reluctant to accept, but the duke's detailed oration, held kneeling, seems to have changed her mind, even if some doubts remained.[5] Finally, Jane also gave a speech in

---

1   Harbison 1940 p. 45
2   Harbison 1940 pp. 46–47
3   Ives 2009 pp. 202, 325
4   Sil 2001 p. 83. Bishop John Goodman claimed this exchange was overheard by John Throckmorton, one of the four brothers of Sir Nicholas Throckmorton and a servant in the Dudley household.
5   Chapman 1962 pp. 104–106; Ives 2009 p. 187; de Lisle 2008 p. 305. The story that she refused the crown, insisting it was Mary's, and that her parents and Guildford bullied her into accepting the crown is from the Abbé Vertot's 18th century introduction to Noailles' despatches (see above pp. 65–66). It is not a primary source, nor a 16th century text, although it has been quoted as such: Chapman 1962 pp. 106–108 and Ives 2009 pp. 187, 321 wrongly give Vertot's *second* volume, page 211, as the source, while it is from page 211 of the *first* volume. De Lisle 2008 p. 305, while citing no source, also presupposes the story is contemporary, but dismisses it as French propaganda. Intriguingly the Imperial ambassadors reported on 22 July 1553 that Jane had said, at what could be called her abdication, that "she knew that the right belonged to Queen Mary, and the part she had played had been prepared for

which she asked of the Lord "such grace as to enable me to govern … to his glory."[1] A banquet ensued to celebrate the accession of Queen Jane.[2]

*

On Monday, 10 July, the royal party proceeded to the Tower of London, to reside their until the coronation. "At her proclamation, the people neither made any great feasts, nor expressed any great satisfaction, neither was one bonfire made",[3] a French tourist described the absence of cheering masses. The silence was only interrupted by "a young man" who was duly arrested for saying that Mary "had the right title." The young man's name was Gilbert Potter, an apprentice, and he was unfortunate enough to have his ears cut off the next morning, with a herald reading aloud his offence and "a trumpeter blowing". His misfortunes did not stop there, for the same day his master drowned in the Thames in a boat accident.[4] – But Gilbert would soon be famous.

Meanwhile, an Italian letter writer and possible eyewitness to some of the scenes at the Tower, was scandalized by the reversal of the natural order in having the parents serve their children: Guildford, "*un bello adolescente*",[5] "stood with hat in hand, not only in front of the Queen, but in front of father and mother, all the other Lords making a show of themselves putting the knee on the ground."[6]

Other revealing scenes were going on on the *Greyhound* and a couple of other royal ships that "rode before the town of Leigh in the River Thames". The ship's captain, Gilbert Grice, a servant of her without her knowledge".

1   de Lisle 2008 p. 101
2   CSP Span 20 July 1553
3   Antiquarian Repertory IV p. 506
4   Machyn pp. 36–37
5   "A handsome youth".
6   Lettere f. 223 recto; Lettere f. 222 verso. There is no evidence for the notion that Guildford was blond. The claim in Davey 1909 pp. 253, 317 that he was "a very tall strong boy with light hair" is a 20th century forgery, as are descriptions of his black velvet suit or that he was dressed "all in white and gold". The same goes for the description of Jane as a tiny person with light brown hair and freckles (de Lisle 2009; Edwards 2013).

Northumberland, "and a man by him specially put in trust for the furtherance of his devilish purpose", went on board the *Hart* "and there with the other captains consulted togethers". As Grice returned on board the *Greyhound* he was asked by the ship's master, John Hurlocke, "what news, and whether the King were then on live". – He replied "that King Edward was dead, but, praised be God ... the realm had another King, being the Duke's his lord and master's son the Lord Guildford, who was married unto the Duke of Suffolk's daughter, then also Queen."[1]

Meanwhile, Mary, aware of her half-brother's death, had moved to East Anglia – where she was the greatest landowner[2] – and began to assemble an armed following. On 10 July a letter from her arrived at the Tower saying she was now Queen of England. It arrived as the council had dinner, and the duchesses of Suffolk and Northumberland burst into tears.[3] They clearly saw into the abyss, but the men decided to continue with what they had started. Mary's messenger was thrown into prison and the council's answer was penned. Addressed to "my Lady Mary", they informed her of Jane's accession and took exception to "your supposed title which you judge yourself to have". They also reminded her of her bastardy, citing Henry VIII's acts of parliament. Intriguingly, they also promised to do her any service so that together they might "preserve the common state of this Realm" – provided she quietly and obediently submit to Jane, "as you ought".[4] Were they alluding to some previous arrangement that she would agree to "live in quiet order", as Edward had called it?[5]

Mary was putting up unexpected resistance, something Northumberland had not prepared for. He needed a week to build up a force to lead against her. Meanwhile, a circular letter was to be sent to the lords lieutenant in the counties – it was to proclaim Jane as the "rightfull Quene of this realme" and speak of the "untrue clayme of the Lady Mary basterd daughter to our grete

---

1 Knighton and Loades 2011 pp. 287–288
2 Loades 1996 pp. 257–258
3 CSP Span 11 July 1553. In the 16th century dinner was served at midday or earlier.
4 Whitelock 2009 p. 168
5 See above pp. 186, 190.

uncle Henry the Eight of famous memory". Secretary Cecil point-blank refused to draft it, so John wrote it himself in a "hurried, almost furious hand". His daughter-in-law signed the ready copies as "Jane the Quene".[1]

On 13 July 1553[2] the streets of London were bustling with preparations for the departure of the duke's army of 1,500 men and some artillery. Northumberland had been appointed by Jane to lead the troops who were being recruited from his retainers and the king's gentlemen pensioners, as well as by the generous payment of up to 20 pence per day for volunteers.[3] Jane's father, the Duke of Suffolk, had been the council's first choice of general, but apparently he did not feel fit. He was possibly unwell,[4] or he may have suffered from nerves or even some diplomatic illness.[5] Northumberland had misgivings, too. It was crucial which duke stayed and which duke went: Suffolk was a political lightweight lacking authority and so Northumberland was needed to keep Jane's council in line. He was perfectly aware of that. But "the council persuaded with the duke of Northumberland to take that voyage upon him, saying that no man was so fit therefore" – "Well (quoth the duke then) since ye think it good, I and mine will go". The assembled lords then went to Jane's presence chamber where she "humbly thanked the duke for reserving her father at home, and beseeched him to use his diligence, whereto he answered that he would do what in him lay." Before his departure, John felt like reminding his colleagues of what was at stake; he did not trust them an inch: If they thought they could now jump ship, "hoping therby of life and promotyon," they were mistaken, for God "shall not ... counte you innocent of our bloodes". Nor should they forget their oath to "this vertuouse lady the quenes highenes, who by your and our enticement is rather of force placed therin then by hir owne seking and request." – And why did they all embark on this venture in the first place?

---

1 Ellis First Series II pp. 184, 185; Alford 2011 p. 58; de Lisle 2008 p. 104
2 MacCulloch 1984 p. 297
3 Ives 2009 p. 200
4 de Lisle 2008 p. 107
5 MacCulloch 1984 pp. 261–262

> "[T]he fear of papistry's re-entrance, hath been as ye have herebefore always said, the original ground whereupon ye even at the first motion granted your goodwills and consents thereunto. ... And think not the contrary, but if ye mean deceit ... God will revenge the same. I can say no more; but in these troublesome time wish you to use constant hearts, abandoning all malice, envy, and private affections."
>
> Therewith-all the first course for the lords came up. Then the duke did knit up his talk with these words: "I have not spoken to you on this sort upon any distrust I have of your truths, of the which always I have ever hitherto conceived a trusty confidence; but I have put you in remembrance thereof, what chance of variance soever might grow amongst you in mine absence; and this I pray you, wish me no worse good speed in this journey then ye would have to yourselves." "My lord, (sayeth one of them), if ye mistrust any of us in this matter, your grace is far deceived; for which of us can wipe his hands clean thereof? And if we should shrink from you as one that were culpable, which of us can excuse himself as guiltless? Therefore herein your doubt is too far cast." "I pray God it be so (quod the duke); let us go to dinner."[1]

After dinner,

> as the duke came through the council chamber, he took his leave of the earl of Arundel, who prayed God be with his grace; saying he was very sorry it was not his chance to go with him and bear him company, in whose presence he could find in his heart to spend his blood, even at his foot. Then my lord of Arundel took also my lord's boy Thomas Lovell by the hand, and said, "Farewell, gentle Thomas, with all my heart."[2]

---

1 Chronicle of Queen Jane pp. 6–7
2 Chronicle of Queen Jane p. 7

With John Dudley went his sons John, Ambrose, and Henry, as well as his son-in-law Lord Hastings. His fellow commanders were the Earl of Huntingdon, the Marquess of Northampton, and Lord Grey de Wilton; the last one in contrast to Northampton a renowned soldier. Andrew Dudley had assembled a force of 500 men at Ware, Hertfordshire, waiting for his brother to join him.[1] On the first day of campaigning, the army plundered Swaston Hall where Mary had found refuge on her flight to Norfolk;[2] they proceeded to Cambridge, expecting to be joined there by additional contingents under Lord Admiral Clinton and the Earl of Oxford. Clinton indeed turned up, with less men than expected, while Oxford went over to Mary, having been forced to do so by his retainers.[3]

On arrival, at Cambridge, Northumberland as chancellor of the university ordered a sermon in support of Queen Jane for the next morning. He then went to supper with the Vice-Chancellor, Dr. Sandys, and Dr. Parker, who had been Anne Boleyn's chaplain. John's confidence was not overwhelming, and he jocularly exhorted his dining partners: "Masters, pray for us, that we speed well: if not, you shall be made bishops, and we deacons." – To be made a deacon was to be beheaded.[4] Hours later, Dr. Sandys, who was to preach in the morning, in the hope of inspiration dropped the Holy Book to open at random. The theme he found there, from the book of Joshua, was agreeably ambiguous and comforting: "All that though commandest us we will do, and withersoever thou sendest us we will go."[5]

*

The court having settled in the Tower, the Marquess of Winchester (William Paulet) came with the crown and asked Jane to try it on, "that I might put it on my head, in order to prove, whether it stayed

---

[1] Löwe 2004
[2] MacCulloch 1984 pp. 262–263
[3] Loades 1996 p. 263; MacCulloch 1984 pp. 263–264
[4] Foxe VIII p. 590. "And even so it came to pass. Dr. Parker and Dr. Sands were made bishops, and he and sir John Gates, who was then at the table, were made deacons, ere it was long after, on the Tower-hill."
[5] Foxe VIII p. 590

on me well." The marquess then said that there was one for Guildford, too, or that one could be commissioned, words that did not please her.[1] Jane discussed the matter with her husband – both were 16 years old – and explained to him that only parliament could make him king; he was content with that. Later she told the earls of Arundel and Pembroke that she had decided to make Guildford a duke, but never a king:

> The which being related to his mother, she angered herself with me in every way, and persuaded her son, that he should not sleep with me anymore: the which he obeyed, declaring to me that he did not desire to be a Duke, but King.[2]

Now, once again, his mother seems to have sensed where the wind was blowing: Guildford was to leave the dangerous court and go home, to Syon House. Queen Jane insisted on etiquette, though, and so Guildford had to stay to play the role of consort: "I was forced, as lady, and loving of my husband, to send to the Earl of Arundel, and the Earl of Pembroke, that they should work [it] so that he should come to me, which they did."[3] However much Jane may have opposed her spouse's pretensions, she did embrace her married status and any ill feeling was gone in a few days. On 19 July she agreed to act as godmother to the new-born son of Edward Underhill, a soldier at the Tower who had refused to march with the duke: Jane chose the name Guildford, "after her husband".[4] Allegedly, this husband was now presiding at the council board and "had himself addressed as 'Your Grace' and 'Your Excellency' … and was served alone."[5]

So, did Guildford Dudley play the king? Could he expect the crown matrimonial? Did he want even more? The notion of a female sovereign existed in theory but was not considered to be a very practical solution, and it would have been assumed that a

---
1 Rosso ff. 56b–57; Ives 2009 p. 189
2 Rosso f. 57
3 Rosso ff. 57–57b
4 Tudor Tracts p. 181; Ives 2009 pp. 205, 215
5 CSP Span 22 July 1553

queen's husband would at least share in the power. Even women, if they were the wives of kings, were known as queens and considered of equal rank to their reigning husbands, sharing some powers with them. It would thus have been perfectly normal for Guildford to expect to be made a king of some sort. When the French ambassador informed Henry II of Edward's death he wrote of "*le nouveau roy*" – referring to Guildford.[1] The Habsburg court at Brussels also believed in the reality of King Guildford; Don Diego de Mendoza was quick to congratulate the English ambassadors, reminding them that "I was his godfather, and would as willingly spend my blood in his service as any servant he hath."[2] – He probably really meant it, and when he visited England in the wake of Queen Mary's victory she was unwilling to grant him an audience.[3]

It was certainly Jane's reaction that was unusual when she decided not "to make my husband King, nor ever to consent to it." – And yet it was in keeping with the official documents. Her proclamation as queen "made it clear that Jane alone was to reign; Northumberland did not attempt to make … his … son … co-sovereign."[4] Accordingly, while several letters have survived signed by "Jane the Quene", no such letters were signed by Guildford or issued in his name.[5] Likewise, the letters patent issued under the personal supervision of Edward VI made no mention of Guildford, although they did list the risk of marriage with a foreigner as a reason for barring the ladies Mary and Elizabeth from the succession. Accordingly, in his speech before the lawyers Edward stressed that Guildford had married Jane with his royal consent.

Supported by gentry and nobility in East Anglia and the Thames Valley, Mary's military camp was gathering strength daily

---

1 Vertot II p. 55. "The new king".
2 Higginbotham 2011a, Ives 2009 p. 189
3 Loades 1989 p. 201
4 Knighton and Loades 2011 p. 288
5 de Lisle 2008 p. 110. The last of these letters, calling for the punishment of rebels in Buckinghamshire, was issued on 18 July, five days after John Dudley left town. He could not have pressurized Jane into signing these documents therefore, nor is it likely that Guildford or his mother did, as Jane would have mentioned that in her exculpatory letter to Mary of August 1553.

and, through luck, came into possession of powerful artillery from the royal navy. This seems to have convinced John that fighting a campaign was hopeless. Having spent a day at Bury St. Edmunds, he retreated back to Cambridge.[1]

Even the day before John had started out with his troops, on 12 July, a handful of privy councillors had met behind his back with one of the newly arrived Imperial ambassadors, Simon Renard – perhaps to sound out their prospects in case they changed sides. The clever Renard had made them suspicious about Northumberland's real motives, having "disclosed" the duke's alleged collusion with French plans to replace Queen Jane with Mary Stuart.[2] By 19 July 1553 they had made up their minds that Northumberland was a tyrant and informed the ostensibly surprised ambassadors. On the same day, revenge and liberty were on the mind of Henry Fitzalan, 19th Earl of Arundel, as he addressed his fellow councillors at dinner. Having left the Tower under a pretext, the group had decided to leave the sinking ship of Queen Jane's government and "look to the Lady Mary". Arundel expostulated how he was "only hereto induced for the common wealth and liberty of this kingdom", and that he

> might well be thought too bold and too little regardful of myself; ... to speak against the person of the Duke of Northumberland, a man of great authority ... thirsting after blood as a man of very small or no conscience at all. ... Whereunto I am not drawn by any passion either of ambition, as desirous to rule, or desire of revenge, albeit he most unjustly kept me a prisoner almost a year, practising my death by many wicked devices."[3]

To underline the message, the Earl of Pembroke during the whole speech held his hand on the hilt of his sword.

Guildford Underhill's baptism turned out to be the last thing to happen under the rule of Queen Jane. On the same afternoon

---

[1] Ives 2009 pp. 209–212
[2] Loades 1996 p. 262
[3] Nichols 1833 pp. 119, 120

Queen Mary was proclaimed in London to universal joy. The Duke of Suffolk personally tore down his daughter's state canopy at the Tower, Jane commenting she would gladly give up the crown, "as gladly as she had accepted it". The Duke and Duchess of Suffolk managed to get out of the fortress, accompanied by some ladies-in-waiting, but the Duchess of Northumberland stayed behind with Jane and Guildford. Now "the Tower jailor serves him at table", de Scheyfve commented gleefully.[1]

The next day a letter from the council in London arrived at Cambridge, declaring that they had proclaimed Queen Mary and commanding Northumberland to disband the army and not to come within 10 miles of the capital, "or els they wolde fight with him."[2] He did not contemplate resistance. He "called for a trumpetter and an Heralt, but none could be founde", so he decided to proclaim Mary himself[3] and went to the market-place with Dr. Sandys.

> The duke cast up his cap with others, and so laughed, that the tears ran down his cheeks for grief. He told Dr. Sands, that queen Mary was a merciful woman, and that he doubted not thereof; declaring that he had sent unto her to know her pleasure, and looked for a general pardon.[4]

John then explained to his fellow commanders that he had acted on the council's orders all the time and that he did not now wish "to combat the Council's decisions, supposing that they have been moved by good reasons ... and I beg your lordships to do the same."[5] The Imperial ambassadors found this to be "a marvellous spectacle," for the duke in his despair might have thrown "England into a tumult."[6] Indeed, the bulk of the troops he had brought from London were with Northumberland until the news of Mary's proclamation in London spread and he proclaimed her himself, and

---

1 CSP Span 22 July 1553
2 Chronicle of Queen Jane p. 10
3 Holinshed IV 1.22
4 Foxe VIII p. 591
5 CSP Span 22 July 1553
6 CSP Span 22 July 1553

he could have made trouble if he had wanted to.[1] A good general, he knew when the war was over.

His colleagues on the council, meanwhile, after setting "a fellow" in the pillory for speaking against Queen Mary,[2] were busy issuing proclamations saying that they would persecute Northumberland and his people "to the uttermost portion" and "to their utter confusion".[3] They were modelling their words on Mary's earlier pronouncement about

> her most false traitor, John, duke of Northumberland and his complices who, upon most false and most shameful grounds, minding to make his own son king by marriage of a new found lady's title, or rather to be king himself, hath most traitorously by long continued treason sought, and seeketh, the destruction of her royal person, the nobility and common weal of this realm.[4]

The council also sent Arundel and Paget to Mary at Framlingham Castle, which, so recently given to her by Edward, she had made her headquarters. Arundel and Paget brought her the good news and knelt before her, begging forgiveness.[5] The town of Cambridge, which only days ago had welcomed the duke splendidly, was equally nervous to please the new queen: The mayor and a large force of university and town's men surrounded King's College, where Northumberland and his party were lodged. They sent a delegation to the duke's apartments; he gave no resistance, but his son Warwick and the Earl of Huntingdon "did not surrender as easily".[6] At the other end of the campus "certain grooms of the stable" busied themselves with apprehending the Vice-Chancellor: "But sir John Gates, who lay then in Dr. Sands'

---

1 Loades 2004 p. 127; Ives 2009 p. 203
2 Machyn p. 37
3 Ives 2009 p. 242
4 Porter 2007 p. 209
5 CSP Span 22 July 1553
6 MacCulloch 1984 p. 266; Chronicle of Queen Jane p. 10

house, sharply rebuked them, and drave them away. Dr. Sands, by the advice of sir John Gates, walked in the fields."[1]

Another missive had meanwhile arrived from London, saying that "all men should go each his way." Seeing the light at the end of the tunnel, John reminded his captors:

> "Ye do me wrong to withdraw my liberty; see you not the council's letters, without exception, that all men should go whither they would?" At which words they than set them again at liberty, and so continued they all night; in so much that the earl of Warwick was booted ready to have ridden in the morning.[2]

Alas, they had tarried too long, for Arundel arrived to arrest them. As soon as John heard that the earl had appeared in his chamber he came out of his bedroom

> and as soon as ever he saw the Earl of Arundel he fell down on his knees and desired him to be good to him, for the love of God. "And consider (saith he) I have done nothing but by the consents of you and all the whole council." "My lord (quod he), I am sent hither by the queen's majesty, and in her name I do arrest you." "And I obey it, my lord (quod he), and I beseech you, my lord of Arundel (quod the duke), use mercy towards me, knowing the case as it is."

Arundel's answer was stern: "My lord (quod the earl), ye should have sought for mercy sooner; I must do according to my commandment."[3] Northumberland was committed into the keeping of "some gentlemen"; he was denied his bedroom, where he would have had his personal things and his body servant, Coxe, and his boy, Tom. So, he "continued walking up and down in the outer chamber almost two hours". – "Then was Tom and Coxe from him." – To a 16th century nobleman the personal servant was the

---

1 Foxe VIII p. 591
2 Chronicle of Queen Jane p. 10
3 Chronicle of Queen Jane p. 10

closest companion, much closer than family members. It is revealing that in his hour of need John did not ask to see his sons, but his servant.

> At last the duke, looking through the window, spied the earl of Arundel pass by; then he called to him, and said, "My lord of Arundell; my lord, I pray a word with you." "What would ye have, my lord?" said he. "I beseech your lordship", quod he, "for the love of God, let me have Coxe, one of my chamber, to wait on me." "You shall have Tom and your boy", quod the earl of Arundell. "Alas, my lord!" quod the duke, "what stead can a boy do me? I pray you let me have Coxe"; and so both Tom and Coxe were with him.[1]

*

Robert Dudley, meanwhile, had been securing several Norfolk towns for Jane and even taken King's Lynn on 18 July. However, when the townsmen heard of Mary's proclamation in London they seized him and the rest of his small army and sent him to Framlingham Castle.[2] It is possible that Robert had a glimpse of his brother-in-law Sidney there, as Northumberland seems to have sent him to Queen Mary before his own arrest to plead for the family.[3]

Meanwhile, John Dudley's nephew, Charles Stourton, 8th Baron Stourton, was sitting on the fence in Wiltshire. A staunch Catholic, he claimed on 22 July that Mary had appointed him Lord Lieutenant, but his rivals pointed out that he "had nothing done" against the proclamation of Jane in the county – and that despite him receiving one of Mary's letters asking for support. Stourton's "nereness of blode to th'arche traitor" Northumberland – the author "of all this mischieve" – was the problem. Charles Stourton, a troublesome man with a violent temper, replied that "ther is nether

---

1 Chronicle of Queen Jane pp. 10–11
2 Ives 2009 p. 209; Haynes 1987 pp. 23–24
3 CSP Span 22 July 1553

the blood of uncle nor brother which shall make me forgett my naturall aleageaunce."[1]

The Earl of Arundel also had the honour and satisfaction to escort John Dudley to the Tower of London. The hatred of the fallen duke was now great: A pamphlet, by "Poore Pratte", appeared in the honour of Gilbert Potter which claimed that "the great devil Dudley ruleth, Duke I should have said".[2] The French and Imperial ambassadors could hardly believe what they saw: Simon Renard had presumed – as had the emperor – that Northumberland would prevail, expressing the view that "[t]he actual possession of power is a matter of great importance, especially among Barbarians like the English".[3] – Days later, he rejoiced that "God has turned to nought the will of men and the designs of the French, whose deceitful practices have been converted into smoke."[4] Antoine de Noailles, indeed, was dumbfounded: "I have witnessed the most sudden change believable in men, and I believe that God alone worked it."[5] When it was all over, the London businessman Henry Machyn summed up:

> The vj day of July, as they say, dessessyd the nobull Kyng Edward …, sune and here to the nobull kyng Henry the viij; and he was poyssoned, as evere body says, wher now, thanke be unto God, ther be mony of the false trayturs browt to ther end, and I trust in God that mor shall folow as thay may be spyd owt.[6]

---

1 Bellamy 2005 p. 151; Ives 2009 pp. 220–221, 235
2 Alford 2002 p. 7
3 CSP Span 13 July 1553; Loades 1996 p. 257
4 CSP Span 22 July 1553
5 Loades 1996 p. 265
6 Machyn p. 35

16.
My Deadly Stroke

The prisoners were escorted through London on 25 July. John Dudley rode last, and "alle the pepulle revyled hym and callyd hym traytor and herytycke, and woulde not seyse for alle the[y] ware spokyn unto for it." Interestingly, he was not just called a traitor but a heretic, an indication of how unpopular the Reformation had been. Arundel told Northumberland, whom he treated "worshyppfully as he ... deservyd", to remove his cap and his conspicuous red cloak; he wished to deliver his prisoner safely. Among the other captives were "the erle of Warwyke, Ambrose Dudley, Henry Dudley, Andrew Dudley, the erle of Huntyngtone, lorde Hastynges, sir John Gattes that was captayne of the garde, and sir Henry Gattes hys brother, sir Thomas Palmer, doctor Saunder."[1] Charles V's ambassadors noted that "the duke preserved a quite good countenance" the whole way, but that his youngest son, Henry, wept as the group approached the Tower.[2] He was 14 or 15 years old.[3]

John was imprisoned in St. Thomas Tower, in apartments located right above Traitor's Gate, the Tower's entrance from the

---

1 Greyfriars Chronicle pp. 80–81. "Doctor Saunder" is Dr. Sandys.
2 CSP Span 27 July 1553
3 Henry Dudley was almost certainly born in 1538 or 1539 (see above p. 20). It was not uncommon for boys of his age to have their first military experience; Sir Robert Dudley, Robert Dudley's son, on his 14th birthday was with his father at Tilbury Camp at the time of the Armada in 1588.

waterside. His sons were lodged in the Beauchamp Tower.[1] Having reached his room, the facade broke: "[T]hey say his only care was to have nobles to judge him, as is the custom in England, and that his remorse and evil conscience were astonishing."[2] – What could be called a nervous breakdown is not surprising, nor should be John's insistence on the accustomed legal procedure in the form of a trial by his peers: He was very sensitive about status,[3] but he was also aware of the possible Spanish-Italian influence on the regime of Queen Mary, who, it was to be feared, would rely on Habsburg advice. He perhaps feared to be dispatched by poison or *garrote*.

"So now the Duke, his wife and five sons, … and the Lady Jane are all prisoners together".[4] Only his son-in-law Sidney and his two daughters, one of whom a child of 10, were still at liberty. The duchess was released almost immediately, having served as a kind of hostage until John was safely behind bars. She immediately headed towards Framlingham "to meet the Queen to move her to compassion towards her children; but when she had arrived at a spot five miles from this place, the Queen ordered her to return to London, and refused to give her audience." As they reported to Charles V, his ambassadors passed her on the road.[5]

The queen had already received Lady Jane's mother, the Duchess of Suffolk, who lost no time to blacken the Dudleys: She told Mary "that her husband had been the victim of an attempt to poison him, and that the Duke of Northumberland had done it. She then prayed for her husband's release from the Tower, where he had been imprisoned two days previously."[6] It was a matter of a few more days and the Duke of Suffolk was out of the Tower again.

That Northumberland had poisoned King Edward was now widely believed. "Poore Pratte" claimed that Mary "would have been as glad of her brother's life, as the ragged bear is glad of his death".[7] In a letter from Strasbourg to Zürich, from Johannes

---

1 Chronicle of Queen Jane pp. 27, 33
2 CSP Span 27 July 1553
3 Ives 2009 pp. 123–124
4 CSP Span 27 July 1553
5 CSP Span 29 July 1553
6 CSP Span 2 August 1553
7 Alford 2002 p. 8

Burcher to Heinrich Bullinger, it was described how "[t]hat monster of a man, the duke of Northumberland, has been committing a horrible and portentous crime."[1] Disfigured from poison, Edward's body could not be displayed in public, so they had to murder another youth as a replacement and bury Edward "privately in a paddock adjoining the palace".[2] – Burcher added that "one of the duke of Northumberland's sons" was to have "acknowledged this fact", which seems extremely unlikely to say the least.[3]

As Grand Master, the principal officer of Edward VI's household, John Dudley should have been present at his master's funeral at Westminster Abbey on 8 August 1553. And indeed in a sense he was: an expenditure of nil was recorded for the duke's and his entourage's mourning blacks. Richard Cox, Edward's former tutor, even managed to be released from prison to attend.[4] Northumberland (and thus his putative entourage) was absent, of course, for he was otherwise busy:

> Sonday the 6 of August ... the Duke of Northumberland was twise examined by the Quenes Counsell in the Tower, with other prisoners. The 7 of August the Duke of Northumberland was examined againe, with other prisoners.[5]

The procedure cannot have been unfamiliar to him, for, as we have seen, he had grilled one or two high-profile prisoners himself. Charles V's ambassadors were pleased to report that "inquiries are being conducted into the nature of the late King Edward's illness. It is found that his big toes dropped off, and that he was poisoned", and that "the proceedings against the Duke of Northumberland and

---

1 Original Letters II p. 684
2 Original Letters II p. 684
3 This has not prevented some authors from validating the story (Chapman 1962 pp. 100–101; Weir 2008 p. 159). Weir even converts *Burcher's* letter into one "written ... by one of Northumberland's sons". Burcher's letter is also the source for the often repeated "fact" that Edward lost his nails and hair before his death.
4 MacCulloch 1996 p. 547
5 Wriothesley II p. 96

his accomplices ... are being pursued with diligence. He was confronted with them and examined, and he has confessed generally most of the indictments against him. He has not yet declared who was the author and instigator of his practices." Some, perhaps most, of the members of the board of examiners might well have known a lot about this last point; understandably their interest was limited, though. The emperor was by now very impatient: "Send us every detail that comes to your knowledge of the depositions made by the Duke of Northumberland, especially on the death of the King and on the intrigues, correspondence and intelligence between him and France or other countries."[1] Charles had convinced himself that King Edward had been poisoned and that there had been not one, but "two plots". One was about depriving Mary of the crown, the other was "to bring about her brother, the late King's, death".[2]

It was now eagerly anticipated who would be punished for the enthronement of Lady Jane – and when. About the time Queen Mary reached London on 3 August a letter-writer reported: "I hard saye this daye that the duke of Northumberland, the marques of Northampton, the earle of Huntingdon, sir John Gates, and Mr. Palmer, wear alredie condemned to dye."[3] – On her grand entrance to the city, Mary stopped at the Tower gate and greeted the Duke of Norfolk, Edward Courtenay, Bishop Stephen Gardiner, and the Duchess of Somerset, all of whom ex-prisoners; they knelt and she "came unto them and kissed them", announcing: "These are my prisoners."[4]

The Imperial ambassadors noted that before the end of the first week of August Queen Mary also took care of her most important

---

1 CSP Span 14 August 1553
2 CSP Span 23 August 1553
3 Chronicle of Queen Jane p. 15
4 Chronicle of Queen Jane p. 14. The prisoners could almost certainly go free if they wished so after the regime change on 20 July: "The Bishop of Winchester had his liberty offered to him; but he did not wish to leave the Tower except by the Queen's authority. ... The Duke of Norfolk ... is not yet out of the Tower, and is awaiting the Queen; but every one who desires to speak with him is allowed to do so." (CSP Span 22 July 1553). Possibly, some of the former prisoners came back to the Tower on 3 August to be ostentatiously released.

prisoner's soul: "[F]or fearing that the Duke of Northumberland might fall a prey to despair in his prison, she thought that a priest should be sent to comfort him".[1] This surely helped him to recover from his nervous breakdown. In the interrogations by the council he was also asked "if he had promoted the marriage of his son to the said Jane, and why he had done so," to which he gave no reply except that the match had been "pushed forward" by the Earl of Pembroke, the Marquess of Northampton, and the Duke of Suffolk.[2] Though being repeatedly questioned, Northumberland, the Habsburg servants wrote, "made no confession as to the French intrigues or as to the charge of poisoning".[3]

A week after Edward's death, Northumberland had sent his second cousin once removed, Sir Henry Dudley,[4] to France. He was to make sure of French assistance in the case of an Imperial invasion in support of Mary. Having met with Henry II, Henry Dudley was arrested on his return to Calais and questioned in the Tower in mid-August. He revealed – "without torture"[5] – that King Henry had assured to come in person should the emperor dare to intervene. This story was confirmed by the French king's congratulations to Queen Jane, which Dudley brought with him. All this fitted excellently into Habsburg paranoia about everything French; it was all too clear: Northumberland had promised Calais as well as Ireland to the French![6] On a separate note the ambassadors were full of disbelief and indignation that Northumberland had also sent embassies to the King of Denmark, Maurice of Saxony, and even to King Ferdinand, the emperor's brother.[7]

The indictment against John Dudley comprised three items, all committed after Edward VI's death, namely that he had been in the field against the queen (i.e. Mary), that when in the field he had

---

1 CSP Span 16 August 1553
2 CSP Span 4 September 1553
3 CSP Span 4 September 1553
4 Intriguingly, Sir Henry Dudley was also a first cousin of Henry Grey, Duke of Suffolk. His parents were John Dudley, 3rd Baron Dudley, and his wife Cicely Grey, daughter of Thomas Grey, 1st Marquess of Dorset.
5 CSP Span 16 August 1553
6 CSP Span 5 September 1553
7 CSP Span 27 August 1553

proclaimed her a bastard and Jane queen, and himself captain-general of the kingdom.[1] Had there been any substance in the poison theory or in the suspicion that he was about to trade English territory for French help, the government would not have hesitated to charge him for these crimes, too, nor would John have denied them. Everything indicates that he was ready to confess his actual misdeeds, but he was not prepared to make absurd statements. Henry Dudley was set free very soon. – He went to France to become a conspirator against Queen Mary's government.

*

The prisoners having "confessed all the crimes imputed to them, except the poisoning",[2] all was ready for the great tribunal. The Spanish resident merchant Antonio de Guaras was an eyewitness:

> On the eighteenth of this month of August, the Duke of Northumberland was brought to trial, and as your Lordship knows, these proceedings are here conducted with great dignity. A stage was erected in the great hall of Westminster, very majestic and richly tapestried, and in the midst of it a rich canopy, and under this a bench with rich cushions, and carpets at its foot.[3]

Guaras obviously wondered at these English niceties; he still noticed the farcical element in the proceedings, however, for the "judges, or the most of them" had themselves been members of Jane Grey's government.

Northumberland, "making three reverences down to the ground, … came with a good and intrepid countenance, full of humility and gravity." His peers, among whom were the Duke of Norfolk presiding as High Steward of England and the Earl of Arundel on the bench, "beheld him with a severe aspect, and the greatest

---

1 Guaras pp. 102–103
2 CSP Span 5 September 1553
3 Guaras p. 101

courtesy shown him of any was a slight touch of the cap."[1] As he confessed the misdeeds he was accused of, however, many "out of compassion at beholding him in the misery into which he had brought himself by the ambition of reigning, and all grieving for their own sakes for the stain they had contracted by the offence they had committed against the Queen by consenting to his treason, even though by constraint, as has been said, many could not refrain from tears."[2] – Northumberland pleaded guilty to the charges but managed to make two good points. He asked the judges:

> Whether a man doing any act by authority of the Prince and Council, and by warrant of the Great Seal of England, and doing nothing without the same, may be charged with treason for any thing he might do by warrant thereof.

As well as:

> Whether any such persons as were equally culpable in that crime, and those by whose letters and commandment he was directed in all his doings, might be his judges, or pass upon his trial as his peers.[3]

Unsurprisingly, Norfolk was unimpressed, evading the issue by pretending that Northumberland was referring to Jane's Great Seal, the seal of a usurper, and not to Edward's, and by pointing out that none of the peers sitting in judgment were attainted of treason at the time of sitting.

> After which answer, the Duke using a few words, ... he saw that to stand upon uttering any reasonable matter ... would little prevail ... & without further answer confessed the indictment.[4]

---

1 Guaras p. 102
2 Guaras p. 103
3 Tytler II p. 224
4 Holinshed IV 1.22

He asked the judges "to be humble suitors unto the Queen's Majesty, and to grant me four requests." These were that he might die by the axe – "that I may have that death which noblemen have had in times past, and not the other" – and that "her Majesty may be gracious to my children, which may hereafter do good service, considering they went by my commandment who am their father, and not of their own free wills". The third point was that he desired "some learned man for the instruction and quieting of my conscience"; and finally, that "two or three of the Council would come to confer with him in prison upon important secrets". – He also asked his peers to pray for him.[1]

The Marquess of Northampton, William Parr, and John Dudley's son, the Earl of Warwick, were tried on the same occasion. The marquess must have surprised his fellow accused with the statement that "he was not himself ever in government" and that he had been away hunting throughout Jane's reign. When reminded that he was caught in arms with the Duke of Northumberland at Cambridge, he confessed his guilt, "weeping openly". It was then the Earl of Warwick's turn, who pleaded his youth and his obedience to his father, "without knowing much else", which was doubtless true.[2] However, "finding that the judges, in so great a cause, admitted no excuse of age," he

> with great resolution heard his condemnation pronounced against him, craving only this favour, that, whereas the goods of those who are condemned for treason are totally confiscated, yet her majesty would be pleased, that out of them his debts might be paid. After this they were all returned again to the Tower.[3]

The next day, 19 July, saw more trials on the same spot. Sir Andrew Dudley, Sir Thomas Palmer, and Sir John Gates and his brother Henry stood accused on the same charges. Thomas Palmer, like Andrew Dudley a military bachelor, pleaded not guilty, calling the judges traitors and telling them that they deserved to die as

---
1   Tytler II p. 225
2   Rosso f. 31
3   Chronicle of Queen Jane p. 121

much as he, "and more"![1] Andrew Dudley pleaded guilty and asked that his jewels that were in the keeping of his wardrobe colleague should not be lost.[2] If he meant lost to the public he needed not to bother, for Mary's council had already ordered Mr. Sturton, his joint keeper and a possible relation of Andrew's, to bring "to the Towere a casket with jewells and money apperteininge to Sir Andrew Dudley, knight, wherof he gave him custodie".[3]

Jane Dudley, in view of the axe, was desperate to save her husband. The frantic directness and grammar of her letter reveal the terror she was going through, but also her passionate nature which made her literally sick. She implored Lord Paget, and Lady Paget her old friend, to enlist the help of two of Mary's most trusted ladies, the Marchioness of Exeter and Susan Clarencius:

> Nowe good madame for the love youe bere to God foregett me nott: & make my lady markes of Exiture my good lady & to remembere me to Mestres Clarencyous to contynewe as she haythe begone fore me: & good madame desyre your lord as he may doe: in spekynge fore my husbondes lyff: in way of cheryte I crave hyme to doe ytt madame I have held upe my hed fore my grett hevynes of hartt that all the world knowes canott be lyttyll: tyll nowe that inded I doe begyne to growe in to weke seknes: & also seche a ryssyng in the nyghte frome my stomake upe to ward that in my jugmentt my brethe ys lyke clene to goe away as my wemen cane full say ytt as they knowe ytt to be trewe by there owene payne they take with me: good madame off your goodnes remembere me: so God to kepe your ladyshep longe lyff with your lord & yours
>
> your ladyshepes powrest frynd Jane Northumland as longe as pleys the quene

---

1   CSP Span 27 August 1553
2   CSP Span 27 August 1553
3   APC IV p. 310

& good madame dysere my lord to be good lord unto my powere [poor] v sones: nayture cane noe othere wyss doe butt sue fore theme althoughe I doe nott so meche care fore theme as fore there fathere who was to me & to my mynd the moste beste gentylmane that evere levynge womane was mached withall: as nethere thos abowtt hyme nore abowtt me canott say the contrary & say trewly: howe good he was to me that owre lord & the quenes maygeste shewe there merssy to theme[1]

*

Whether Mistress Clarencius and Lady Exeter tried or not, Mary was not inclined to be merciful towards Northumberland. She even asked the pope's special envoy to stay his return to Italy for a few days so that he could witness the duke's punishment.[2] But first she sent him her Lord Chancellor, Stephen Gardiner, just released from the Tower. The outcome of their encounter was that John agreed to be reconciled to the Catholic Church. By their very nature the details of such confidential meetings must remain secret, yet a French contemporary reported that John was sorry "that he had entered the Protestant sect ... [and] that if God gave him the grace of longer life he would endeavour to amend these past faults", and that he pleaded with Gardiner to "intercede with the queen to grant him life in some low and vile condition".[3] Strikingly, as we shall see, the very last point appears also in his last letter, as it would have in another to Gardiner, now lost. A late Elizabethan tale spread by the Jesuit Robert Parsons repeats as much when it has the duke say to the bishop: "I would do penance all the days of my life, if it were but in a mouse-hole – is there no hope of mercy?" This story, designed to stress the saintliness of the "gentle Gardiner", ends with both men in tears.[4]

---

1   Gunn 1999 pp. 1270–1271
2   Tytler II p. 227
3   Ives 2009 p. 118
4   Chapman 1962 p. 165; Ives 2009 pp. 118, 310

Executions had been scheduled for 21 August, but were suddenly postponed. Instead an assembly of invited onlookers saw the Duke of Northumberland, Sir Andrew Dudley, Sir Thomas Palmer, the Marquess of Northampton, and Sir Henry Gates take the sacrament in the Tower Chapel St. Peter ad Vincula, with "all the ... rites and accidents of old time appertaining". – To the great delight of Queen Mary, John was willing to abjure his Protestant faith:

> When the time came the prisoners should receive the sacrament, the duke turned himself to the people and said, first, these words, or such like, "My masters, I let you all to understand that I do most faithfully believe this is the very right and true way, out of the which true religion you and I have been seduced these 16 years past, by the false and erroneous preaching of the new preachers, the which is the only cause of the great plagues and vengeance which hath light upon the whole realm of England, and now likewise worthily fallen upon me and others here present for our unfaithfulness. And I do believe the holy sacrament here most assuredly to be our Saviour and Redeemer Jesus Christ; and this I pray you all to testify, and pray for me."[1]

John also used the occasion to personally ask forgiveness from the Lord Protector's sons, the teenagers Edward and Henry Seymour; he confessed to have "falsely procured" their father's death.[2]

In the evening of that day John Dudley sat in his cell writing a letter to the Earl of Arundel. He begged him to intercede with Queen Mary for his life. He was struggling to be resigned to his fate; but neither had he lost his nerve, nor had he given up yet:

> Honourable lord, and in this my distress my especial refuge; most woeful was the news I received this evening by Mr. Lieutenant, that I must prepare myself against tomorrow to receive my deadly stroke. Alas

---

1 Chronicle of Queen Jane pp. 18–19
2 CSP Span 27 August 1553

my good lord, is my crime so heinous as no redemption but my blood can wash away the spots thereof? An old proverb there is and that most true that a living dog is better than a dead lion. O that it would please her good grace to give me life, yea, the life of a dog, that I might live and kiss her feet, and spend both life and all I have in her honourable service, as I have the best part already under her worthy brother and her most glorious father. O that her mercy were such as she would consider how little profit my dead and dismembered body can bring her, but how great and glorious an honour it will be in all posterity when the report shall be that so gracious and mighty a queen had granted life to so miserable and penitent an object. Your honourable usage and promises to me since these my troubles have made me bold to challenge this kindness at your hands. Pardon me if I have done amiss therein and spare not I pray your bended knee for me in this distress, ye God of heaven it may be will requite it one day on you and yours. And if my life be lengthened by your mediation and my good Lord Chancellor's (to whom I have also sent my blurred letters) I will vow it to be spent at your honourable feet. O my good lord remember how sweet life is, and how bitter ye contrary. Spare not your speech and pains for God I hope hath not shut out all hope of comfort from me in that gracious, princely and womanlike heart; but that as the doleful news of death hath wounded to death both my soul and body, so that comfortable news of life shall be as a new resurrection to my woeful heart. But if no remedy can be found, either by imprisonment or confiscation, banishment and the like, I can say no more but God give me patience to endure and a heart to forgive the whole world.

> Once your fellow and loving companion, but now worthy of no name but wretchedness and misery,
> JD[1]

It might be asked why John Dudley chose to address the Earl of Arundel of all people – a man on whose sympathy he certainly could not count. Arundel was well-placed to intervene with the queen, however, and on a more personal level John may have believed the earl owed him some consideration; after all, while Arundel had twice plotted John's "removal", John had never sought Arundel's life.

John probably did hope for a pardon. As we have seen, at Cambridge, having finally proclaimed Mary himself, he was hopeful of a pardon. However, when he entered the Tower a few days later he was under no illusions about his fate. Nearly a month later, though, he could see that only very few people were being prosecuted for their part in elevating Jane to the throne, that many had climbed back into favour, and that even of those condemned so far only three men were scheduled to die – he being the only one of high rank. It is no wonder that hope replaced realism. This does not necessarily mean, however, that he was looking out for a reprieve until the very last moment of his life, as is so often implied. Between writing the letter and his performance in the next morning there lies a night of many hours, and he delivered an elaborate scaffold speech from which it appears that he had made his peace with God and the world. Catholic observers like the

---

1 Loades 1996 p. 269. Historians have often criticized this letter as pathetic or abject. Like many sources of the era it survives only as a copy and is generally thought to be genuine. A forgery cannot be ruled out entirely, though. It is intriguing that the transcript is believed to have been made from a letter found in the study of Mr. Dell, secretary to Archbishop Laud, the anti-Puritan primate during the English Civil War. This might be significant because Robert Dudley was the most notable patron of the Elizabethan Puritan clergy and had been a *bête noire* to the very conservative Archbishop Whitgift. The episcopal Anglican High Church also developed "a direct interest in discrediting" Leicester's posthumous reputation (Adams 2008b), which would explain the interest of churchmen in an embarrassing letter written by the earl's notorious father. However, the style of the letter, while forceful and florid, is not untypical of John Dudley's unquestionably authentic letters.

foreign ambassadors had no doubts about the "Christian death of the Duke".[1]

Of the seven men convicted, only the young Earl of Warwick and Sir John Gates had been missing from the performance in the Tower chapel. It seems plausible that the two needed a day longer to convince themselves to reject the "new doctrine" and go to mass. Gates was known to be a fanatical Protestant. The younger John Dudley on the other hand, had grown up in a climate of religious reform. For him to accept the old ways of religion would have presented a much greater challenge than for his father, who after all returned to the faith of his childhood.

On Tuesday, 22 August 1553, at nine o'clock, Sir John Gates and the Earl of Warwick went to mass in St. Peter ad Vincula. Quite possibly they were still unaware that they had escaped death. They had to "openly acknowledge" their "abuse and error", John Gates confessing:

> "we have been out of the way a long time, and therefore we are worthily punished; and, being sorry therefore, I ask God forgiveness therefore most humbly; and this is the true religion." In much like sort said the Earl of Warwick; and then one asked the other forgiveness, and required all men to forgive them as they forgave every man freely.[2]

Next, Gates turned to Edward Courtenay, only just released from the Tower after a stay of 15 years, asking to pardon him for holding him a state prisoner as Captain of the Guard, "not for any hatred towards you, but for fear that harm might come thereby to my late young master." Everyone being in forgiving mood, Warwick likewise asked Courtenay's pardon. It is possible that, like his father the day before, he also asked his young brothers-in-

---

1 CSP Span 27 August 1553. Vertot II p. 117–118. Noailles, hours after witnessing the execution, felt an urge to inform the Connétable Montmorency how, "miraculously, the Duke of Northumberland, in the end, recognized the true religion." ("ne voulant au surplus obmettre à vous dire comme miraculeusement le duc de Northomberland, sur sa fin, a reconnu la vraye religion.")
2 Chronicle of Queen Jane p. 20

law Edward and Henry Seymour (who were standing by) for forgiveness. The service then continued, the priest explaining:

> "I would ye should not be ignorant of God's mercy, which is infinite; and let not death fear you, for it is but a little while, to wit, ended in one half-hour. What shall I say? I trust to God it shall be to you a short passage (though somewhat sharp), out of innumerable miseries into a most pleasant rest; which God grant." The priest having spoken these or much like words, gave them the host, which being finished, and the mass ended, they came forth again; and the Earl of Warwick was led to his lodging, and Sir John Gates to the lieutenant's house, where he remained about half an hour and more.[1]

He remained there until Sir Thomas Palmer and the Duke of Northumberland were led out of their cells, the three men proceeding towards the scaffold after a short farewell chat. There was no farewell between father and son on this morning,[2] and it can be ruled out that Northumberland would have been allowed visits from family members during his imprisonment; he would have been able to write farewell letters, though.

The last exchange of words between John Dudley and John Gates, "at the garden gate", did not lack a certain edge:

---

1 Chronicle of Queen Jane p. 20
2 It is often claimed that the young Earl of Warwick accompanied his father to mass before execution, and that the two took leave of each other with an embrace. However, from the Chronicle of Queen Jane, an eyewitness account, it is clear that Northumberland "came forth" only after his son was back in the Beauchamp Tower; it is also clear from that account that Northumberland and Palmer did not hear mass on that morning. The misconception of a farewell between the duke and his son or sons is probably due to the forger Richard Davey (see above p. 193), who claimed to have seen a manuscript in the "Brussels Archives, entitled, *Les evenements en Angleterre, 1553-4*" (Davey 1909 p. 307). According to this the Duke of Northumberland was allowed to take leave of his son Guildford, "whom he pressed again and again to his breast, sighing and weeping a deluge of tears, as he kissed him for the last time." No-one except Davey seems ever to have seen this manuscript.

"Sir John," saieth the duke, "God have mercy upon us, for this daie shall ende bothe our lives. And I praye you forgeve me whatsoever I have offended; and I forgeve you with all my harte, althoughe you and your counsaill was a great occasion herof." "Well, my lorde," saithe sir John Gates, "I forgive you as I wolde be forgeven; and yet you and your auctoritye was the onely originall cause of all together; but the Lorde pardon you, and I praie you forgeve me." So, ether making obeasaunce to other, the duke preceded.[1]

For his last performance John had dressed up, only to undress again on the scaffold minutes later: "first, he put off his gown of crane-coloured damask ... at the last he put off his jerkin and doublet".[2] As was customary, the duke's costly gown seems to have served as the executioner's fee, and he and his fellows Sir John Gates and Sir Thomas Palmer had also received £10 14s. 4d. in cash "to give alms at their execution."[3] – The money-obsessed Imperial ambassadors misunderstood this ritual when they said Northumberland gave up all the money he had supposedly stolen from the crown on the scaffold![4]

The eagerly anticipated event was watched by a crowd of an estimated 10,000 people. The French ambassador was among the spectators, and so was Antonio de Guaras, who understood English well. He was duly impressed:

> And the Duke ... having taken place upon the scaffold, approaching the railing, begged with much humility and great dignity to speak to the people, as is the custom. And amid profound silence he spoke in substance these words, which I heard from being very near him.[5]

---

1   Chronicle of Queen Jane p. 21
2   Chronicle of Queen Jane pp. 21–22. "Crane-coloured" means a light grey.
3   Bayley 1830 p. 424
4   CSP Span 27 August 1553
5   Guaras p. 106

A considerable number of independent versions of the scaffold speech survive; differing only slightly in contents, they testify to Northumberland's celebrity status at the time, however unpopular he may have been. His return to the old faith and his denunciation of the new was an opportunity not to be missed, so there was an "official" version of the duke's "confession" which was printed by John Cawood on the orders of Queen Mary. It soon became the basis for several Latin, French, German, and Italian editions, and thus the speech came to circulate more widely on the Continent than it ever did in England. A letter by the London merchant William Dalby of 22 August 1553 gave a brief summary of what was said in town about John Dudley's end:

> This present daye the duke of Northumberlande, sir John Gates, and master Palmere, came to executione, and suffered deathe. The duke's confessyon was in effecte but lytle, as I hard saye; hee confessed himselfe worthie to dye, and that he was a greate helper in of this religion which is false, thearfore God had punished us with the lose of kinge Henry 8, and also with the lose of king Edward 6, then with rebellione, and aftere with the swetinge sicknes, and yet we would not turne. Requiringe them all that weare presente to remember the ould learninge, thankinge God that he would vutsafe to call him nowe to be a Christyane, for this 16 yeares he had byne non. Theare weare a greate nomber turned with his words. He wished every man not to be covetous, for that was a greate parte of his distruction. He was asked further yf he had any thinge moare to saye, and he said nothinge but that he was worthie to dye, and so was mo[r]e than he, but he cam to dye, and not to accuse any mane. And thus bouldly he spak, tyll he layd his head on the block.[1]

*

---

[1] Chronicle of Queen Jane p. 21

The sayinge of John late Duke of Northumberlande, vpon the scaffolde at the tyme of his execution was printed on the government's orders and is the fullest and most beautiful version of the speech. Charles V had specifically requested to be sent John Dudley's words on the scaffold, so it is conceivable that care was taken to record what the duke had to say; some phrases, like his fondness of the word "fancy", and the subtle humour certainly occur also in John's letters. What emerges from this version is Northumberland the patriot and statesman. He speaks of a universal church, for all people and peoples; he neither cares for the mass, nor for cantankerous preachers. He also insisted that he was not the "original doer" of Edward's "devise", that it originated with others, but that he would now accuse no man, "as he desired the forgiveness of God."[1]

> Good people, all you that be here present to see me dye. Though my death be odyouse and horrible to the flesh, yet I pray you iudge the beste in goddes workes, for he doth all for the best. And as for me, I am a wretched synner, & have deserved to dye, and moost iustly am condempned to dye by a law. And yet this acte Wherefore I dye, was not altogither of me (as it is thoughte) but I was procured and induced therevnto by other. I was I saye induced thereunto by other, howbeit, God forbyd that I shoulde name any man unto you, I wyll name no man unto you, & therfore I beseche you loke not for it.
>
> I for my parte forgeve all men, and praye God also to forgeve them. And yf I have offended anye of you here, I praye you and all the Worlde to forgeve me: and moost chiefly I desire fogevenes of the Quenes highnes, whome I have most grevouslye offended. Amen sayde the people. And I pray you all to witness with me, that I depart in perfyt love and charitie with all the worlde, & that you wyll assiste me with youre prayers at the houre of death.

---
1 Guaras p. 106; Tytler II p. 231

And one thinge more good people I have to saye unto you, whiche I am chiefly moved to do for discharge of my conscience, & that is to warne you and exhorte you to beware of these seditiouse preachers, and teachers of newe doctryne, which pretende to preache Gods worde, but in very deede they preache theyr owne phansies, who were never able to explicate themselves, they know not to day what they wold have to morowe, there is no stay in theyr teaching & doctryne, they open the boke, but they cannot shut it agayne. Take hede how you enter into straunge opinions or newe doctryne, whiche hath done no smal hurt in this realme, and hath iustlye procured the ire and wrath of god upon us, as well maye appeare who so lyst to call to remembraunce the manyfold plages that this realme hath ben touched with all synce we dissevered oure selves from the catholyke church of Christ, and from the doctryne whiche hath ben receaved by the holy apostles, martyrs, and all saynctes, and used throughe all realmes christened since Christ.

And I verely beleve, that all the plagues that have chaunced to this realme of late yeares synce afore the death of kynge Henrye the eyght, hath iustly fallen upon us, for that we have devyded ourselfe from the rest of Christendome wherof we be but as a sparke in comparison: Have we not had warre, famyne, pestylence, the death of our kinge, rebellion, sedicion amonge ourselves, conspiracies? Have we not had sondrye erronious opinions spronge up amonge us in this realme, synce we have forsaken the unitie of the catholyke Churche? and what other plagues be there that we have not felt?

And yf this be not able to move you, then loke upon Germanye, whiche synce it is fallen into this scysme and division from the unitie of the catholike church, is by continuall dissention and discorde, broughte almoost to utter ruyne & decaye. Therfore, leste an utter ruyne come amonge you, by provokynge to muche the iuste vengeaunce of God, take up betymes these contentions, & be not ashamed to returne home agayne, and ioyne youre selves to the rest of Christen realmes, and so shall you brynge your selves againe to be membres of Christes bodye, for he cannot be head of a dyfformed or monstruous body.

Loke upon your crede, have you not there these wordes: I beleve in the holy ghost, the holy catholik churche, the communion of saynctes, which is the universall number of all faythfull people, professynge Christe, dispersed throughe the universall worlde: of whiche number I trust to be one. I could bryng many mo[re] thinges for this pupose, albeit I am unlearned, as all you knowe, but this shall suffice.

And heare I do protest unto you good people, moost earnestly, even from the bottome of my harte, that this which I have spoken is of my selfe, not beynge required nor moved therunto by any man, nor for any flattery, or hope of life, and I take wytnes of my lord of Worcestre here, myne olde frende and gostely father, that he founde me in this mynde and opinion when he came to me: but I have declared this onely upon myne owne mynde and affection, for discharge of my conscience, & for the zeale and love that I beare to my naturall countreye. I coulde good people reherse muche more even by experience that I have of this evyl that is happened to this realme by these occasions, but you knowe I have an other thyng to do, wherunto I must prepare me, for the tyme draweth awaye.

And nowe I beseche the Quenes highnes to forgeve me myne offences agaynst her maiestie, wherof I have a singular hope, forasmuch as she hath already extended her goodnes & clemency so farre upon me that where as she myghte forthwith without iudgement or any further tryall, have put me to moste vyle & cruell death, by hanging drawing, and quartering, forasmuch as I was in the field in armes agaynst her highnesse, her maiestie nevertheles of her most mercyfull goodnes suffred me to be brought to my iudgement, and to have my tryall by the lawe, where I was most iustly & worthelye condempned. And her highnes hath now also extended her mercye and clemencye upon me for the manner and kynde of my death. And therefore my hoope is, that her grace of her goodnes wyl remyt al the rest of her indignation and displeasure towardes me, whiche I beseche you all moost hartely to praye for, and that it maye please God longe to preserve her maiestie to reigne over you in muche honour and felicitie. Amen, sayd the people.

And after he hadde thus spoken he kneeled downe, sayinge to them that were about: I beseche you all to beare me wytnesse that I dye in the true catholyke fayth, and then sayde the Psalmes of Miserere, and De profundis, and his Pater nostre in Latin, and sixe of the fyrste verses of the psalme, In te domine sperant endynge with this verse, Into thy handes O lorde I commend my spirite. And when he had thus finished his prayers, the executioner asked him forgevenes, to whom he sayde: I forgeve you with all my harte, and doo thy parte without feare. And bowynge towarde the block he sayd, I have deserved a thousand deaths, and therupon he made a crosse upon the strawe, and kyssed it, and layde his head upon the blocke, and so dyed.[1]

Antonio de Guaras reported a rather similar speech with similar points, like the warning against German conditions and the appeal

---

1 Sayinge; Jordan and Gleason 1975 pp. 44–48

to return to the true faith. – "Withdrawing himself from the rail," John Dudley "knelt in the middle of the scaffold" and Bishop Nicholas Heath, his confessor, assisted him in his prayers. Finally, he was ready and his eyes bandaged and he "cast himself upon the beam where his head should be cut off with an axe". But his bandage slipped as it "was not well fitted" and "he rose again upon his knees, and surely figured to himself the terrible dreadfulness of death." – Slapping his hands together, "as who should say, this must be," he "cast himself upon the said beam, where the executioner struck off his head at a blow, and may our Lord be pleased to have him in His holy glory!"[1]

Another spectator in the crowd was a traveller from France, the friar Stephen Perlin; he evidently had some trouble with English names, listing "milor Notumbellant", "milor Arondell", and "milor Suphor" as the powerful men of England.[2] He described the executioner as lame on one leg and wearing "a white apron, like a butcher",[3] and he also observed "little children" mopping up John Dudley's blood under the scaffold.[4]

John Dudley's head was not displayed on a pole at Tower Bridge, for Queen Mary allowed it to be buried complete with the rest of the body. Lancaster Herald, "sometime servant" to Northumberland, had asked as much and saw to it that the duke was laid to rest in St. Peter ad Vincula next to the Duke of Somerset's remains.[5] In April 1554, at the next session of the Knights of the Garter at Windsor, the plaque with John Dudley's coat of arms was ceremoniously pulled down and hurled into the Thames. On 4 September 1553 Charles V's ambassadors summarized:

---
1 Guaras pp. 108–109
2 Antiquarian Repertory IV p. 503
3 Antiquarian Repertory IV p. 507
4 Antiquarian Repertory IV p. 508. The same was observed at the Duke of Somerset's execution, misleading modern commentators to interpret it as proof of the duke's popularity. This was a common ritual after executions, however; the blood of executed criminals had mystical connotations and was treated like relics, regardless of guilt or innocence (Schild 1980 p. 72).
5 Wilson 1981 p. 62

We have not been able to find out more ... and it appears that it was thought best not to inquire too closely into what had happened, so as to make no discoveries that might prejudice those who assisted in the trial and the rendering of the sentences. We are informed that the execution of the sentences passed on the rest of the prisoners was delayed in the hope of obtaining a pardon; and that the Marchioness of Exeter, ... Dame Clarentius and the Marquess [of Northampton's] first wife have sued for his pardon. They have told the Queen, in order to move her to pity, that he never ceases weeping. ... We have been told that the Duke of Northumberland's sons will not be executed.[1]

*

The reckoning of the Dudleys' earthly possessions took place between 28 August and 13 September 1553, under the supervision of Richard Rich, 1st Baron Rich. In Northumberland's town palace, Durham Place, the sum of "ready money found" was "nil", yet at Cambridge his war treasure of nearly £1,999 of cash had been secured for "her Highness's use". An amazing 10,180 ounces of plate of all sorts were found at his houses, of which 234½ oz. of gilt plate and 417 oz. of silver plate were graciously delivered to the Duchess of Northumberland. So was her entire wardrobe.[2]

An inventory of the duke's wardrobe was made by one John Empson and most items went to the queen, via her best friend Mrs. Clarencius (who habitually kept such stuff for her own benefit[3] – but equally may well have helped Jane Dudley to keep hers). The Earl of Devon received some of the rest, together with the fallen duke's rapier. The Duke of Norfolk received Northumberland's coronet, Garter collar, and parliament robes, and one wonders what the London jewellers were thinking of this perpetual recycling.

---

1 CSP Span 4 September 1553
2 Loades 1996 pp. 304, 307–308
3 Porter 2007 p. 249

One gown in Empson's list was "with the duke at the Tower";[1] just one – and was it the "crane-coloured"?

Much household stuff was sold or given away "to divers persons", and some stuff had been stolen, such as 2¼ yards of white sarcenet; a collection of stable equipment had been "taken away by the Duchess". John's widow was also granted carpets and tapestries from Syon House, as well as the "contents of the duke's bedchamber" there. She was also allowed kitchen stuff. – "A butt of malmsey and a butt of sack half wasted" had to be "spent", though.

The commissioners also found "the Earl of Warwick's his goods … at Mr. Jobson's house at Westminster", Francis Jobson being of course his uncle, and despite his heavy involvement in Jane Grey's government now a free man. "The Lord Robert Dudley's goods" were equally found at Jobson's house and sold for £6 13s. 4d. Lord Ambrose, on the other hand, had "the contents … of his chamber [at Syon] delivered to him for his furniture at the Tower":[2] John Dudley's five sons were to stay for quite a while. From the Beauchamp Tower they would have observed with interest that, on 14 September 1553, "the busshope of Canterbury was brought into the Tower as prysoner, and lodged in the Tower over the gate anenst the water-gate, wher the duke of Northumberland laye before his death."[3]

---

1   Loades 1996 pp. 307–308
2   Loades 1996 pp. 308–310
3   Chronicle of Queen Jane p. 27

17.

There Hath Lacked a Northumberland

John Dudley's Black Legend originated in the last years of his life, when people started to make out the bear and ragged staff on English coins. Only a week after Northumberland's death Antonio de Guaras described to his patron in Spain how the monstrous duke had not only engineered the downfall of the Howards, the executions of the Earl of Surrey, of Thomas Seymour, and the Duke of Somerset, but how in the end he had also poisoned the king: "The poor innocent languished for seven months."[1]

John Dudley also served as an indispensable scapegoat:[2] Mary could not afford to punish all men who had engaged in the enthronement of Jane, or she would have had no government. It was the most practical thing for her to believe that Northumberland had been acting all alone and it was in nobody's interest to doubt it. Edward's move to leave the crown to Jane also presented Mary with a constitutional problem. As questionable as the letters patent to make Jane queen may have been, they passed the Great Seal,[3] and would almost certainly have been enshrined in law had the

---
1 Ives 2009 p. 107
2 Beer 1979 p. 2
3 Hoak 2015 p. 27

king not died before parliament could assemble. This was such a horrible prospect to the pro-Marian chronicler Robert Wingfield that he had God intervene directly: Taking "pity of his most devoted servant Mary", He cuts through Edward's thread of life just in time, for "the most godly king indeed died without waiting for parliament".[1]

Juridically, responsibility lay with the head of state. That is why no-one was ever charged with anything that had occurred under Edward VI. Mary under no circumstances could acknowledge that Edward had been involved in making his own will, as this could have touched her own title to the crown. Accordingly, Charles V's ambassadors implied that Edward's will had been manipulated,[2] and they advised Mary to hold a parliament before her coronation and "declare the late King Edward's testament null and void."[3] Mary did nothing of the kind, of course, she ignored Edward's will and perhaps chose to believe it was a forgery. James I certainly did so. In 1611 he charged the antiquarian Robert Cotton to deliver up "the originall" of Edward VI's letters patent so that it could be destroyed or "canseled".[4] If it had not been a potentially dangerous precedent,[5] it need not have been destroyed. Thankfully, a copy was made before of the supposed forgery, of the "counterfet wille forged and published under the Great Seale of Englande by the confederacie of the dukes of Suffolke and Northumberlande".[6]

*

John Dudley's greatest PR blunder was to renounce Protestantism and return to popery at the end of his life.[7] The Protestant outrage at his "apostasy" appeared from Lady Jane Grey's remarks about

---

[1] MacCulloch 1984 p. 249. Wingfield's account, composed in Latin, is both highly rhetorical and highly partisan.
[2] CSP Span 22 July 1553
[3] CSP Span 19 September 1553
[4] Hoak 2015 p. 27
[5] Mortimer 2013 p. 130
[6] Hoak 2015 p. 27
[7] Loades 2008a

her father-in-law, which she made a week after his execution, at dinner:

> "I pray you," quod she, "have they mass in London?" "Yay, forsooth," quod I, "in some places." "It may so be," quod she, "it is not so strange as the sudden conversion of the late duke; for who would have thought," said she, "he would have so done?" It was answered her, "perchance he thereby hoped to have had his pardon." "Pardon?" quod she; "wo worth him! He hath brought me and our stock in most miserable calamity and misery by his exceeding ambition."

But Jane could not really believe the duke could seriously have "hoped for life by his turning": "[T]hough other men be of that opinion, I utterly am not". How could he have hoped to save his life, "being in the field against the queen in person as general" and, after his arrest, "so hated and evil spoken of by the commons"? "And at his coming into prison so wondered at as the like was never heard?" – That Jane believed his unpopularity to have sprung up with his downfall is revealing. Perhaps she had not found him so obnoxious as a person before? Perhaps he had not been so universally hated as the emperor's hostile ambassadors were thinking? Perhaps only in defeat his "life was odious to all men?"[1]

> But what will ye more? Like as his life was wicked and full of dissimulation, so was his end thereafter. I pray God, I, nor no friend of mine, die so. Should I, who [am] young and in my few years, forsake my faith for the love of life? Nay, God forbid! Much more he should not, whose fatal course, although he had lived his just number of years, could not have long continued. But life was sweet, it appeared; so he might have lived, you will say, he did [not] care how.[2]

---

1 Chronicle of Queen Jane p. 25
2 Chronicle of Queen Jane pp. 25–26

Jane had decided that her late father-in-law was damned, while she was happy to be among the elect; quoting Scripture she pointed to those who deny "Him before men".[1] Jane's interpretation, that John had tried to save his life by going to mass was also indignantly reported by the Imperial ambassadors: "[T]he heretics ... say he did as he did out of hypocrisy, in the belief that he might incline the Queen to show him mercy."[2] Within the next few years this motif was taken up by Protestant polemicists until John Foxe, in his *Acts and Monuments*, claimed that Mary's government had promised Northumberland his life for his return to popery, "the Papists ... rejoicing not a little at his conversion, or rather subversion, as it then appeared."[3] Some Catholic writers, like Antonio de Guaras, indeed rejoiced: "And although his treasons were many and notorious, his end was that of a true and catholic Christian, and he took his death most patiently."[4] Others, those who really hated John Dudley, were apparently annoyed by his conversion and simply ignored it, like Robert Wingfield.[5]

*

Seven weeks after John's execution it was reported that his widow was "doing her utmost to secure a pardon for her children", but that so far the queen had not decided on anything.[6] Other than almost all the adult plotters, Jane and Guildford and his four brothers remained in prison; all were tried at some point. Jane and Guildford Dudley's turn came on 13 November 1553. They were led on foot from the Tower to the Guildhall with their co-accused, Archbishop Cranmer and Guildford's brothers Ambrose and Henry. Importantly, and in spite of all the gossip, Guildford was not accused of having tried to usurp the crown or of assuming undeserved titles. His crime had been to "compass to depose"

---

1 Chronicle of Queen Jane p. 26
2 CSP Span 27 August 1553
3 Loades 1996 p. 271; Beer 1973 p. 159
4 Guaras p. 109
5 It is inconceivable that he should not have known about John Dudley's return to the Catholic faith, as the news was widely promulgated and he included other details of John's time in custody.
6 CSP Span 9 October 1553

233

Queen Mary by sending troops to his father, and the "receiving, honouring, and proclaiming" of his wife as queen. Jane's own treason consisted in having signed certain documents as "Jane the Queen".[1] The Imperial ambassadors summarized:

> To-day three sons of the Duke of Northumberland, Jane of Suffolk and the Bishop of Canterbury were taken to the hall at Cheapside, and were there condemned to death. The only one of the Duke's sons who has not been condemned is now my Lord Robert. When execution is to take place is uncertain, for though the Queen is truly irritated against the Duke of Suffolk, it is believed that Jane will not die.[2]

In the end it was indeed Jane's father who caused the young couple's undoing by his decision to participate in Wyatt's Rebellion against Mary's Spanish marriage. His actions are quite inexplicable; he must have seen himself as a freedom fighter. His rebel army never materialized and he had to hide in an old oak tree, where he was captured.[3] Henry Grey arrived in the Tower as a prisoner on 10 February 1554, two days before Jane and Guildford were scheduled to die. Both wrote short messages to the duke in a prayerbook, in the hope that it would ultimately reach him:

> the lorde comforte youre grace and that in his worde whearen all creatures onlye are to be comforted and though it hathe pleased god to take awaye ij of youre children yet thincke not I moste humblye besech youre grace that you have loste them but truste that we by leavinge this mortall life have wanne an immortal life and I for my parte as I have honoured youre grace in thys life will praye for you in this life

---

1 Bellamy 1979 p. 54
2 CSP Span 14 October 1553
3 Ives 2009 p. 263

youre gracys humble daughter
Jane Duddley[1]

youre lovyng and obedyent son wishethe vnto your grace long lyfe in this world wth as muche ioy and comforte, as dyde I wyshte to my selfe, and in the world to come ioy euer lasting

your most humble son to his dethe
Gduddley[2]

On 12 February 1554 Guildford Dudley was beheaded on Tower Hill. William Parr, "the lord marques", watched the execution from the roof of his prison.[3] Guildford's body was brought to St. Peter ad Vincula, where it was buried a few yards from his father's. His wife followed him within an hour. "Jane of Suffolk who made herself queen and her husband have been executed", Simon Renard reported with satisfaction. – There was also much sympathy for the young couple, though: Many gentlemen had come to take leave of Guildford and shake hands with him outside the Tower, and the chronicler Grafton claimed that "even those that never before the time of his execution saw him, did with lamentable tears bewail his death." John Knox, writing in 1554, saw Jane and Guildford as "innocents ... such as by just laws and faithful witnesses can never be proved to have offended by themselves".[4]

On 18 October 1554 the younger John Dudley was released from the Tower, with his brothers Robert and Henry, leaving behind only Ambrose. John died three days later, "at midnight", in the house of his brother-in-law Henry Sidney at Penshurst.[5] His teenage widow, Anne Seymour, who had been allowed to pay him visits in the Tower, remarried the following year; she continued to be styled Countess of Warwick.

---

1 BL Harleian MS 2342 ff. 78–80
2 BL Harleian MS 2342 ff. 59v–60
3 Chronicle of Queen Jane p. 55
4 Ives 2009 pp. 275, 268
5 Machyn p. 72

On 30 November 1554 a son was born to Mary and Henry Sidney. He was named Philip after his illustrious godfather, King Philip of Spain. His godmother was his grandmother, Northumberland's widow. The queen had allowed her to continue living at the house in Chelsea, where she died in January 1555. In her will, written in her own hand, she remembered John as "my lord, my dear husband" and left her daughter Mary a favourite clock – the one "that was the lord her father's, praying her to keep it as a jewel."[1] Mary was also to have two velvet gowns, one furred with sables, one "with a high back". Her youngest daughter, Katherine Hastings, who was not yet 12, was to have "a gown of new purple velvet, a summer gown, and a kirtle of purple velvet to it and sleeves."[2] Jane Dudley's old friend, "Elizabeth, daughter of the Lord Cobham" (as she was again), received another velvet gown together with other clothes and "a chair, two cushions, and a new bed of black velvet."[3] Elizabeth Brooke was now the former wife of the former Marquess of Northampton, who had had to take back his first wife as a condition of his pardon. He was also plain William Parr again. The bequest to Elizabeth Brooke appears under those to close family members, indicating that Jane did not bear her any grudges, despite all that had happened since the marchioness had suggested the marriage between Guildford and Jane Grey.

Jane Dudley also thanked Queen Mary, assuring her that she had always borne her a "faithful poor heart … although it was little in value for such a personage"; and she asked Philip and Mary to look after her sons: "And my sons all three I leave them all to the King's Majesty and her Highness beyond me."[4] She did not forget Mary's favourite lady, nor her only old friends at court:

> I give Mistress Clarencius my tawny velvet jewel coffer; I give to my Lady Paget my high-backed gown

---

1 Collins 1745 pp. 34–35
2 Collins 1745 p. 34
3 Higginbotham 2011b; Collins 1745 p. 34
4 Collins 1745 p. 35

of wrought velvet; to my Lord Paget one of my black enamelled rings I did use to wear.[1]

She also remembered "her brother, Sir Francis Jobson", and "her sister his wife", another indication, if any were needed, that the Jobsons had been part of the closer family circle. John Dudley's brother, Jerome, was apparently in some institution now: "I give to my Lord, my husband's brother Jerome Dudley, his board and his apparel, as [my] executors shall think proper for him, considering the state of him." Finally, Jane stipulated that "in no wise let me be opened after I am dead." For, "I have not loved to be very bold afore women, much more I should be loath to come into the hands of any living man, be he physician or surgeon." She did not say anything about religion, which only weeks before the start of the Marian burnings is perhaps no surprise; but she confessed that "who ever doth trust to this transitory world, as I did, may happen to have an overthrow, as I had".[2]

Ambrose Dudley and his uncle Andrew were finally released in January 1555. Going to mass on 21 August 1553 may have saved Andrew Dudley his life, and in April 1555, after his official pardon, Philip and Mary granted him a pension of £100 p.a.[3] He was also allowed to retain certain possessions he had managed to conceal before Mary's government so far. Moving to Tothill Street, London, he in vain tried to reclaim the jewels and other stuffs he had sent to his bride in the north of England. Margaret Clifford soon married the heir of the Earl of Derby, but her father kept Andrew's jewels. Andrew Dudley died in 1559,[4] at a time his nephew Robert had become a powerful presence at court. Jerome Dudley was still alive in 1556, when Andrew left him £200 in his will.[5]

Mary proved less merciful to Andrew's nephew, Charles Lord Stourton, who was executed for murder in 1557. One night in

---

1 Collins 1745 p. 35
2 Collins 1745 p. 35; Higginbotham 2011b. For Jerome Dudley see above p. 22.
3 Loades 1996 p. 273
4 Löwe 2004
5 Collins 1745 p. 30. This could point to Jerome's independence, but then Andrew also left £200 to his one-year-old nephew, Philip Sidney.

January of that year, Stourton had ordered his servants to kidnap his neighbours, the Hartgills, father and son, wealthy gentlemen of the shire, with whom the Stourtons had been feuding for decades and who had given shelter to Charles' mother when she had fled from her violent husband. Charles had the Hartgills put away in an earth-hole, but then grew nervous and had them killed when a search was instituted for the men. He personally oversaw the murder, giving orders to his unfortunate servants who had to do the dirty work. He was soon found out, though, and imprisoned in the Tower. It was not unusual for noblemen to avoid punishment in similar cases, but this time Mary would not grant a pardon. Apart from the brutality of the crime, the fact that Stourton was John Dudley's nephew did not help him.[1] He was tried by his peers at Westminster Hall with the Earl of Arundel as presiding judge and convicted of felony. He was hanged at Salisbury on 6 March 1557. Like his uncle he gave a scaffold speech, a speech that bore some resemblance to Northumberland's and was likewise printed.[2]

*

Protestant clerics who wanted to avoid the stake went into exile under Mary. Among them were John Knox and John Ponet. Knox was less complimentary about John Dudley than he was about Jane and Guildford: "And who, I pray you, ruled the roste in the courte all this tyme by stoute corage and proudnes of stomack but Northumberland?"[3] John Ponet, meanwhile, made a bishop by John Dudley, declared him to have been "the ambitious and subtle Alcibiades of England".[4] John Ponet, in 1556, also invented the "good duke" of Somerset. It followed that there had also to be a bad duke.[5]

---

1 Bellamy 2005 p. 162
2 Bellamy 2005 ch. 5
3 Literary Remains I p. clxx
4 Beer 1979 p. 2. Alcibiades, an Athenian general and politician notorious for changing sides several times during the Peloponnesian War.
5 MacCulloch 2001 p. 42. Ponet in *A short treatise of politicke power*. According to Hoak 2008 it was William Harrison who invented the "good duke" in 1587.

The Elizabethan historians Grafton, Holinshed, and Stow managed to be both sympathetic to Somerset and fair to Northumberland – Robert Dudley, Earl of Leicester, after all, was a powerful patron.[1] Raphael Holinshed, in his 1577 edition, dedicated his book on Scotland to the Earl of Leicester; it seemed as though the reign of Queen Jane had never happened:

> It resteth (right noble Earle) that it may please your Honor to accept my doinges in good parte, to whom I offer this parcell of my travayles in this Historie of Scotlande, in regarde of the honour due to your noble Father, for his incomparable valure well knowen and approved, aswel within that realme as els where in service of two Kings of most famous memory, Henry the viij. and Edward the sixte, sounding so greatly to his renowme as the same can not passe in silence, whilest any remembraunce of those two most perelesse Princes shall remain in written Histories.[2]

John Hayward's *The Life and Raigne of King Edward the Sixth* (1630) modelled its characters on notorious Romans.[3] It essentially portrayed two bad dukes who manipulated a precocious but helpless king. Naturally, Northumberland is the really wicked duke. Of "ancient nobility" and "great courage", he destroys his rival Somerset, a weakling encumbered with a wicked wife. Northumberland's lust for power makes him "sottishly mad with over great fortune" in the pursuit of absolute power.[4] Hayward's portrait of Northumberland, which influenced countless later works, clearly took some inspiration from *Leicester's Commonwealth*, the 1584 libel which depicted Robert Dudley as the murderous and all-powerful monster of the Elizabethan court. Accordingly, in Hayward it is *Robert* Dudley who poisons the

---

1 Beer 1998 pp. 110–113
2 Holinshed IV To The Right Honourable etc.
3 Alford 2002 pp. 16–17
4 Hayward p. 20

king, Edward enjoying "his health not long" after Robert's appointment to Edward's privy chamber.[1]

The Victorians firmly re-established the good duke/bad duke model, and Somerset became an even better duke: Not just the champion of Protestantism, he was now the champion of civil liberties as well.[2] Northumberland, meanwhile, became ever more wicked. To A. F. Pollard – Somerset's greatest admirer among historians – he was "the subtlest intriguer in English History".[3] Pollard also emphasized the alleged "violence and iniquity of Northumberland's rule".[4] His interpretation gained currency in textbooks and thus in schools, universities, and in popular works. In Hester Chapman's 1958 biography of Edward VI, Northumberland appeared as a Iago-like devil alongside an angelic Somerset. As relentlessly wicked but less brilliant, Northumberland, in the Whiggish *Oxford History of England*, was "desperate and drunk with his own 'auctoritye'" and "knew no restraints", while his "arbitrary rule" was a short-lived aberration from England's liberal destiny.[5] In W. K. Jordan's two volumes on Edward VI's reign (1968/1970) there was again a good and a bad duke, the pages reeking with Somerset's "gentleness" and "idealism" set against Northumberland's "dark and possibly twisted mind". Radically departing from tradition, however, Jordan ascribed the "devise" to Edward's initiative, Northumberland playing the part of a reluctant, even tragic, enforcer of the king's last will.[6]

The mid-1970s, finally, saw the deconstruction of the Duke of Somerset. G. R. Elton gleefully pronounced "The demolition of the good duke" in a book review.[7] The work under review was M. L. Bush's *Government Policy of Protector Somerset*, which indeed demolished the notion that the duke was motivated by his social conscience. Somerset's diminished prestige with historians automatically raised Northumberland's. It was now Somerset's rule

1 Hayward p. 20
2 Alford 2002 pp. 20–21
3 Beer 1979 p. 4
4 Pollard 1900 p. 312
5 Mackie 1963 pp. 523, 530
6 Jordan 1970 pp. 531–532
7 Elton 1976 p. 130

that was arbitrary, while Northumberland restored the privy council to its function and even reformed it.[1] It could now be said that John Dudley "took the necessary but unpopular steps to hold the minority regime together",[2] and that he seemed to have been "one of the most remarkably able governors of any European state during the sixteenth century."[3] – The plot against Mary's succession was still a plot, but it increasingly became a plot of *king and minister*. The "incompetent way the plot was carried out" clearly pointed to Edward, G. R. Elton believed.[4] Eric Ives in 2009 believed there was no plot, but, technically, a successful rebellion by Mary. Still, John Dudley the pantomime villain survives to this day, even in academic essays.[5]

*

"But ... I had rather beg my bread than procure any hurt to the commonwealth",[6] John Dudley assured William Cecil in one of his letters. The discrepancy between his own letters on one side and reports and memoirs by his contemporaries on the other is obvious. Unfortunately, the latter were mostly written at the time of his downfall or later, and – as the years 1945 and 1989 in European history have shown – people do change their minds, past, and memories within hours in times of regime change. Most historians have been inclined to believe the judges, diplomats, and chroniclers rather than John Dudley's own words. While usually not doubting the beliefs of Edward Seymour, Thomas Cranmer, William Cecil, or even Henry VIII, they could not believe that John changed his mind or that he saw the hand of God in Mary's success. It has usually been implied that he had no faith whatsoever – although some historians have conceded that he really may have believed what he said, or that he conformed to save his family, or that he finally found comfort in the faith of his

---

1 Hoak 1980 p. 50; Hoak 2008
2 Loades 1996 p. vii
3 Hoak 1980 p. 51
4 Elton 1977 p. 375
5 For example, Hoak 2015.
6 Knighton 1992 p. 278

childhood. John himself addressed these doubts minutes before his death: "but I tell you what I feel at the bottom of my heart, and as ye see I am in no case to say aught but truth ."[1]

John Dudley's lifestyle was appropriate to his rank. He acquired, sold, and exchanged lands as a business model, but never managed to build himself a territorial power base with a large armed force of retainers.[2] He achieved a maximum income of £4,300 p.a. from land and a £2,000 p.a. from fees and annuities – which figured still below the annuity of £5,333 p.a. Edward Seymour had granted himself while in office, reaching an income of well over £10,000 p.a.[3] John was certainly a very ambitious and proud nobleman, very sensitive on what he called "estimacion", status.[4] He was, however, not personally vindictive regarding slurs upon his honour from more humble slanderers.[5]

A tall figure, "about six feet in height",[6] he was a handsome man with dark eyes.[7] According to a minor French diplomat, who may or may not have accompanied the French ambassador on his social calls to Northumberland, the duke effused charm and was "affable, gracious and kind in speech". He was "an intelligent man who could explain his ideas and who displayed an impressive dignity. Others, who did not know him, would have considered him worthy of a kingdom." – He commanded a "great presence" and was of "great courage". As the report was written in late 1553, we are not really surprised to read that all this affability and generosity was staged, and that "inwardly he was a proud *felon* and as vindictive as one ever was." One may wonder how the anonymous writer, who cannot have come close to John Dudley,

---

1 Guaras p. 106
2 Loades 1996 pp. 285–286, 258
3 Loades 1996 pp. 222–223; Beer 2009 estimates Somerset's yearly income as £12,800.
4 Loades 1996 p. 73
5 Beer 1973 pp. 137–138
6 Bell 1877 p. 29. Description of his remains, excavated and reburied in the 1870s.
7 No contemporary portrait of John Dudley survives. The portrait at Knole, painted around 1600 as part of a set, and a similar picture in Penshurst, are probably good likenesses copied from a contemporary prototype. Both paintings also show some family resemblance with portraits of Robert and Ambrose Dudley.

could read his mind. The answer is that he too used reports by others ("those who knew him could well see ...").[1] What can undoubtedly be gleaned from this report is that John possessed considerable charisma and intelligence.

His wife deeply loved him. For her, he was "the most best gentleman" she could have wished for in an arranged marriage. She was keen to point out "how good he was to me", perhaps aware of how common ill-treatment was even in aristocratic marriages. Her remarks though suggest that "all the world" and "those about him", and about her, knew how psychologically dependent she was on her husband (the evidence not suggesting she was an otherwise dependent person). She also treasured his memory, of which his clock was the last physical evidence. We do not know in what measure John reciprocated her feelings, but he was certainly a considerate husband.

John without doubt loved his children; they saved him from his depression, as he saw it, and he died in the hope of their pardon, having asked the queen "to be gracious to my children" (they had, after all, only obeyed their father's commandments).[2] John could not foresee Henry Grey's folly to rebel against Mary for a second time, nor is he responsible for a regime that specialized in executing teenagers.[3]

Of the seven children left by John Dudley only four survived into the reign of Elizabeth: Ambrose, Robert, Mary, and Katherine. Robert Dudley, the greatest Elizabethan art collector, did not display his parents' portraits on his walls, nor did he keep them in storage. The Duke of Northumberland may have been too politically unacceptable to be present in Robert's household, but it is as likely that any pictures still in the family's possession would have belonged to Ambrose's collection. As the family heir he would have inherited any family heirlooms. Unfortunately, his papers have disappeared completely,[4] so there is no way of

---

[1] Ives 2009 pp. 104, 105. He described Northumberland as *comte*, when the latter had been a duke for some years (Quelques particularitez f. 211). "[T]he author is reporting *'ce que l'on dict'*, what the talk was at court in August 1553 about events of the past few months." (McDiarmid 2015 p. 188).
[2] Tytler II p. 225; Rosso f. 30
[3] Mary's youngest victim was a 12-year-old boy burnt for heresy.
[4] Adams 2008a

knowing whether he reserved a place for Mum and Dad on his walls. It is intriguing, though, that two portraits believed to show John Dudley can be found at Penshurst, the residence of his daughter, Mary Sidney.

As to what Robert and Ambrose Dudley thought about their father, we have very few clues. They did not hesitate to proudly describe themselves as "sons of the most mighty Prince, John, late Duke of Northumberland",[1] on the epitaph of Robert's little son, who died in 1584. More intriguingly, Robert, decades earlier, seems to have sought the friendship of Bishop Nicholas Heath, who as we have seen heard John's last confession. In early 1561 Robert told Philip II's ambassador that he was a "great friend" of Heath, now imprisoned as Mary's former Archbishop of York.[2] Heath had refused to accept Elizabeth's Act of Supremacy, but was treated much better than his imprisoned colleagues[3] and this very likely had to do with Robert Dudley's favour. Perhaps Robert really needed to know more about his father's last hours.

Elizabeth seems not to have held a serious grudge against the Dudleys for the attempt to remove her from the succession (perhaps she knew details lost to us). When, in November 1560, it was pointed out to her how unworthy Lord Robert was of her hand because of "his race" she was also told that "the Duke's hatred was rather to her than to the Queen her sister" – "she laughed, and forthwith turned herself to the one side and to the other, and set her hand upon her face."[4] Elizabeth may even have remembered Northumberland with some sympathy or, at least, respect. When, 25 years later, she was displeased with Robert Dudley's conduct of the war in the Netherlands she praised John Dudley's superior skills; the point, of course, was to give Robert a snub (she could be sure it was reported to him). He took it stoically, and with a degree of satisfaction:

---

1 A standard address for dukes, who ranked as princes.
2 CSP Simancas I p. 197; Rodriguez-Salgado and Adams 1984 p. 339
3 Rodriguez-Salgado and Adams 1984 p. 339
4 Hardwicke SP I p. 165. It is sometimes said that Elizabeth, on slashing a patent for the ennoblement of Robert Dudley, remarked that "the Dudleys had been traitors for three generations." (Jenkins 1961 p. 73; Wernham 1966 p. 193). This is an invention of Elizabeth's modern biographers, however; in the original report of the incident she says no such thing (Hardwicke SP I p. 168).

because her majesty said, there hath lacked a Northumberland in my place; indeed I shall always give place to him, and I pray God able me for her majesty's service sake to be as able to serve her.[1]

Sir Philip Sidney, Robert's nephew and John's grandson – whose "chiefest honour" was to be a Dudley[2] – dared openly to defend his family against unfair, and unending, criticism:

> But our house received such an overthrow; and hath none else in England done so? I will not seek to wash away that dishonour with other honorable tears. I would this island were not so full of such examples ... but this I may justly and boldly affirm let the last fault of the Duke be buried.[3]

*

A year after Mary's triumph over the duke, the Venetian ambassador returned to his republic and, as was customary, wrote a long *relazione* that summarized his mission and gave an assessment of the current state of England. The ambassador diagnosed that Marian England lacked a true statesman or general, an assessment John would have shared:

> The most important deficiency in the great naval and military forces of England, is, that in the whole realm they have no persons, neither sailor nor soldier, capable of commanding either fleet or army. The only man they had was the Duke of Northumberland, who by his bravery distinguished himself in both capacities, and from the grade of a private gentleman (his father indeed was beheaded for treason by Henry VIII) rose step by step through his abilities to the eminent position at length attained by him; but in like

---

[1] Leycester Correspondence p. 388
[2] Adlard 1870 p. 70
[3] Adlard 1870 p. 75

manner as the punishment of his rashness was well merited, so must the friends of England lament the loss of all his qualities with that single exception.[1]

---

1 CSP Ven 18 August 1554

Tables

Table 1: The sons of John Dudley and Jane Guildford.

1. Henry Dudley, c.1525 – 1544, "died at the siege of Boulogne being xix years old"*

2. Thomas Dudley, "second son died at the age of two years"*

3. John Dudley, Earl of Warwick, 1530 – 21 October 1554, "third son died without issue xxiii years old"*; "died Anno. 1554. skarce 24 years of age"**

4. Ambrose Dudley, Earl of Warwick, 1531(?) – 21 February 1590, "fourth son"*

5. Robert Dudley, Earl of Leicester, 24 June 1532 – 4 September 1588, "fifth son"***

6. Guildford Dudley, died 12 February 1554, "sixth son married the Lady Jane and died with her"*

7. Henry Dudley, died 1557, "seventh son slain at the siege of St. Quentin's"*

8. Charles Dudley, "eighth son died at the age of viii years"*

Table 2: The daughters of John Dudley and Jane Guildford.

1. Mary, Lady Sidney, eldest daughter, died 9 August 1586

2. Margaret, "died at the age of iiii years"*

3. Temperance, "died at the age of one year"*

4. Katherine Hastings, Countess of Huntingdon, "third or fourth" daughter,**** c.1543(?)**** – 14 August 1620

5. Katherine, "fifth daughter",**** 1545(?)**** – 1552(?), "died at the age of vii years"*

**Genealogies of the Erles of Lecestre and Chester.* U Penn Ms. Codex 1070. f. 18r–18v.
**John Dee: *The Mathematicall Praeface.*
***Epitaph of Robert Dudley, Earl of Leicester at Beauchamp Chapel, St. Mary's Church, Warwick.
****Simon Adams (ed.) (1995): *Household Accounts and Disbursement Books of Robert Dudley, Earl of Leicester.* Cambridge University Press. p. 44.

Table 3: John Dudley and some of his children with their marriages during his lifetime.

John Dudley, Viscount Lisle, Earl of Warwick, Duke of Northumberland 1504/5 – 1553, m. c.1525 Jane Guildford 1508/9 – 1555	son of Edmund Dudley 1471/2 – 1510, grandson of John Sutton, 1st Baron Dudley	son of Elizabeth Grey c.1481/3 – 1525, daughter of Edward Grey, 4th Viscount Lisle, m. 1511 Arthur Plantagenet
Henry Dudley c.1525 – 1544		
John Dudley c.1530 – 1554	m. 1550 Anne Seymour, daughter of Edward Seymour, Duke of Somerset	
Ambrose Dudley c.1531 – 1590	m. c.1549 Anne Whorwood, daughter of Sir William Whorwood, Attorney-General	m. c.1552 Elizabeth Tailboys, Baroness Tailboys
Robert Dudley 1532 – 1588	m. 1550 Amy Robsart, daughter of Sir John Robsart	
Guildford Dudley d.1554	m. 1553 Lady Jane Grey, daughter of Henry Grey, Duke of Suffolk	
Henry Dudley d.1557		
	m. before July 1553 Margaret Audley, daughter of Thomas Audley, 1st Baron Audley of Walden	
Mary Dudley d.1586	m. 1551 Henry Sidney, son of Sir William Sidney	
Katherine Dudley d.1620	m. 1553 Henry Hastings, son of Francis Hastings, 2nd Earl of Huntingdon	

Table 4: The common descent of Jane Grey and Guildford Dudley from Edward Grey and his wife Elizabeth Ferrers, Baroness Ferrers of Groby.

Reginald Grey, 3rd Baron Grey de Ruthyn	
Sir Edward Grey .... married to	Elizabeth Ferrers, Baroness Ferrers of Groby
Sir John Grey of Groby	Edward Grey, 1st Viscount Lisle
Thomas Grey, 1st Marquess of Dorset	Elizabeth Grey, Baroness Lisle
Thomas Grey, 2nd Marquess of Dorset	John Dudley, Duke of Northumberland
Henry Grey, Duke of Suffolk	Lord Guildford Dudley
Lady Jane Grey	

Table 5: The descent of John Dudley, Duke of Northumberland from Richard Beauchamp, 13th Earl of Warwick, and John Talbot, 1st of Shrewsbury.

Richard Beauchamp, 13th Earl of Warwick	
Margaret Beauchamp .... married to	John Talbot, 1st Earl of Shrewsbury
	John Talbot, 1st Viscount Lisle
	Elizabeth Talbot, Baroness Lisle
	Elizabeth Grey, Baroness Lisle
	John Dudley, Duke of Northumberland

Table 6: Sample of grants by Edward VI to courtiers and noblemen, April – July 1553.[1]

- 17 April

  Henry Neville, 5th Earl of Westmorland
- 22 May

  John Cheke, royal tutor, lands worth £100 p.a.
- June

  Lord Edward Clinton
  Lord Thomas Darcy
  Thomas West, 9th Baron De La Warr
- 12 June

  Henry Gates, brother of Sir John Gates, lands worth £102 12s 7d p.a.
  Francis Hastings, 2nd Earl of Huntingdon, £158 8s 5d p.a.
- 23 June

  Sir Henry Sidney, privy chamber, lands worth £160 6s 11½d p.a.
- 26 June

  William Herbert, 1st Earl of Pembroke, Dnyate, Somerset
  John Russell, 1st Earl of Bedford, lands worth £78 16s 7d p.a.
  George Talbot, Earl of Shrewsbury, mansion of Coldharbour, London, and lands worth £66 13s 1½d p.a.
- 1 July

  Thomas Gresham, financier, lands worth £201 14s 9½d p.a.
- 3 July

  Sir Henry Sidney, keepership of Sheen (Palace of Placentia)
  John Dudley, Earl of Warwick, lands worth £158
- 4 July

  Thomas Wroth, privy chamber, lands worth £87 3s 8½d p.a.

---

1 Skidmore 2007 pp. 264, 327; Ives 2009 p. 317; Gammon 1973 pp. 185, 275; Loach 2002 p. 165; Loades 1996 p. 224

Bibliography

Primary sources

Acts of the Privy Council of England. http://www.british-history.ac.uk/search/series/acts-privy-council

Adams, Simon (ed.) (**1995**): *Household Accounts and Disbursement Books of Robert Dudley, Earl of Leicester, 1558–1561, 1584–1586.* Cambridge University Press.

Adams, Simon; **Archer**, Ian; **Bernard**, G. W. (eds.) (**2003a**): "Certayne Brife Notes of the Controversy betwene the dukes of Somerset and Nor[t]humberland" in: Ian Archer (ed.): *Religion, Politics, and Society in Sixteenth-Century England.* Cambridge University Press.

Adams, Simon; **Archer**, Ian; **Bernard**, G. W. (eds.) (**2003b**): "A 'Journall' of Matters of State happened from time to time as well within and without the Realme from and before the Death of King Edw. the 6th untill the Yere 1562" in: Ian Archer (ed.): *Religion, Politics, and Society in Sixteenth-Century England.* Cambridge University Press.

Adlard, George (**1870**): *Amye Robsart and the Earl of Leycester.* John Russell Smith.

*The **Antiquarian** Repertory.* (ed. Francis Grose and Thomas Astle, 1809).

*The Whole Works of Roger **Ascham**.* (ed. J. A. Giles, 1864).

Bayley, J. W. (**1830**): *History and Antiquities of the Tower of London. Second Edition.*

Bell, D. C. (**1877**): *Notices of the historic persons buried in the chapel of St. Peter ad Vincula, in the Tower of London.* J. Murray.

Brigden, Susan (ed.) (**1990**): "The Letters of Richard Scudamore to Sir Philip Hoby, September 1549 – March 1555". *Camden Miscellany.* Volume XXX. Royal Historical Society.

*Calendar of State Papers, **Dom**estic Series, of the Reigns of Edward VI, Mary, Elizabeth, 1547–1580.* (ed. Robert Lemon, 1856). Longmans.

*Calendar of State Papers, **Foreign**.* http://www.british-history.ac.uk/search/series/cal-state-papers--foreign

*Calendar of the State Papers relating to **Scotland** and Mary, Queen of Scots 1547–1603.* (ed. Joseph Bain).
*Calendar of State Papers, **Span**ish. 1485–1558.* http://www.british-history.ac.uk/search/series/cal-state-papers--spain
*Calendar of ... State Papers Relating to English Affairs ... in ... **Simancas**, 1558–1603.* (ed. by Martin Hume, 1892–1899). HMSO.
***Chronicle of the Greyfriars** of London.* (ed. J. G. Nicholls, 1852). Camden Society.
*The **Chronicle of Queen Jane** and Two Years of Queen Mary.* (ed. J. G. Nichols, 1850). Camden Society.
Cameron, Annie (ed.) (**1927**): *The Scottish Correspondence of Mary of Lorraine.* Scottish History Society.
Cranmer, Thomas: *Miscellaneous Works.* (ed. J. E. Cox, 1846).
Ellis, Henry (ed.) (1825): *Original Letters Illustrative of English History.* **First Series**.
Feuillerat, Albert (ed.) (1914): *Documents Relating to the Revels at Court in the Time of King Edward VI and Queen Mary.*
*The Acts and Monuments of John **Foxe**.* (ed. S. R. Cattley, 1839).
Fuller, Thomas: *The Church History of Britain.* (ed. J. S. Brewer, 1845).
***Genelogies of the Erles of Lecestre** and Chester*: U Penn Ms. Codex 1070.   http://dla.library.upenn.edu/dla/medren/detail.html?id=MEDREN_4218616
Gentlemen's Magazine
Antonio de **Guaras**: *The Accession of Queen Mary.* (ed. Richard Garnett, 1892).
Gunn, S. J. (ed.) (**1999**): "A Letter of Jane, Duchess of Northumberland, 1553". *English Historical Review.* Vol. CXIV pp. 1267–1271.
Edward **Hall**: *The Union of the Two Noble and Illustre Families of Lancastre and Yorke.* (1809).
*The **Hamilton Papers**.* (ed. Joseph Bain, 1890).
***Hardwicke** State Papers.* (1778).
Hayward, John: *The Life and Raigne of King Edward the Sixth.* (ed. B. L. Beer, 1993). The Kent State University Press.
Jordan, W.K. **and** M.R. **Gleason** (eds.) (**1975**): *The Saying of John Late Duke of Northumberland Upon the Scaffold, 1553.* Harvard Library.
*Report on the Manuscripts of Lord **Montagu** of Beulieu.* (ed. Historical Manuscript Commission, 1900).
*Report on the **Pepys** Manuscripts Preserved at Magdalen College, Cambridge.* (ed. Historical Manuscript Commission, 1911).
***Second Report** of the Royal Commission on Historical Manuscripts.* (1874).

*Calendar of the Manuscripts of ... The Marquess of **Salisbury** ... Preserved at Hatfield House, Hertfordshire.* (ed. **H**istorical **M**anuscripts Commission). HMSO.
Holinshed, Raphael: *Chronicles of England, Scotland, and Ireland.* (1577). http://www.english.ox.ac.uk/holinshed/toc.php?edition=1577
Hoyle, R. W. (ed.) (**1992**): "Letters of the Cliffords, Lords Clifford and Earls of Cumberland, c. 1500–c. 1565". *Camden Miscellany.* Volume XXXI. Royal Historical Society.
*Manuscripts of The Marquess of **Bath**.* (**H**istorical **M**anuscripts Commission, 1907).
*Notes of **P**ost **M**ortem Inquisitions Taken in **Sussex**.* (ed. F. W. T. Attree, 1912)
Jackson, J. E. (**1878**): "Amye Robsart". *The Wiltshire Archaeological and Natural History Magazine.* Volume XVII.
Knighton, C. S. (ed.) (**1992**): *Calendar of State Papers, Domestic Series, of the Reign of Edward VI, 1547–1553.* Revised Edition. HMSO.
Knighton, C. S. **and** David **Loades** (eds.) (**2011**): *The Navy of Edward VI and Mary I.* The Navy Records Society.
Lady Jane Grey's Prayer Book BL Harleian MS 2342 http://www.bl.uk/catalogues/illuminatedmanuscripts/record.asp?MSID=7220&CollID=8&NStart=2342
Lefèvre-Pontalis, Germain (ed.) (**1888**): *Correspondance Politique de Odet de Selve, Ambassadeur de France en Angleterre (1546–1549).* Fèlix Alcan.
Lettere *di Principi, le quali si scrivono o da principi, o ragionano di principi.* (ed. J. S. Edwards, 2013) http://www.somegreymatter.com/lettereengl.htm
*Letters & **P**apers of Henry VIII.* http://www.british-history.ac.uk/search/series/letters-papers-hen8
Correspondence *of Robert Dudley, Earl of **Leycester**, during his Government of the Low Countries, in the Years 1585 and 1586.* (ed. John Bruce, 1844). Camden Society.
Literary Remains *of King Edward the Sixth.* (ed. G. J. Nichols, 1857). Roxburghe Club.
MacCulloch, Diarmaid (ed.) (**1984**): "The Vita Mariae Angliae Reginae of Robert Wingfield of Brantham". *Camden Miscellany.* Vol. XXVIII. Royal Historical Society.
*The Diary of Henry **Machyn**.* (ed. G. J. Nichols, 1848). Camden Society.
John Dee: *The **Mathematicall Praeface**.* http://www.gutenberg.org/files/22062/22062-h/main.htm

Murray J. T. (1910): *English Dramatic Companies, 1558–1642.* Houghton Mifflin.
Nares, Edward (1828): *Memoirs of the Life and Administration of the Right Honourable William Cecil, Lord Burghley.* Colburn and Bentley.
Narratives of the Days of the Reformation. (ed. J. G. Nichols, 1859). Camden Society.
Nichols, J. G. (ed.) (**1833**). "Life of the last Fitz-Alan, earl of Arundel". *Gentlemen's Magazine.* Vol. 103/2.
Original Letters Relative to the English Reformation. (ed. Hastings Robinson, 1847). Cambridge University Press.
Potter, D. L. (ed.) (**1984**): "Documents concerning the Negotiations of the Anglo-French Treaty of March 1550". *Camden Miscellany.* Vol. XXVIII. Royal Historical Society.
Quelques particularitez d'Angleterre. BNF MS Français 15888 http://gallica.bnf.fr/ark:/12148/btv1b9061305c/f214.item.r=15888.lang
Rodriguez-Salgado, M. J. **and Adams**, Simon (eds.) (1984): "The Count of Feria's Dispatch to Philip II of 14 November 1558". *Camden Miscellany.* Volume XXVIII. Royal Historical Society.
Giulio Raviglio **Rosso**: *History of the Events that Occurred in the Realm of England in Relation to the Duke of Northumberland after the Death of Edward VI.* (ed. J. S. Edwards, 2011). http://www.somegreymatter.com/rossointro.htm
*The **Sayinge** of John late Duke of Northumberlande, vpon the scaffolde at the tyme of his execution.* http://www.tudorplace.com.ar/Bios/JohnDudley%281DNorthumberland%29.htm
*Mémoires de la vie de François de **Scépeaux**, Sieur de Vieilleville.* (ed. C. B. Petitot, 1822)
*Chronicle of King Henry VIII of England ... written in **Spanish** by an unknown hand.* (ed. M. S. Hume, 1889)
Starkey, David (ed.) (**1998**): *The Inventory of King Henry VIII: The Transcript.* Harvey Miller.
St. Clare Byrne, Muriel (ed.) (**1983**): *The Lisle Letters: An Abridgement.* Secker & Warburg.
Stopes, C. C. (**1918**): *Shakespeare's Environment.* Bell.
Stow, John. *Annales of Englund.* (1601).
Strype, John (ed.) (1822): *Ecclesiastical **Memorials**.* Clarendon Press.
Strype, John (ed.) (1824): ***Annals** of the Reformation.*
Thomas, William: *The History of Italy (1549).* (Folger Shakespeare Library, 1963).

Tudor Tracts, 1533–1588. (ed. A. F. Pollard and Thomas Seccombe, 1903). E.P. Dutton.
Tytler, P. F. (1839): *England under the Reigns of Edward VI. and Mary.* Richard Bentley.
Ambassades de Messieurs de Noailles en Angleterre. (ed. Abbé **Vertot**, 1763).
Wilson's Arte of Rhetoricke. (ed. G. H. Mair, 1909). Clarendon Press.
Wriothesley, Charles: *A Chronicle of England During the Reign of The Tudors, from A.D. 1485 to 1559.* (ed. W. D. Hamilton, 1877).

Secondary sources

Ackroyd, Peter (2006): *Shakespeare: The Biography.* Vintage.
Ackroyd, Peter (2012): *The History of England II: Tudors.* Macmillan.
Adams, Simon (2002): *Leicester and the Court: Essays in Elizabethan Politics.* Manchester University Press.
Adams, Simon (2008a): "Dudley, Ambrose, earl of Warwick (c.1530–1590)". *Oxford Dictionary of National Biography.* Online edition.
Adams, Simon (2008b): "Dudley, Robert, earl of Leicester (1532/3–1588)". *Oxford Dictionary of National Biography.* Online edition.
Adams, Simon (2008c): "Sidney, Mary, Lady Sidney (1530×35–1586)". *Oxford Dictionary of National Biography.* Online edition.
Akrigg, G. P. V. (1968): *Shakespeare and the Earl of Southampton.* Harvard University Press.
Alford, Stephen (2002): *Kingship and Politics in the Reign of Edward VI.* Cambridge University Press.
Alford, Stephen (2011): *Burghley: William Cecil at the Court of Elizabeth I.* Yale University Press.
Alford, Stephen (2014): *Edward VI: The Last Boy King.* Allen Lane.
Beer, B. L. (1973): *Northumberland: The Political Career of John Dudley, Earl of Warwick and Duke of Northumberland.* The Kent State University Press.
Beer, B. L. (1979): "Northumberland: The Myth of the Wicked Duke and the Historical John Dudley". *Albion.* Vol. 11, No. 1.
Beer, B. L. (1982): *Rebellion and Riot: Popular Disorder in England during the Reign of Edward VI.* The Kent University Press.
Beer, B. L. (1998): *Tudor England Observed: The World of John Stow.* Sutton.
Beer, B. L. (2009): "Seymour, Edward, duke of Somerset (c.1500–1552)". *Oxford Dictionary of National Biography.* Online edition.

Bellamy, John (1979): *The Tudor Law of Treason: An Introduction*. Routledge & Kegan Paul.

Bellamy, John (2005): *Strange, Inhuman Deaths: Murder in Tudor England*. Sutton.

Bernard, G. W. (2008): "Seymour, Thomas, Baron Seymour of Sudeley (*b.* in or before 1509, *d.* 1549)". *Oxford Dictionary of National Biography*.

Bernard, G. W. (2010): *Anne Boleyn: Fatal Attractions*. Yale University Press.

Brennan, Michael (2006): *The Sidneys of Penshurst and the Monarchy, 1500–1700*. Ashgate.

Brigden, Susan (2001): *New Worlds, Lost Worlds: The Rule of the Tudors 1485–1603*. Penguin.

Brigden, Susan (2012): *Thomas Wyatt: The Heart's Forest*. Faber & Faber.

Byrne, Conor (2014): *Katherine Howard: A New History*. Made Global.

Chamberlin, Frederick (1939): *Elizabeth and Leycester*. Dodd, Mead & Co.

Chapman, Hester (1958): *The Last Tudor King: A Study of Edward VI*. Jonathan Cape.

Chapman, Hester (1962): *Lady Jane Grey*. Jonathan Cape.

Childs, Jessie (2006): *Henry VIII's Last Victim: The Life and Times of Henry Howard, Earl of Surrey*. Thomas Dunne Books.

Clabby, Simon (2015): "Recovering the Mary Rose – 1545–1552". http://www.maryrose.org/recovery-1545/

Cross, Claire (1966): *The Puritan Earl: The Life of Henry Hastings, Third Earl of Huntingdon 1536-1595*. Jonathan Cape.

Davey, Richard (1909): *The Nine Days' Queen: Lady Jane Grey and Her Times*. Methuen & Co.

Dawson, Ian (1993): *The Tudor Century 1485–1603*. Thomas Nelson & Sons.

Dawson, Jane (2015). *John Knox*. Yale University Press.

de Lisle, Leanda (2008): *The Sisters Who Would Be Queen: Mary, Katherine, and Lady Jane Grey. A Tudor Tragedy*. Ballantine Books.

de Lisle, Leanda (2009). "The Faking of Jane Grey". *BBC History Magazine*. http://www.leandadelisle.com/articles/

de Lisle, Leanda (2013): *Tudor: The Family Story*. Chatto & Windus.

Donaldson, Gordon (1987): *Scotland: James V – James VII*. Mercat Press.

Doran, Susan (2008): "Keys [Grey], Lady Mary (1545?–1578)". *Oxford Dictionary of National Biography*. Online edition.

Edwards, John (2011): *Mary I. England's Catholic Queen*. Yale University Press.
Edwards, J. S. (2013): "The Spinola Letter". http://www.somegreymatter.com/spinola.htm
Elton, G. R. (1976): "The demolition of the good duke". *Times Literary Supplement*. 6 February 1976.
Elton, G. R. (1977): *Reform and Reformation: England 1509–1558*. Hodder Arnold.
Fletcher, Antony and Diarmaid MacCulloch (2008): *Tudor Rebellions*. Routledge.
French, Peter (2002): *John Dee: The World of an Elizabethan Magus*. Routledge.
Goldring, Elizabeth (2014): *Robert Dudley, Earl of Leicester, and the World of Elizabethan Art: Painting and Patronage at the Court of Elizabeth I*. Yale University Press.
Grummitt, David (2008), "Plantagenet, Arthur, Viscount Lisle (b. before 1472, d. 1542)". *Oxford Dictionary of National Biography*. Online edition.
Gunn, S.J. (2008): "Dudley, Edmund (c.1462–1510)". *Oxford Dictionary of National Biography*. Online edition.
Guy, John (1990): *Tudor England*. Oxford Paperbacks.
Guy, John (2013): *The Children of Henry VIII*. Oxford University Press.
Harbison, E. H. (1940): *Rival Ambassadors at the Court of Queen Mary*. Princeton University Press.
Hawkyard, A. D. K. (1982): "Dudley, Sir John (1504/6–53), of Halden, Kent; Dudley Castle, Staffs.; Durham Place, London; Chelsea and Syon, Mdx.". *The History of Parliament Online*.
Haynes, Alan (1987): *The White Bear: The Elizabethan Earl of Leicester*. Peter Owen.
Hayward, Maria (2009): *Rich Apparel: Clothing and the Law in Henry VIII's England*. Ashgate.
Heinze, R. W. (1976): *The Proclamations of the Tudor Kings*. Cambridge University Press.
Higginbotham, Susan (2011a): "How Old Was Guildford Dudley? (BeatsMe)". http://www.susanhigginbotham.com/blog/posts/how-old-was-guildford-dudley-beats-me/
Higginbotham, Susan (2011b): "The Last Will of Jane Dudley, Duchess of Northumberland". http://www.susanhigginbotham.com/subpages/lastwilljanedudley.html

Higginbotham, Susan (2012a): "The Funeral of Jane Dudley, Duchess of Northumberland". http://www.susanhigginbotham.com/blog/posts/the-funeral-of-jane-dudley-duchess-of-northumberland/

Higginbotham, Susan (2012b): "It's A Boy! No, It's A Girl! Some Seymour Birth Dates". http://www.susanhigginbotham.com/blog/posts/its-a-boy-no-its-a-girl-some-seymour-birth-dates/

Hoak, Dale (1976): *The King's Council in the Reign of Edward VI.* Cambridge University Press.

Hoak, Dale (1980): "Rehabilitating the Duke of Northumberland: Politics and Political Control, 1549–53", in Jennifer Loach and Robert Tittler (eds.): *The Mid-Tudor Polity c.1540–1560.* Macmillan.

Hoak, Dale (2008): "Edward VI (1537–1553)". *Oxford Dictionary of National Biography.* Online edition.

Hoak, Dale (2015): "The Succession Crisis of 1553 and Mary's Rise to Power", in Elizabeth Evenden and Vivienne Westbrook (eds.): *Catholic Renewal and Protestant Resistance in Marian England.* Ashgate.

Honan, Park (2000): *Shakespeare: A Life.* Oxford Paperbacks.

Hutchinson, Robert (2006): *The Last Days of Henry VIII: Conspiracy, Treason and Heresy at the Court of the Dying Tyrant.* Phoenix.

Ives, Eric (2005): *The Life and Death of Anne Boleyn.* Blackwell.

Ives, Eric (2009): *Lady Jane Grey: A Tudor Mystery.* Wiley-Blackwell.

Ives, Eric (2012): *The Reformation Experience: Living Through the Turbulent 16th Century.* Lion Books.

James, Susan (2008a): *Catherine Parr: Henry VIII's Last Love.* Tempus.

James, Susan (2008b): "Parr, William, marquess of Northampton (1513–1571)". *Oxford Dictionary of National Biography.* Online edition.

Jenkins, Elizabeth (1961): *Elizabeth and Leicester.* Victor Gollancz.

Jordan, W. K. (1970): *Edward VI: The Threshold of Power. The Dominance of the Duke of Northumberland.* George Allen & Unwin.

Kantorowicz, E. H. (1981): *The King's Two Bodies: A Study in Medieval Political Thought.* Princeton University Press.

Kolehouse, Bobbie (2005): "Dusting Off History to Look at Cocker Hunting Tradition". http://www.spanieljournal.com/bkolehouse.html

Lehmberg, Stanford (2008): "Guildford, Sir Edward (c.1479–1534)". *Oxford Dictionary of National Biography.* Online edition.

Loach, Jennifer (2002): *Edward VI.* Yale University Press.

Loades, David (1989): *Mary Tudor: A Life.* Blackwell.

Loades, David (1991): *The Reign of Mary Tudor: Politics, Government and Religion in England, 1553–1558.* Longman.

Loades, David (1996): *John Dudley, Duke of Northumberland 1504–1553*. Clarendon Press.
Loades, David (2004): *Intrigue and Treason: The Tudor Court, 1547–1558*. Pearson/Longman.
Loades, David (2006): *Mary Tudor: The Tragical History of the First Queen of England*. The National Archives.
Loades, David (2008a): "Dudley, John, duke of Northumberland (1504–1553)". *Oxford Dictionary of National Biography*. Online edition.
Loades, David (2008b): *The Life and Career of William Paulet (c.1475–1575): Lord Treasurer and First Marquess of Winchester*. Ashgate.
Loades, David (2011): *Henry VIII*. Amberley.
Loades, David (2012): *The Tudors. History of a Dynasty*. Continuum.
Loades, David (2013a): *Catherine Howard: The Adulterous Wife of Henry VIII*. Amberley.
Loades, David (2013b): *Jane Seymour: Henry VIII's Favourite Wife*. Amberley.
Loades, David (2013c): *Thomas Cromwell: Servant to Henry VIII*. Amberley.
Loades, David (2015): *The Seymours of Wolf Hall. A Tudor Family History*. Amberley.
Lock, Julian (2004): "Fitzalan, Henry, twelfth earl of Arundel (1512–1580)". *Oxford Dictionary of National Biography*. Online edition.
Lovell, M. S. (2006): *Bess of Hardwick: Empire Builder*. W. W. Norton.
Löwe, J. A. (2004): "Sutton, Henry (d. 1564?)". *Oxford Dictionary of National Biography*. Online edition.
MacCaffrey, Wallace (2008): "Sidney, Sir Henry (1529–1586)". *Oxford Dictionary of National Biography*. Online edition.
MacCulloch, Diarmaid (1996): *Thomas Cranmer: A Life*. Yale University Press.
MacCulloch, Diarmaid (2001): *The Boy King: Edward VI and the Protestant Reformation*. Palgrave.
MacCulloch, Diarmaid (2002): "The Change of Religion", in Patrick Collinson (ed.): *The Sixteenth Century*. Oxford University Press.
McDiarmid, J. F. (2015): "'To content god quietlie': The Troubles of Sir John Cheke under Queen Mary", in Elizabeth Evenden and Vivienne Westbrook (eds.): *Catholic Renewal and Protestant Resistance in Marian England*. Ashgate.
McIntosh, J. L. (2008): *From Heads of Household to Heads of State: The Preaccession Households of Mary and Elizabeth Tudor*. Columbia University Press. http://www.gutenberg-e.org/mcintosh/index.html
Mackie, J. D. (1963), *The Earlier Tudors, 1485–1558*. Clarendon Press.

Mathew, David (1972): *Lady Jane Grey: The Setting of the Reign*. Eyre Methuen.
Merriman, Marcus (2000): *The Rough Wooings: Mary Queen of Scots, 1542–1551*. Tuckwell Press.
Miller, Helen (1982): "Wyatt, Sir Thomas I (by 1504–42), of Allington Castle, Kent". *History of Parliament Online*.
Moorhouse, Geoffrey (2006): *Great Harry's Navy: How Henry VIII Gave England Sea Power*. Phoenix.
Morris, R. K. (2010): *Kenilworth Castle*. English Heritage.
Mortimer, Ian (2013): *The Time Traveller's Guide to Elizabethan England*. Vintage.
Murphy, John (2012): "The Royal Household of Mid Tudor England". http://john-murphy.co.uk/?page_id=1258
Norton, Elizabeth (2011a): *Bessie Blount: Mistress to Henry VIII*. Amberley.
Norton, Elizabeth (2011b): *Catherine Parr*. Amberley.
Penn, Thomas (2012): *Winter King: The Dawn of Tudor England*. Penguin.
Pollard, A. F. (1900): *England Under Protector Somerset*. Kegan Paul, Trench, Trübner.
Porter, Linda (2007): *The First Queen of England: The Myth of "Bloody Mary"*. St. Martin's.
Porter, Linda (2011): *Katherine the Queen: The Remarkable Life of Katherine Parr*. Pan.
Rathbone, Mark (2002): "Northumberland". *History Review*. Vol. 44. December 2002.
Rowse, A. L. (1965): *Shakespeare's Southampton: Patron of Virginia*. Harper & Row.
Rowse, A. L. (1971): *The Elizabethan Renaissance: The Life of the Society*. Macmillan.
Scard, Margaret (2011): *Tudor Survivor: The Life and Times of William Paulet*. The History Press.
Schild, Wolfgang (1980): *Alte Gerichtsbarkeit. Vom Gottesurteil bis zum Beginn der modernen Rechtsprechung*. Callwey.
Sharpe, J. A. (2002): "Economy and Society", in Patrick Collinson (ed.): *The Sixteenth Century*. Oxford University Press.
Sherman, W. H. (1995): *John Dee: The Politics of Reading and Writing in the English Renaissance*. University of Massachusetts Press.
Sil, N. P. (2001): *Tudor Placemen and Statesmen: Select Case Histories*. Rosemont Publishing.

Sil, N. P. (2008): "Jobson, Sir Francis (b. in or before 1509, d. 1573)". *Oxford Dictionary of National Biography.* Online edition.

Skidmore, Chris (2007): *Edward VI: The Lost King of England.* Weidenfeld & Nicolson.

Skidmore, Chris (2010): *Death and the Virgin: Elizabeth, Dudley and the Mysterious Fate of Amy Robsart.* Weidenfeld & Nicolson.

Slack, Paul (1980): "Social Policy and the Constraints of Government, 1547–58", in Jennifer Loach and Robert Tittler (eds.): *The Mid-Tudor Polity c. 1540–1560.* Macmillan.

Smith, L. B. (2013): *Anne Boleyn: Queen of Controversy.* Amberley.

Starkey, David (2003): *Six Wives: The Queens of Henry VIII.* Chatto & Windus.

Stevenson, Jane (2004): "Seymour, Lady Jane (1541–1561)". *Oxford Dictionary of National Biography.* Online edition.

Virgoe, Roger (2004): "Tailboys, Sir William (c.1416-1464)". *Oxford Dictionary of National Biography.* Online edition.

Warnicke, R. M. (2012): *Wicked Women of Tudor England: Queens, Aristocrats, Commoners.* Palgrave.

Weir, Alison (2008): *Children Of England: The Heirs of King Henry VIII 1547-1558.* Vintage.

Wernham, R. B. (1966): *Before the Armada: The Growth of English Foreign Policy 1485–1588.* Jonathan Cape.

Whitelock, Anna (2009): *Mary Tudor: England's First Queen.* Bloomsbury.

Williams, Penry (1998): *The Later Tudors: England 1547–1603.* Oxford University Press.

Wilson, Derek (1981): *Sweet Robin: A Biography of Robert Dudley Earl of Leicester 1533–1588.* Hamish Hamilton.

Wilson, Derek (2005): *The Uncrowned Kings of England: The Black History of the Dudleys and the Tudor Throne.* Carroll & Graf.

Wood, Andy (2007): *The 1549 Rebellions and the Making of Early Modern England.* Cambridge University Press.

Index

Aglionby, Edward 91
Alcibiades 238
Anne of Cleves 31–32, 142
d'Albon, Jacques, Sieur de St. André, Marshal of France 113
d'Annebault, Claude, Admiral of France 39, 40, 42, 45, 47–50, 97
Arundel, Thomas 124, 133
Ascham, Roger 15, 91
Askew, Anne 49–50
L'Aubespine, Monsieur de 176–177
Audley, Thomas, 1st Baron Audley of Walden 152
Basset, Anne 26
Basset, Katherine 26
Beauchamp, Richard, 13th Earl of Warwick 53
Beaumont, John 146
Beaton, David, Cardinal 56
Bellingham, Edward 34
Berteville, Jean 133
Boleyn, Anne 21, 23, 28, 106, 171, 182, 197
Boleyn, George, Viscount Rochford 23
Borgia, Lucrezia 169
Bourbon, Charles III, Duke of 16
Bourbon, Nicholas 23
Bourg, Antoine du, Chancellor of France 30
Brandon, Charles, 1st Duke of Suffolk 16, 17, 36, 38, 39, 40, 43–44
Brandon, Henry, 2nd Duke of Suffolk, 98, 108
Brandon, Katherine, née Willoughby, Duchess of Suffolk 20, 45, 59, 60, 89, 95, 98, 108
Brandon, Mary, Duchess of Suffolk 181
Brereton, William 23
Bromley, Thomas 182
Brooke, Elizabeth, m. Parr, Marchioness of Northampton 94, 177, 236
Brooke, George, 9th Baron Cobham 139, 140
Browne, Anthony 134
Bullinger, Heinrich 208
Burcher, Johannes 208
Bush, M. L. 240
Cabot, Sebastian 99, 100
Calvin, John 135–136
Camden, William 20
Cardano, Girolamo 144
Carew, George 31, 40
Carew, Peter 41
Catherine de Medici 111, 114–115
Cavendish, Elizabeth, née Hardwick 60
Cavendish, Henry 60
Cavendish, William 60
Cawarden, John 133–134, 177
Cawood, John 222
Cecil, Richard 146
Cecil, William 60, 61, 66, 75, 80, 85, 93, 95, 96, 106, 109, 116–119, 121, 123, 126,139–140, 146, 155, 160–165, 175, 177, 183, 184, 195, 241
Chamberlain, Thomas 168
Chancellor, Richard 99
Chapman, Hester 240
Chapuys, Eustace, Imperial ambassador 27, 52, 60
Charles V, Holy Roman Emperor 16, 27–30, 34, 40, 54, 101, 105–108, 111, 112, 154–155, 165–170, 190, 206–211, 223, 227, 231
Cheke, John 100, 123, 181, 187
Christian III, King of Denmark 210
Clarencius, Susan 189, 214, 215, 230, 236
Clifford, Eleanor, née Brandon, Countess of Cumberland 180
Clifford, Henry, 2nd Earl of Cumberland 153, 237

Clifford, Margaret, *m.* Stanley 152–153, 180–181, 183, 237
Clinton, Edward, 9th Baron Clinton 22, 58, 98, 151, 177, 182, 188, 197
Clinton, Ursula, *née* Stourton, Lady Clinton 22, 151
Coligny, Gaspard de, Admiral of France 97–98
Commendone, Giacomo, Papal envoy 215
Cotton, Robert 231
Courtenay, Gertrude, *née* Blount, Marchioness of Exeter 214, 215
Courtenay, Edward, Earl of Devon 209, 228
Cox, Richard 91, 208, 219
Crane, William 124, 130, 148
Cranmer, Thomas 21, 32, 61, 78–79, 82, 84, 94, 100, 101, 105, 119, 120, 156, 159, 172, 173, 182–183, 229, 235, 236, 241
Croft, James 147
Cromwell, Elizabeth, *née* Seymour, Lady Cromwell 136
Cromwell, Gregory 32
Cromwell, Richard 31
Cromwell, Thomas 10, 21, 24, 25, 28, 32, 94
Darcy, Thomas, 1st Baron Darcy of Chiche 81, 110, 114–116, 140, 141
Dalby, William 222
Davey, Richard 220
Dee, John 19–20, 99–100, 188
Delft, François van der, Imperial ambassador 40, 45, 52, 54, 71, 76–78, 82, 88, 89, 93, 97, 100, 117
Digby, Anthony 134
Dudley, Ambrose 19, 70, 75, 91, 140, 141, 151, 153, 197, 206, 207, 229, 233, 235, 237, 243
Dudley, Amy, *née* Robsart 70, 89, 91, 109
Dudley, Andrew 9, 12, 22, 33, 34, 39, 45, 46, 56–59, 68, 81, 84, 91, 134, 147, 149–151, 153, 165–169, 176–177, 183, 197, 206, 213–214, 216, 237
Dudley, Anne, *née* Seymour, Countess of Warwick 89–90, 135–137, 179, 190, 235
Dudley, Anne, *née* Whorwood 91, 140, 141
Dudley, Anne, *née* Windsor 9
Dudley, Arthur 24
Dudley, Charles 20, 92
Dudley, Edmund 9–15, 51, 162–163, 245
Dudley, Elizabeth, *née* Grey, Baroness Lisle 9, 11, 14–15, 19, 21, 33, 179
Dudley, Elizabeth, *m.* Stourton 9–10, 22, 238
Dudley, Elizabeth, *née* Tailboys, Baroness Tailboys 151
Dudley, Guildford 20, 27, 91, 92, 151, 153, 166, 176, 177, 179, 182, 183, 192, 193, 198–199, 201, 207, 220, 229, 233–236, 238
Dudley, Henry, eldest son of *John Dudley* 19, 23, 38, 39
Dudley, Henry, youngest son of *John Dudley* 20, 92, 151, 197, 206, 207, 229, 233, 235
Dudley, Henry, soldier of fortune 210–211
Dudley, Jane, *née* Guildford, Viscountess Lisle, Countess of Warwick, Duchess of Northumberland 19–21, 24, 26, 31, 39, 45, 48–49, 60, 61, 85, 88–89, 96, 99–100, 106, 144–145, 147, 170, 193, 198, 199, 201, 207, 214–215, 228–229, 233, 236–237, 243–244
Dudley, Jerome 9, 12, 22, 237
Dudley, John, 1st Baron Dudley 9
Dudley, John, 3rd Baron Dudley 24
Dudley, John, of Atherington 9
Dudley, John, Viscount Lisle, Earl of Warwick, Duke of Northumberland *passim*; birth 9; Black Legend 65–66, 71, 230, 238–241; and body servants 197, 203–204; at Calais

15–16, 21, 23; chattels 228–229; and children 19–20, 39, 89–92, 108–109, 113, 137–138, 140–142, 151–153, 164, 243, 244; clemency 74, 147; depression 162–164, 207, 210; duke 123–124, 145; earl 53–54; Earl Marshal 109, 128; education 11, 15–16, 143; and Edward VI 27, 100, 110–111, 135, 191, 207–208; and Elizabeth I 21, 61, 106, 179; execution 221–227, 244–245; and exploration 98–100; foreign policy 97–99, 111–115, 154–155, 165–170, 185–186; in France 27–28, 38–39, 41, 45–49; Great Master of the Household 43–44, 86, 93, 94, 208; historiography 239–241; ill health 60, 68, 76, 82–83, 87, 93, 97, 112, 117, 161–163, 178; Irish affairs 147; and Jane Grey 192, 195, 231–233; Knight of the Body 18; Knight of the Garter 37; lifestyle 44, 163, 242; Lord Admiral 36–42, 55, 81, 98; and Mary I 33, 102, 104–106, 170, 192, 194–195, 225–226; and *Mary Rose* 40–41; Master of the Queen's Horse 31–33; military campaigns 16–17, 27, 37–42, 46, 57–59, 68–75, 133, 195–197, 199–202; northern and Scottish affairs 34, 35–38, 57–59, 98, 145–147, 157–161; patronage of arts and letters 18, 91, 143–144, 173; personal attributes 242–243; plots against 83–85, 124, 126–131, 133, 200; fear of poison 90, 126; popularity and unpopularity 55, 147, 151, 162, 205, 232; President of the Council of Wales 61; President of the King's Council 86, 92–93, 105, 110–111, 115–122, 129, 146–147, 185–186, 190; religion 23, 36, 60, 61, 78, 82, 101, 156, 160, 215–216, 218–219, 233, 241–242; religious policy 100–106, 156–161, 172–173; residences 21, 24–25, 60, 61, 75, 76, 142–143, 163; scapegoat 228, 230; and siblings 9–10, 14, 22, 33, 147; social policy 67, 118, 120–122; in Spain 28–30; sports 18, 134; and stepfather 21–22, 33; and Stratford-upon-Avon 190; and succession plot 173–174, 178–179, 181, 183, 185–190, 210; trial 211–213; Vice-Admiral 27; viscount 33; and wife 15, 19, 26, 48–49, 60, 88–89, 147, 179, 214–215, 243

Dudley, John, Viscount Lisle, Earl of Warwick, son and heir of *John Dudley* 19–20, 39, 54, 85–87, 89–92, 98, 100, 112, 134–138, 142, 143, 153, 170, 171, 179, 182–184, 190, 197, 202, 206, 207, 213, 219–220, 231, 233

Dudley, Katherine, *m.* Hastings, daughter of *John Dudley*, died 1620 20, 177, 207, 236, 243

Dudley, Katherine, daughter of *John Dudley*, died 1552 20, 45, 140–142

Dudley, Margaret, daughter of *John Dudley* 20

Dudley, Margaret, *née* Audley 151–152

Dudley, Mary, *m.* Sidney 19, 20, 108–109, 144, 151, 192, 207, 236, 243

Dudley, Robert, Earl of Leicester 19–20, 23, 33, 70, 89, 91, 92, 109, 125, 134–135, 138, 142–144, 151, 192, 204, 206, 207, 218, 229, 233–235, 237, 239–240, 243–245

Dudley, Robert, illegitimate son of Robert Dudley, Earl of Leicester 206

Dudley, Thomas 19

Dudley, Temperance 20

Dugdale, William 9

Edward IV, King of England 151

Edward V, King of England 151

Edward VI, King of England 15, 20, 27–29, 33, 35, 53, 54, 56, 59, 60, 62, 64–66, 73, 76, 77, 79–82, 89–90, 93, 98–105, 107–116, 121, 123,

265

125, 128, 130–134, 144, 147–149, 153–159, 161, 163, 165, 168–185, 187–189, 191–193, 199, 202, 205, 208–210, 212, 217, 222, 223, 230–231, 239, 240
Eleanor of Austria, Queen of France 48
Elisabeth de Valois, Princess of France 111–112, 114–115
Elizabeth I, Queen of England, Princess, Lady 20, 21, 33, 45, 59, 61, 65, 112, 122, 125, 142, 177–178, 181, 184, 189, 199, 244–245
Elton, G. R. 240, 241
Empson, John 228–229
Empson, Richard 10, 12, 13
d'Este, Ercole II, Duke of Ferrara 170
d'Este, Ippolito, Cardinal of Ferrara 47
d'Eyck, Sieur 44
Ferdinand I, King of the Romans, Holy Roman Emperor 210
Fisher, Thomas 75
Fitzalan, Henry, 19th Earl of Arundel 76–77, 81–83, 87, 93, 105, 124, 127, 130, 188, 192, 198, 200, 202–206, 211, 216–218, 229, 238
Fitzpatrick, Barnaby 130
Fitzroy, Mary, née Howard, Duchess of Richmond 96
Flamock, Andrew 25, 75
Florio, Michelangelo 144
Foxe, John 160, 233
Francis I, King of France 16, 21, 29–30, 45–48, 57
Gardiner, Stephen 39, 49, 50, 157, 209, 215
Gates, Henry 187, 206, 213, 216
Gates, John 109, 110, 115–116, 119, 134–135, 141, 181, 187, 192, 197, 202–203, 206, 209, 213, 219–222
Goodman, John 192
Goodrich, Thomas 84, 181
Gordon, George, 4th Earl of Huntly 35, 57, 58, 142
Grafton, Richard 239
Granado, Mr. 91
Gray, Patrick, 4th Lord Gray 57, 59

Gresham, Thomas 70, 121–122, 145, 188–189
Grey, Arthur, 13th Baron Grey de Wilton 177
Grey, Edward, 4th Viscount Lisle 9
Grey, Frances, née Brandon, Duchess of Suffolk 170, 180–181, 190, 193, 201, 207
Grey, Henry, 3rd Marquess of Dorset, Duke of Suffolk 61, 65, 84, 120, 123, 145, 152, 170, 179, 186, 190, 195, 201, 207, 212, 227, 231, 234–235, 243
Grey, Jane, *m.* Dudley, Lady 61, 125, 176–177, 179–183, 185, 187, 188, 190–195, 197–202, 204, 207, 209–212, 218, 230–236, 238, 239
Grey, Katherine 177, 180, 181, 183
Grey, Mary 177
Grey, William 13th Baron Grey de Wilton 123, 197
Grice, Gilbert 193
Grimaldi, Battista 11, 12
Guaras, Antonio de 66, 211, 221, 226, 233
Guidotti, Antonio 111–113, 115
Guildford, Edward 14–17, 19–21
Guildford, Eleanor, née West 15
Guildford, Henry 14, 18
Guildford, John 21
Guildford, Richard 15, 16, 21
Haddon, Walter 143
Hales, John 63, 67
Hamilton, James, 2nd Earl of Arran, Duke of Chatelherault, Regent of Scotland 35–37, 56, 58
Hamilton, James, 3rd Earl of Arran 56–57
Hartgill, John 238
Hartgill, William 238
Hastings, Francis, 2nd Earl of Huntingdon 142, 177, 182, 188, 192, 197, 202, 206, 209
Hastings, Henry, 3rd Earl of Huntingdon, Lord Hastings 142, 177, 197, 206

Hayward, John 239
Heath, Nicholas 62, 190, 227, 244
Henry II, King of France 47–48, 57, 65, 97, 111–113, 154–155, 167, 169–170, 186–187, 191–192, 201, 212
Henry VI, King of England 54
Henry VII, King of England 10–12, 122
Henry VIII, King of England 12, 14, 16, 18, 19, 21, 24, 27–48, 50–53, 59, 60, 81, 98, 129, 136, 142, 143, 152, 154, 156, 157, 176, 180, 181, 183, 193, 205, 217, 222, 224, 239, 241, 245
Hepburn, Patrick, 3rd Earl of Bothwell 59
Hepburn, James, 4th Earl of Bothwell 59
Herbert, Henry, 2nd Earl of Pembroke, Lord Herbert 177
Herbert, William, 1st Earl of Pembroke 94–95, 117, 121, 123, 130–132, 177, 188, 192, 198, 200, 210
Heywood, John 92
Hilliard, Nicholas 20
Hoby, Philip 85–86, 106, 186
Holinshed, Raphael 239
Home, John, Abbot of Jedburgh 35
Hooper, John 100–101, 156
Horne, Robert, Dean of Durham 157–158
Howard, Elizabeth, *née* Stafford, Duchess of Norfolk 96
Howard, Henry, Earl of Surrey 32, 50–52, 66, 232
Howard, Katherine 32–33
Howard, Thomas, 3rd Duke of Norfolk 23, 33–34, 38, 39, 50, 52, 96, 209, 211–212, 228
Howard, Thomas, 4th Duke of Norfolk 96
Howard, William, 1st Baron Howard of Effingham 32
Huggones, Elizabeth 152–153
Ives, Eric 241
James V, King of Scotland 34–35

James I, King of England 231
Jobson, Francis 22, 92, 229, 239
Jordan, W. K. 240
Juan, Prince of Spain 28
Katherine of Aragon 12, 28, 143, 182
Kett, Robert 68, 70–73
Kingston, Anthony 31
Knollys, Francis 134–135
Knox, John 146–147, 159–161, 235, 238
Knyvett, Edward 72
Latimer, Hugh 66
Laud, William 218
Laval, René de, Sieur de Boidaulphin, French ambassador 98, 112–114, 133, 155, 169, 170, 179
Leland, John 18, 39, 76
Lorraine, Jean de, Cardinal 47
Machiavelli, Niccoló 110
Machyn, Henry 205
Mary I, Queen of England, Princess, Lady 27, 29, 33, 45, 59, 71, 76–77, 101–106, 119, 122, 125, 128, 135, 145, 147, 157, 166, 170, 172–174, 176, 181, 182, 184, 186–190, 192–195, 197, 199, 201, 202, 204, 207, 209–218, 222, 225–226, 230–231, 233, 234, 237–238, 241, 243–245
Mary of Guise, Queen of Scotland, Regent of Scotland 34, 124–125
Mary of Hungary, Regent of the Low Countries 45, 107, 166, 186
Mary Stuart, Queen of Scots 34, 35, 37, 56, 59, 111–112, 202
Mason, John 113
Maurice of Saxony 210
Melanchthon, Philip 173
Mendoza, Diego Hurtado de, Imperial ambassador 20, 27, 166–168, 199
Mexía, Pedro 109
Mildmay, Walter 121
Montague, Edward 54, 182–184
Montmorency, Anne de, Constable of France 155, 219
Morison, Richard 106, 114, 145, 166–168

Neville, Henry 123, 134
Neville, Henry, 5th Earl of Westmorland 188
Noailles, Antoine de, French ambassador 65–66, 186, 190–192, 199, 205, 219
Norris, Henry 23
Occhino, Bernardino 92
Page, Richard 62
Paget, Anne, *née* Preston, Lady Paget 148–149, 236
Paget, William, 1st Baron Paget of Beaudesert 41–43, 45, 46, 49–54, 65, 76–78, 81–82, 97, 124, 148–149, 202, 214, 237
Palmer, Thomas 72, 124, 130, 145, 206, 209, 213, 216, 220–222
Parker, Matthew 197
Parr, Anne, *née* Bourchier 94, 228
Parr, Anne, *m.* Herbert, Countess of Pembroke 45
Parr, Katherine 45, 49, 60–62
Parr, William, Baron Parr, Earl of Essex, Marquess of Northampton 37, 49, 54, 61, 68–69, 81, 93–95, 112, 125, 127, 130–132, 139, 197, 209, 210, 216, 235, 236
Parsons, Robert 215
Partridge, Miles 133
Patten, William 57
Paulet, William, Baron St. John, Earl of Wiltshire, Marquess of Wiltshire 37, 44, 76, 81, 83, 98, 123, 125, 136, 197
Perlin, Stephen, Friar 194, 227
Perrot, John 134–135
Peto, William, Friar 143
Petre, William 46, 118, 155, 175, 184
Philip II, King of Spain, Prince 176, 236, 244
Pickering, William 155
Plantagenet, Arthur, Viscount Lisle 14–15, 21–23, 26, 33
Plantagenet, Bridget 22
Plantagenet, Elizabeth, *m.* Jobson 22, 237

Plantagenet, Frances 22
Plantagenet, Honor, *née* Grenville, Viscountess Lisle 23, 145
Pollard, A. L. 240
Ponet, John 71, 156, 173, 238
Potter, Gilbert 193, 205
Poynings, Thomas 31
Quadra, Álvaro de la, Spanish ambassador 244
Radcliffe, Anne, *née* Calthorpe, Countess of Sussex 151
Radcliffe, Thomas, 3rd Earl of Sussex, Lord Fitzwalter 134
Renard, Simon, Imperial ambassador 111, 112, 192, 200, 205–207, 210, 227–228, 231, 233, 235
Rich, Richard, 1st Baron Rich 110, 117, 228
Richard II, King of England 92
Richard III, King of England 79
Richard of Shrewsbury, Duke of York 151
Ridley, Nicholas 105
Robsart, John 70, 91
Rogers, Edward 81
Ronsard, Pierre de 90
Rossetti, John 59
Russell, John, 1st Earl of Bedford 33, 68, 79, 81, 188
Sandys, Edwin 197, 201, 202–205, 206
Sanguin, Antoine, Cardinal de Meudon 47
Scheyfve, Jehan de, Imperial ambassador 105–108, 112, 117, 126, 132–133, 135, 154–155, 165, 168–171, 175, 178–179, 186, 190, 201
Scudamore, Richard 85–86
Selve, Odet de, French ambassador 65
Seymour, Anne, *née* Stanhope, Duchess of Somerset 43, 45, 62, 64, 78, 83, 88–89, 95, 128, 130, 132, 135–136, 152–153, 209
Seymour, Edward, Earl of Hertford, Duke of Somerset, Lord Protector 17, 21, 32–38, 43–45, 49–59, 61–

68, 71, 75–80, 83–84, 87–91, 93–96, 101, 106–108, 110, 113, 117, 118, 123–124, 126–133, 135–136, 143, 148, 152–153, 171, 188, 216, 227, 230, 239–241
Seymour, Edward, 1st Earl of Hertford, son of Protector Somerset 136, 216, 219–220
Seymour, Henry, brother of Protector Somerset 62, 136
Seymour, Henry, son of Protector Somerset 136, 216, 219–220
Seymour, Jane 26, 28, 129
Seymour, John, father of Protector Somerset 129
Seymour, John, son of Protector Somerset 136
Seymour, Margaret, née Wentworth 128–129
Seymour, Mary 95–96
Seymour, Thomas, Baron Seymour of Sudeley 31, 42, 54, 55, 59, 61–66, 81, 94–96, 132, 136, 230
Sheffield, Edmund, 1st Baron Sheffield 68, 74
Shute, John 144
Sidney, Henry 108–110, 123, 134–135, 142, 147, 165, 170, 187, 191, 204, 207, 235, 236, 245
Sidney, Philip 236, 244
Sidney, William 109, 142
Smeaton, Mark 23
Smith, Thomas 78, 80, 118
Soranzo, Giacomo, Venetian ambassador 170, 174, 175, 177, 245
Southwell, Richard 34, 71
Stanhope, Elizabeth, née Bourchier 135
Stanhope, Michael 62, 77, 80, 124, 126, 130, 133
Stanley, Edward, 3rd Earl of Derby 105
Stanley, Henry, 4th Earl of Derby 237
Stewart, James, Earl of Moray 35
Stourton, Charles, 8th Baron Stourton 22, 204–205, 237–238
Stourton, William, 7th Baron Stourton 22, 238
Stow, John 239
Stukeley, Thomas 155
Sturton, Mr. 214
Talbot, John, 1st Earl of Shrewsbury 54
Talbot, Francis, 5th Earl of Shrewsbury 128, 187
Thirlby, John 61
Thomas, William 110, 143–144
Throckmorton, John 192
Throckmorton, Nicholas 192
Thynne, John 65–68, 80
Tournon, François, Cardinal 30
Tunstall, Cuthbert 35, 46, 157
Tytler, P. F. 141
Underhill, Edward 198
Underhill, Guildford 198, 200
Unton, Edward 136
Vane, Ralph 124, 133, 142
Vendome, François, Vîdame de Chartres 98, 114
Vere, John de, 16th Earl of Oxford 197
Vergil, Polydore 12
Verney, Richard 91
Vertot, René Aubert de, Abbé 66, 192
Wentworth, Thomas, 1st Baron Wentworth 81
West, Thomas, 8th Baron West and 9th Baron De La Warr 15
West, Thomas, 9th Baron West and 10th Baron De La Warr 19, 188
Weston, Francis 23
Whalley, Richard 93, 127
Wharton, Thomas, 1st Baron Wharton 160–161
Whitgift, John 218
Willoughby, Hugh 99
Willoughby, William, 1st Baron Willoughby of Parham 147
Wilson, Thomas 91
Windsor, Thomas, of Stanwell 9
Wingfield, Robert 231, 233
Wolfe, Edward 126
Wolsey, Thomas, Cardinal 16, 19
Woodville, Elizabeth 129
Wotton, Nicholas 47

Wriothesley, Thomas, 1st Earl of
  Southampton 33, 51, 52, 54, 76–77,
  82–84, 87, 93, 96

Wroth, Thomas 81, 187, 191
Wyatt, Thomas 17–18, 28–31, 33
Yorke, John 78, 85, 99, 121